TWICE DELIVERED

TWICE DELIVERED

JEANETTE MEADE AND TED HASKINS

Library of Congress Control Number:		2015900720
ISBN:	Hardcover	978-1-5035-3535-0
	Softcover	978-1-5035-3536-7
	eBook	978-1-5035-3531-2

This book was printed in the United States of America.

Rev. date: 01/31/2015

To order additional copies of this book, contact:
Xlibris
1-888-795-4274
www.Xlibris.com
Orders@Xlibris.com
536947

CONTENTS

PROLOGUE

Our story is a collection of Jeanette's experiences then mine as well as testimonials we've gathered from friends and family. Some are rather dark, but were used to demonstrate how life really was for our family and the harsh conditions of the times. Beginning in the mountains of Virginia, it spans from the 1930s to present day.

Jeanette and two younger sisters, Dinah and Darlene, grew up on the east bank of the Blue Ridge Mountains of Virginia during the 1950s and 60s. They continue to live within a few miles of their childhood home to this day.

Having had an abusive childhood, Jeanette's single saving grace was her loving Granny. She endured and survived hardships and violations to pursue a lifelong, needle-in-a-haystack search without so much as a name to aid her. She credits her faith for keeping her dream alive even though life's distractions pulled her in other directions countless times.

These stories are meant to convey the remarkable contrasts and parallels in our lives. They are so implausible that if this had not happened to me, I would not have believed them myself.

We hope that you will walk away with a positive feeling of faith and a better understanding of how the choices we make can impact not only the rest of our lives, but the lives of those around us for ever. Family should always be the most important thing in everyone's lives -- a structure of support and unconditional love. When we have nothing else in the world, we have family.

I am Jeanette and I will tell my part of the story in chapters one through three. Two different font styles are used to help you keep track of who is telling the story. This font style represents me. I will begin with some family background and continue until I hire a private investigator.

I am Ted and at that point, I will take over in this font style with my part of the story in chapters four through six.

We both share in Chapter seven.

Some of the names in our story have been changed. All else is as close to the truth as we know it to be.

Dedicated to the loving memory of

Evelyn "Granny" Jackson

I

THE JACKSONS

Granny and Granddaddy

In 1903, escape artist, Harry Houdini was making headlines in Europe after escaping from an Amsterdam jail. Teddy Roosevelt was president and the first Teddy Bear was introduced in the United States.

Whippoorwill Park is located on the eastern outskirts of Virginia's Appalachian Mountains, in Madison County. Ohmer Jackson, my granddaddy, was born there. Living in Madison County his entire life, Granddaddy was a well liked and respected man throughout the county.

Widespread fear of bolshevism and anarchism blanketed America as she went to war in 1917. At fourteen years of age, Granddaddy left his Wolftown, Virginia home, his parents, four sisters and two brothers behind. Too young to fight for his country, he found work in a logging camp, in nearby Wallace's Gap.

Growing into adulthood, he became one of the more vibrant characters of Madison County. Some knew him as Mountain Man, while others knew him as the SOB. He was as proud as he was colossal in stature, standing every bit of six feet tall and tipping the scales at two hundred and fifty pounds or more in his prime, I reckon. His large hands were one and a half times wider than most other men's and he was as strong as a mule. Like him or not, everyone who knew him would tell you that he was one very hardworking farmer and logger who could spin a tale better than most.

His skills were many. There was nothing he couldn't do. When Granddaddy wasn't farming, he was logging. When he wasn't logging, you could find him mending a fence or breaking horses that others would bring from miles around. He was the one man in Madison who could break a horse that seemed otherwise unbreakable. When he was nowhere to be found, he was most likely tending his still, making some of the best moonshine in the county. Peaches were the primary ingredient that made his shine as distinctive as it was exceptional. At forty dollars a gallon, it's easy to see that making shine was where he and the other farmers got the best value for their crops.

Granddaddy's voice was gruff and unique. His presence was commanding, surpassed only by his legendary feats of strength. Among those stories was the time he lifted the front end of a loaded-down logging truck off its wheels and turned it around on a narrow, impassable mountain road. When the county sponsored an annual strongman contest, Granddaddy, who had been used to lifting hogs all by himself, didn't see much of a challenge in the competition and decided to give it a try. After performing all the tasks leading up to the barrel-lifting finale without breaking a sweat, everyone watched in amazement as he walked up to the fifty-gallon barrel full of water. With a shiver from head to toe, like a wet dog shaking dry, he stood steadfast over the barrel. The crowd stood silently with anticipation, and Mother Nature seemed to pause as well. He squatted down. With hardly a strain, and to no one's surprise, Granddaddy lifted the barrel and carried it across the finish line as everyone cheered him on. He not only was crowned the strongest man in the county, the stories of my granddaddy, Ohmer Jackson, spread throughout and may very well have been the inspiration of many a lumberjack tale.

Coming from a large family, Granddaddy had a bounty of cousins and nephews. One of his favorite nephews was Charles Berry. They palled around a lot and often played jokes on one another. Each gag was an attempt to top the last one. One of Charles' favorites was the time he grabbed a' hold to an old black rubber hose and tossed it in Granddaddy's direction while shouting, "Say, Ohmer, look at this here snake."

Startled, Granddaddy yelled back at him, "Gawd damn it, Charles, you caused me to mess all over myself!" Charles got a lifetime of laughs from that one gag and he always delighted in sharing it with others.

It was while working in the logging camp that Granddaddy met and befriended a fellow logger named John Will. One day he invited Granddaddy to come home with him on the weekend. It was there that he met John Will's younger sister, Evelyn.

❖ ❖ ❖ ❖

Granny

A Madison County native, my granny, Evelyn, was a very vivacious young lady with light colored hair, slender frame, and very petite. A most generous and loving person, she never spoke a discouraging word. She was as well educated as anyone in Madison, meaning that she often earned straight A's on her report cards even though I don't reckon she graduated high school. Most were lucky to get through the seventh grade. High school required most of us to travel and without transportation, there weren't many who continued their education beyond the 7th grade. Those who were fortunate enough to do so usually moved in with other families who lived near the county high school. I don't reckon she was ever without an anecdote for any situation. One of her favorites was "There's a lot of truth in a joke."

Granny loved to dance and she had a great ear for music. She played numerous instruments including the piano, guitar, and accordion, but it was the harmonica that she often played in church. It wasn't unusual to find her singing hymns, not only in church, but while doing her chores, which usually lasted from early predawn hours well into the night.

They say that opposites attract, and there was no better proof of that than Granny and Granddaddy. A God-fearing lady, she was the most affectionate woman on God's green earth and everything that Granddaddy wasn't. A living angel perhaps.

Upon learning that their daughter had taken a liking to Granddaddy, Granny's parents became very disappointed in her obvious attraction to him, believing that she could do better with her life. When Granddaddy proposed to her, Granny accepted and was determined to be a Jackson, even against her father's expressed wishes.

May 11, 1929, was a beautiful spring day. The air was clear, and the land transformed with gorgeous, renewed plant life as far as the eye could see. The trees, as green as the grass on the ground, were surrounded with colorful wildflowers in bloom. Inside the Circuit Court of Madison County, a joyous twenty-six-year-old Ohmer and seventeen-year-old Evelyn were getting hitched. It was a brief and private affair that was over nearly as fast as it had begun when they were pronounced husband and wife.

Most of the people born in Madison County remained there for their entire lives, raising their children and working the land day in and day out. Except on Sundays, of course, when most took time out for church. Later that year, what became known as Black Tuesday took America into the Great Depression. Granddaddy and Granny seemed undaunted by what Wall Street was doing -- after all, they were already poor. They had the advantage of knowing how to survive hard times and live off the land.

Granny was always the first to rise each morning from her twin bed on one side of the living room. She was the one who prepared the fire in the kitchen wood stove. While waiting for it to get hot, she sat quietly, reading her Bible. She knew it well and could quote any passage upon request. Granddaddy was rarely far behind. He was the one who started the fire in the pot belly stove in front of the fireplace after rising from his twin bed, opposite Granny's twin bed.

When the stove was hot enough, she'd cook breakfast, which usually consisted of eggs, pork, potatoes, and batter cakes for the entire household. Of course, they had coffee with breakfast and they had a very unusual way of drinking it. After the coffee came to a boil, they poured it into a cup. From the cup, the coffee was poured into the saucers so it could cool faster. As it cooled, they would loudly slurp the coffee from the saucers.

Batter cakes were used in place of bread since we grew nearly everything we ate. Granny only went to the store for the staples—flour and sugar. Granddaddy planted four to five hundred pounds of potatoes every year, so there were not only always plenty of potatoes to go around, they were served with every meal.

Weather permitting, laundry was done outdoors on the porch. Granny used a large metal washtub and washboard to wash the clothes. She boiled the water that was used to wash the white clothes. Scrubbing clothes for hours, Granny didn't stop even though her knuckles sometimes bled. When the weather wasn't accommodating, she did the laundry in the kitchen. During the winter months, it would be so cold that the clothes would freeze before she got them hung up to dry. When the tub wasn't being used to wash clothes, it doubled as the bathtub.

The irons that we ironed our clothes with pulled double duty during the cold winter months. After being warmed on the wood stove, we wrapped them in rags and placed them at the foot of the bed to keep our feet warm. We grew up in a large white house in the hollow. It had no electricity so we used nature as best we could, especially when it came to storing perishables. Tomatoes, cucumbers, and watermelons were kept as cold as ice in the spring box. This was a thick cement slab with a pipe that fed cold water from the spring. It kept our food very cold during the summer as well as during the winter months. Crock pots full of food were stored there, in the water. They were topped with a rock to prevent creatures such as the ever present frogs and lizards from getting inside. Adjacent to the spring box was a huge tree with a split in it. A black snake made its home there and when my sister, Darlene, went to dip water for drinking, it would sometimes peer out at her. She never paid any attention to it. I reckon that's why she was the one who usually fetched the drinking water for the house, but I'm getting ahead of myself. That story is actually much later.

Some of the pre-daylight chores included making sure there was enough water in the house to last the day or until we got home from school. The cows, however, had to be milked before breakfast. At the end of the day, kerosene lamps provided light in the house after it started getting dark. Before going to bed, Granddaddy would always tell us, "Blow them lamps out and save that damn lamp oil." I'd like to have a nickel for every time he said that.

Granddaddy's garden was next to the house and covered at least two acres. The garden-grown foods included potatoes, tomatoes, corn, and green beans, among other vegetables, all of which Granny canned as part of her daily chores. What we couldn't use, we gave to our neighbors and other family members.

Separate from the garden was a huge corn field where he grew corn to feed the animals. So huge was this field that oftentimes he asked other family members to help maintain them as it was more than any single person could handle. On one occasion, John Will volunteered his two children to help. Granddaddy showed little Charles and his sister Jane how to use the thinning stick to thin out the crowded rows of corn stalks.

Disappearing for a while, Granddaddy left Charles and Jane to their work. They would have preferred doing something else, of course, and the long rows of corn looked never-ending. Digging in at the beginning of the first row, they methodically worked to the opposite end together. Each hill that contained three stalks was thinned down to two, always leaving the healthiest to grow and be productive. Upon reaching the end of each row, they sat down in the dirt and took what they thought was a well deserved break, just like they had seen the adults do many times before.

After getting all liquored up, Granddaddy returned, curious to see how much they had achieved. Finding them sitting in the dirt, at the end of the row, they were laughing and giggling as though they were having a grand ole time. Not very pleased at their carrying on, Granddaddy began shouting at the top of his lungs. He called them lazy and demanded more from them. When John Will returned he asked Granddaddy how his kids had done.

"Those kids are worthless!" Granddaddy said, "They're not doing anything and they ain't makin' no progress." John Will smelled liquor on Granddaddy's breath and told Charles and Jane that he thought it was time that they should be getting back home.

Liquor seemed to turn Granddaddy into a very different person. He would become very crude and often cruel. After he had been drinking, he once walked over to the stove while Granny was cooking and lifted the lid of the pot she was cooking in. Without provocation, he spat inside and covered it right back up. On yet another occasion, without warning and while Granny wasn't looking, he worked up a copious amount of phlegm, then expelled it onto the firewood in the wood box. Unaware, Granny reached down into the wood box and got a handful of more than just firewood. Wiping her hand on her apron, she would say, "Oh, dear Lord," and continue with her chores without ever saying anything to Granddaddy. To further amuse himself, he'd sit next to the hot wood stove and repeatedly spit on it while watching as it sizzled down the side.

One day, Granny went to church without telling Granddaddy. When he discovered she was gone, he rode his horse to the church. Instead of tying it up out front, he rode it in and directly to the pulpit, where he made an even more dramatic scene. Rearing the horse up on its back legs, Granddaddy shouted loud enough to be heard throughout the entire county, ordering her to get back home. Even though many of the things he did caused her a lot of grief, her vows didn't allow her to act out against him. She remained faithful and obedient to her Lord and her husband alike.

During the 1930s and 1940s, the United States struggled through the great depression and was dragged into World War II. As the 1940s drew near an end, GIs returned home from the war that was followed by the baby boom. Granny and Granddaddy had eleven children, not all of whom survived to adulthood. I reckon you could say they had their own baby boom going on, but it was Granddaddy's sister, Aunt Paige who outdid them. She had twenty of her own. Surviving childhood was one of the biggest challenges that faced families back then. Home remedies were commonplace, partly because medicines weren't readily available and money was scarce. People didn't go to the doctor unless they were seriously ill. Some of the home remedies included turpentine for a sore throat and cornmeal and onions to ease chest congestion.

Momma was Granny and Granddaddy's second born, ten months after her older brother, Randolph, died before his first birthday. Momma was named for

Granny's younger sister who died a tragic death just shy of her twelfth birthday, when she was struck by a vehicle walking home from school. Even though Momma was named for Granny's sister, everyone always called her Sugarloaf.

As a young girl, Momma was as inquisitive as she was audacious, becoming increasingly hardened and bitter as she matured. I reckon that was due in part to the way Granddaddy treated her, but what's confusing is the rift that existed between Momma and Granny. Momma often received beatings from Granddaddy, who didn't hesitate to use the first thing he could get his hands on to strike her. The only other one of Granddaddy's children that fell victim to his abuse was Aunt Suzie who was eight years younger than Momma. Granddaddy had unsuccessfully attempted to smother her with a pillow behind the wood stove in the kitchen on one occasion. No one ever knew why nor did they know how she survived the malicious attack.

Momma at nine or ten year old

Momma learned to stand up for herself at a very young age. No one did anything to her without getting it right back. Her cousin, Charles Beahm, was two years older than Momma. He had been teasing her on the school playground when she bolted through the schoolyard, chasing him with a fierce vengeance. A barefooted Charles jumped off the schoolhouse porch steps, onto a broken bottle, slicing his heel wide open. Of course, there was no school nurse or doctor nearby, so he walked on tiptoe, all the way home, where his Papa, John Will, put some yellow sulfur on it and bandaged it up. Charles didn't soon forget that incident as he spent the next twenty years picking pieces of glass out of his foot as they surfaced from the ugly scar.

Shortly after giving birth to one of her children, Granny had a bout with depression. Afraid that she'd try to run away, Granddaddy tied her to the bed. When John Will brought his family by for a visit, Charles began to wander around the house. The adults were talking amongst themselves and not paying him much attention. Coming across one of the bedrooms, he peered through a partially opened door and was shocked to discover his Aunt Evelyn tied to the bed with heavy plow lines. As he looked on, she muttered softly, words he couldn't make sense of. As shocking as it must have looked to Charles, he didn't express any concern and continued on his way, playing throughout the house.

Roy was Aunt Paige's second born. As a young man, he enjoyed helping his Uncle Ohmer make shine. One night, while they were working on a new batch, Granddaddy's goat wandered over to the bucket filled with the dingy whiskey backing that had run off from the still. After lapping it down, the goat backed out and moved away from the now empty bucket. Standing upright, wavering a bit, the goat shivered from head to tail. His eyes bulged and spun so wildly that neither Granddaddy nor Roy would have been surprised to see smoke blowing from its ears. Focusing on a tree a few yards away, the goat put his head down and charged it as fast as he could. He was no match for a big old tree, and as soon as he collided with it, he was stopped cold. Taking a few steps back, the goat fell to the ground like he'd been shot dead. Roy jumped up in a flash to aid the goat, but not before Granddaddy could grab him and pull him back. He said, "Give him some time. He'll be okay." Roy sat back down and he and his Uncle Ohmer continued drinking throughout the rest of the night. The goat eventually recovered, but I reckon its headache was probably greater than the ones Roy and Granddaddy woke up with the following morning.

Granddaddy was very demanding of his animals, and if they didn't perform to his expectations, he would viciously punish them. One afternoon, a chaotic pack of dogs had gathered near the house. Granddaddy picked up an axe and softly walked over and into the commotion until he stood right in the middle of the pack. They seemed completely oblivious to him as they were focused on Momma's dog that was in heat at the time. Standing over her dog with the axe hanging at his ankle,

Granddaddy swung it full circle, up and around, swiftly bringing it down and splitting the female's head wide open like a melon. The happy barking quickly turned into high pitched yelps as all the other dogs scattered with tucked tails, leaving her lying there lifeless in the dirt. Granddaddy turned and walked away without ever showing the least bit of emotion.

His own animals weren't treated any better. Whenever he got a new horse that didn't obey him or just gave him trouble, Granddaddy would show it who was boss. I personally witnessed him breaking a bottle over a rock and placing the jagged edge inside the horse's mouth, proceeding to slice its mouth wide open, one side at a time. As the horse reared back, it shook its head, throwing blood all over Granddaddy. Angered by being bloodied, he gripped the horse's face, placed the bit in its mouth, and shoved it into the gaping flesh that flapped loosely while the horse fought to get away. As cruel as it may have seemed, the horse was spared a much harsher treatment. He'd also wrap heavy chains around his horse's neck. So heavy were those chains that they rubbed the flesh raw and the open wounds would fill with maggots until he eventually cleaned the wounds out to heal. He'd also wrap the chains around its ankles until they too were rubbed raw, believing that these things he did would make the horses obey him and keep them from running away.

Granddaddy once had a mule that presented a great challenge in trying to break him. It seemed that no matter what he tried, the mule was going to prove to him that he had met his match. Nothing he could do would break it. In a rage, Granddaddy threw a pitchfork at its hindquarters. The mule laid its ears back and charged him. In a full sprint, the mule put its head down and knocked him twenty feet, if not more. Standing over Granddaddy, the mule looked down upon him as if daring him to return to his feet. One of Aunt Paige's sons, Bradley, was there and saw everything. I reckon it gave Bradley quite a scare as he thought that his Uncle Ohmer had just been killed. He ran to the house for help. When he found Granny working in the kitchen and singing a hymn, he told her what happened. Hardly daunted, she said, "Oh, Bradley, he'll be alright." Granddaddy laid there motionless for three hours before regaining consciousness and realizing that he was now all alone. Slowly rising to his feet, he gathered himself and tracked down the mule. He then led it over the hill, where he shot and killed it with his shotgun.

Granddaddy knew every inch of those mountains better than most and he could seemingly disappear anytime he wanted to. His elusiveness drove the revenuers crazy. Whenever they began to close in on him, he'd set up decoys to distract them. He'd blend into the countryside and they'd never find him or his stills. It wasn't until Revenuer Birckhead was brought in to get Granddaddy that he felt a real challenge. Birckhead knew that he could make a name for himself if he were the one to bring Granddaddy to justice. Granddaddy initially got the best of his arch nemesis numerous times. Birckhead began to take it personally, which, of course only made him even more determined to find Granddaddy's stills and shut down his operations once and for all. Agent Birckhead figured someone was tipping Granddaddy off, so he decided to keep his plans to himself even if it meant cutting out the local sheriff and offering a reward for information leading to Granddaddy's arrest.

One day Revenuer Birckhead caught up with Granddaddy and his cousin, James Berry in a harvest corn field. Poking around, he noticed a whiskey bottle near Granddaddy's mule. Birckhead ordered him to go over and get it so he could inspect it. Sneering,

Granddaddy said to him, "If you want it, you'll have to get it your own damned self." Birckhead's keen senses told him that something wasn't right. Outnumbered this time, he thought it wiser to back off and bid them good day before leaving. After Granddaddy was sure that Birckhead was out of hearing distance, he began to laugh and explained to James Berry that there wasn't anything but water in that bottle. He'd outsmarted Birckhead, but the revenuer didn't give Granddaddy the satisfaction of walking behind the mule only to be taken out by one swift kick. Granddaddy then revealed to James Berry the real stash was hidden under the corn stalk that his mule was straddling.

Knowing he was under the watchful eye of Revenuer Birckhead, Granddaddy sent his daughters, Suzie, Butter Roll, and Lillie into town to get the sugar for his still. Granny's strong objections fell on deaf ears and she realized that there was little if anything she could do about it. They took the horse and wagon down to Utz's store. All three went into the store and had the large sacks of sugar stacked on the wagon, as the sacks were too heavy for the girls to handle. Not far away, Birckhead noticed the girls taking the large order and decided to follow them. Later, when Granddaddy was in the middle of working his still, Birckhead came down on him, catching him red-handed this time.

Granddaddy was eventually convicted and sentenced to serve one year in jail. However, understanding his home situation, the judge allowed Granddaddy to go home on weekends. Before leaving, Granddaddy arranged for his nephew, John Beahm, to come and live with Granny during his absence. Just shy of one year, he was released and placed on three years' probation as assigned by the Honorable John Paul of Harrisonburg. Because his incarceration created such a hardship on the family, the local officers made a pact to never arrest Granddaddy again, choosing instead to bust up his stills whenever they were discovered.

As Revenuer Birckhead neared the end of his life, Momma ended up sitting with him and his wife until he died. Momma told me that she had discovered Birckhead's stash which consisted of several newspaper articles and photographs of his victory over Granddaddy. She also found some of Granddaddy's moonshine in Birckhead's basement. She never said anything to anyone else about it, but she did get a pretty good laugh over the irony of it all.

The mail was delivered on horseback in that region. One day, the carrier gathered up the mail, mounted his horse, and journeyed back into the mountains on his familiar trails as he had each and every day before. This time, however, he had a considerable amount of extra cash on his person. He'd been carrying it around everywhere he went and wasn't shy about boasting about it. Later in the day, his horse returned to town without him, the mail, and his cash. Granddaddy was the last person seen with him, but charges were never brought against him.

Years later, Granddaddy started to get a loose tongue and often times quite emotional after he'd been drinking. He'd cuss Revenuer Birckhead and blow his own horn about a large sum of money that he had buried under a sassafras tree. The story changed a little each time he told it. When Granddaddy told his son, Bullpuncher, that he had buried a large sum of money under a headstone in the hollow, his curiosity got the best of him. He couldn't wait to find that money. As soon as the opportunity presented itself, he went up on the hill above the house in the hollow to the small family cemetery there and proceeded to overturn every headstone until he found Granddaddy's buried money. Much to his dismay, his frantic search uncovered nothing but discouragement.

Never owning any of the properties they lived on, Granny and Granddaddy rarely stayed in one place very long. He preferred to live away from everyone else so he could be close to his stills. Fires forced them to move at least twice during their lives after the homes they were living in burned to the ground. Oddly enough, both occurrences took place when Granddaddy had been gone for days at a time on logging trips. On one of those occasions, Granny had just purchased a few hundred chickens. All perished in the fire. She always suspected that Granddaddy returned in the middle of the night, while everyone in the house was sleeping and set it ablaze. Momma, even though just a young girl, had been seen by her cousin, John, placing arms-full of straw under the house, earlier in the day. After everyone had gone to sleep, Granny awoke to the crashing noises of the ceiling falling down around her and managed to escape unharmed as Momma had gotten everyone else safely out of the house.

Momma left home at the young age of twelve and rarely came back to visit. She lived with friends and relatives who were willing to lend her a helping hand. Her absence created a void in the household, but she was missed primarily by her younger siblings. After the autumn leaves had fallen, you could see from the mountain, down to the road. Aunt Suzie and the other siblings would sit on the porch, watching the lights of the cars that traveled by in the far distance, all the while wondering when their sister, Sugarloaf was coming back home.

Aunt Paige paid a visit to Granddaddy one day and brought her son, Charles along. As they approached the house, the boy took off running, leaving his mom and dad behind to continue on their own along the rough dirt trail that cut through the hollow. As Charles neared the house in a sprint, he quickly scanned over the property, looking for Granddaddy. Running up, around the corner, Charles discovered his Uncle Ohmer sitting on the porch, intoxicated, and eating from a big jar of homemade sauerkraut. Like the scoop on the end of a crane, his huge fingers dipped into the jar, digging the sauerkraut out. Leaning back in his chair, he hoisted a handful up to his face, tilted his head back, and dropped the dangling glob into his wide-open mouth. Bent over and out of breath, Charles shattered the peacefulness that had blanketed the hollow, by blurting out, "How you doin', Uncle Ohmer?" Startled and nearly falling backward, Granddaddy choked on his sauerkraut.

Pleased to see his little nephew, he said in his gruff voice, "Gawd damn! I'm glad to see ya, Charles, but I think I'm gonna die." Baffled by his response, he asked his Uncle Ohmer why he would say such a thing. Now sucking the tips of his fingers and shaking his head, Granddaddy replied, "Charles, there's a damn chicken walking 'round here in the yard this morning. He looked up at me and said, 'How ya feel?'" As Charles smiled at his Uncle Ohmer, Aunt Paige came around the corner and they all went into the house where Granny welcomed them and fixed them something to eat.

Granddaddy on the porch.

II

THE HOLLOW

The white house in the hollow.

The 1950s marked a new beginning for Americans. It was post World War II, and the American dream was becoming a reality for millions across the nation. Harry Truman was President and a phenomenon known as the baby boom was creating a new generation unlike any before it. Sprawling tract housing began to replace wide, open spaces across the United States, including farmlands. Suburban lifestyles were becoming the norm.

For the isolated people of the Appalachian Mountains, life was very different than it was for the rest of America. For them, it was still a case of "only the strong survive." Physical strength was important, but emotional strength was equally important to survive what they had to endure. To the outside world, their ways would often appear quite brutal. In fact, their lives were simply ruled by "survival of the fittest."

Berry Mountain was located on the outer east bank of Virginia's Shenandoah Valley. The people who made that area home were as rich with pride as they were penny poor. They toiled daily, sunup to sundown, to eke out a meager existence. Some lived in small shacks, while others lived in comfortable homes. Most lived without running water and electricity. Their homes could be as small as one room. Some were log cabins with dirt floors, and others were wood framed structures as large as nine rooms and two stories high. None were ever far from a mountain stream. Fireplaces and stoves were used to heat the homes. Kerosene lanterns provided light after the sun went down. Walking was their primary mode of transportation. Horses were a luxury, with only one in three families having them. Even fewer owned cars or trucks, partly because they couldn't afford them, and mostly because the roads were primitive dirt roads at best. Because of the poor condition of the mountain roads, their economic and social conditions suffered. Neighbors could be miles apart; however, they were drawn together out of necessity. Their lifestyles changed very little, if at all, over the generations. They had their own way of doing things. They bothered no one, and they didn't want to be bothered by outsiders. These were God fearing people and thankful for what they had, while making the most of things no matter how miniscule.

On her own for a number of years now, Momma spent a lot of time with her second cousin, Haywood. They became very close during this time, as I would later learn. Nearing the end of his tour of duty in the army, his enlistment was abruptly extended. Before he knew it, he was driving tanks in South Korea, fighting in what would become known as the forgotten war.

With Haywood gone, I reckon Momma filled much of her time going to dances alone. That seemed to be a good place to yield to her promiscuous spirit that seemed to control much of her life. Like so many women of the time, Momma had an affinity for a man in uniform. Unfortunately, she didn't look far beyond the brass buttons into the character of the man inside the polish and shine. She was quite taken by one blonde, blue-eyed, five-foot eight, handsome man from Illinois the first time she laid eyes on him at a local dance. Gordon's shortcomings were disguised by his charm and the three stripes on the arm of his army green uniform. If it wasn't love at first sight, I reckon she most certainly believed that as a sergeant in the United States Army, he was quite capable of supporting her and a family. Their whirlwind courtship ended in marriage on the fourth day of March, 1950. An already pregnant Momma sat down and wrote Haywood with her exciting news.

Back on the mountain, with Momma gone, Kelly was now the oldest Jackson child living at home. With Granny's musical talent, he loved playing guitar and learned to play it well. Unfortunately, he contracted tuberculosis as a teenager, the same time his brother, Bullpuncher did. This disease put them both in the Charlottesville sanitorium where the two brothers, 16 and 11 years old, could be treated and stood a better chance of surviving the grave illness.

On the mend and back home, Kelly picked up his guitar one evening to play a few songs for Granny. She and Suzie were working in the kitchen as he sat behind the cook stove and strummed a few chords of his favorite song, *Tramp on the Street*. Granny closed her eyes and began to sway to the rhythm before turning to Kelly and telling him how pretty it sounded. She could hardly get the words out when a fury seemed to jump out from nowhere. Unable to play it the way he always had before, he swung the guitar over his shoulder and launched it across the kitchen. Slamming against the wall, the guitar fell to the floor, in pieces, held together only by its six strings as Kelly stormed out of the room. His tuberculosis grew worse and eventually took his life. On the day he died, Granny went from window to window throughout the house, pulling all the green shades down. Granddaddy mounted his horse and went to call on the Madison undertaker.

Pictured left to right: Butter Roll, Slicky, Ruby Lee, Suzie, Poke, and Bullpuncher.

Just before he was to go out on maneuvers, Haywood received the letter that Momma had written. Finding a quiet corner where he could have some privacy, he sat down and began reading it. He was struck by the news that she was pregnant and now married to a man she had met shortly after he left the states. Before having much time to reflect, Haywood was being called to his tank as his company was starting to roll out. It was on those maneuvers that the tank he was driving ran out of fuel in a very dangerous territory. Before supplies could reach them, they found themselves surrounded by the Chinese enemy. He and several others with him were captured and taken prisoner.

On October 30, 1950, I was born in Fort Belvoir, Virginia to Momma and Gordon.

When Gordon received orders to go to Germany, Momma and I remained stateside. I reckon living apart from Gordon and taking care of a toddler must have been a pretty lonely lifestyle for a married woman left behind. We moved in with Momma's good friend, Beulah. Momma managed to go out and party now and then while Beulah looked after me. It wasn't long before Momma found herself not only going to dances and having fun once again, but she also gave into her promiscuous desires.

Momma and I had been visiting with relatives in Indiana for a number of weeks when she decided it was time to return to Berry Mountain. The seclusion of the cabin provided a safe cocoon where only Granny, Granddaddy and a few of her sisters would be around. I wasn't quite three years old then and Momma had managed to keep a secret to herself and a very select few, including her friend and neighbor, Dot Schumaker. No one noticed, not even when she'd gone out dancing, that she was pregnant and ready to deliver at any time.

September 6, 1953, the day after one of those dances, she ran into the outhouse upon going into labor. Granny, Granddaddy, and Momma's younger siblings heard the commotion and went to her aid. Realizing she was in labor, they moved her into the house. Much to everyone's surprise, Momma gave birth to a baby boy. She was later taken to town where Doctor Roberts examined her and the baby, giving them both a clean bill of health.

❖   ❖   ❖   ❖

Dot's brother, Tom Schumaker

Living a few miles down the road, at the base of the mountain was Momma's good friend Dot Schumaker. Dot's younger brother, Tom was a sailor in Uncle Sam's Navy. He was conveniently stationed about two hundred miles away at the U.S. Naval Shipyard in Norfolk. He often went home on the weekends that he had leave. On one of those weekends, Dot told him that Momma had a newborn baby that she couldn't keep. He knew right away who he thought would be the perfect couple. Upon sharing this news with a shipmate and his wife, they became very excited. They loved children dearly and always wanted to have their own, but were unable to conceive after nine years of marriage. The childless couple thought their prayers had at long last been answered. They welcomed the opportunity to finally become the family they had always wanted to be. Without asking any questions, they eagerly agreed to take the baby.

Granny, not Momma, saw to the baby boy's needs initially and even lovingly called him Warner, her own father's name. As she rocked him in her arms, Granny began to get attached. Knowing that she wasn't going to keep him, Momma wouldn't allow herself to do the same. In fact, she didn't pay him much mind at all. Two weeks after delivering her second child, Momma bundled him in a blue blanket with matching cap. Granddaddy pleaded with her not to give her baby away. Her mind was made up and no one, especially Granddaddy, was going to change it. It was useless. All his pleading fell upon deaf ears. Knowing he had to say more to reach her, he blurted out, "Even animals don't give their young away!" As she began to make her way to the door, he told her that she would regret her decision for the rest of her life.

Opening the door, with her best friend and Beulah's sister, Virgie, at her side, Momma somberly walked out of the house and two miles down the dirt road to the base of the mountain. The rough, unpaved road was full of deep holes and large boulders. However, the dirt had begun to firm up in preparation for the cold winter ahead, making the walk a little less hazardous than what it might have otherwise been.

Virgie wanted to keep the boy, as Momma referred to him, but she didn't have the means. She felt her heart break as they got closer to the bottom of the mountain. In the clearing ahead was a car with a man and woman sitting anxiously inside. Virgie stopped a few yards away and watched Momma as she approached the waiting car. The childless couple sat nervously inside, unsure of what might actually happen. The woman sat on the passenger side of the front seat, peering through the window with a smile. Taking her last puff on her cigarette before putting it out in the ashtray, she rolled down the car window. Looking into Momma's eyes, she searched for any emotion that might be there.

Expressionless and without a single word, Momma handed the baby boy through the car window to the woman whose outstretched arms welcomed her new son. Thanking Momma with a smile, the woman held the baby lovingly with one arm against her chest. Reaching down with her other hand, she rolled the window up. The car then slowly drove away. Virgie watched as tears began to fill her eyes. Turning away, Momma, still without emotion, slapped her hands together with an up and down motion and said, "Well, that takes care of that!" She and Virgie solemnly walked back up the mountain road.

Very few people ever knew that Momma was pregnant and ended up having a baby in the seclusion of the cabin on Berry Mountain. It was a well guarded secret for many years as very little was ever said about that turn of events ever again.

Tensions were high on Berry Mountain, so Momma didn't stay much longer. Once back in Indiana with her cousin, life picked up where she left off about a month before. They were none the wiser about her pregnancy. A couple of weeks passed when she received news about

Haywood. After being held prisoner for thirty-three months, he had been released by the Chinese and was on his way home. Rushing to the bus station, Momma boarded the first bus back to Madison.

Arriving at the Jackson place on Berry Mountain at four o'clock in the morning, Haywood was just as anxious to see Momma as she was to be with him. Of course, Granny and Granddaddy were already up and the coffee was on the stove. Pleasantly surprised to see Haywood alive and well at her door, Granny welcomed him and his two buddies with a big hug and kiss before sitting them down at the table where she began to prepare them some hot home cooking.

I don't reckon Haywood was ever happier to be back home. When he asked Granny if she would mind fixing him some chitterlings, she gave him a broad beaming smile and fetched a quart and cooked them up for him and his buddies. She served them a feast fit for a king. It had been years since he had such a meal and they ate every last drop. Haywood was finally discharged shortly thereafter at nearby Fort Meade.

Some years later, wanting Granddaddy to be saved, a conspiring Aunt Suzie, Aunt Slicky, and Aunt Butter

Roll, along with Granny, dared Granddaddy to go to church with them one day. Much to their surprise, he accepted. They walked from the top of the mountain, all the way to the little rock church. Granddaddy and Granny walked not much more than arms length behind the girls. Along the way, the three of them began to cut up. Granddaddy leaned forward and popped them in the backs of their heads with his thumb, telling them that he'd pluck the thunder out of them if they didn't straighten up. Now marching like little soldiers, they walked the rest of the way without another word being spoken. He wasn't saved that day, but it didn't stop them from encouraging Granddaddy to go to church with them afterwards, to no avail.

None the wiser, upon returning home from Germany, everything appeared to be the same as Gordon left it. The three of us moved to the Washington D.C. area where we lived in a large white house. Aunt Butter Roll, came to stay with us for the summer. She helped all she could around the house, babysitting and doing many of the domestic chores.

One day, after locking the doors, Aunt Butter Roll began cleaning the floors. I had been playing outside and needed to come inside and use the bathroom. I reckon she believed that I was only making up an excuse to get into the house and mess up her clean floors. Ignoring me, she continued her chores. Balling up my fist, I drew back and rammed it through the window. Shattered glass, went everywhere, covering Aunt Butter Roll's clean floor. The real damage, however, came from one of the sharp edges as it sliced my thumb wide open.

Aunt Butter Roll opened the door and in I darted, straight to the bathroom. Getting on the phone, Aunt Butter Roll called Momma to tell her what had happened. Sparing no time to get home, Momma rushed me to the hospital. She stood at my side while the doctor stitched up my thumb and wrapped a bandage around it. After leaving the hospital, she took me out for a milkshake. No longer feeling any pain, I sat smugly with Momma in a booth, sipping my milkshake and thinking to myself how well it all had worked out.

Moving to Arlington, we found yet another large white house to live in—this one with large white columns in the front. Momma hired a babysitter to help out at home. Gertrude, an African American woman had a peculiar attraction to the boxwoods in the yard. I couldn't stand the very distinct odor they emitted. Digging up a handful of dirt from the boxwood, Gertrude forced me to eat it. I told Momma when she got home, but my story fell on deaf ears. I reckon Momma thought that I was just trying to get her in trouble.

When I discovered that my crayons were missing, I began searching the house for them. There was Gertrude, outside and bent over near one of the large, white columns. A closer look revealed that she was scribbling all over them with the missing crayons. When Momma came home, she immediately noticed the mess and began beating me without asking questions. After I stopped crying, she ordered me to go out and scrub the columns until I got them clean of all the marks. I scrubbed for hours, but no matter how hard or how long I scrubbed, I was never able to remove all the marks that Gertrude had made.

When I had to have my tonsils removed, Momma took me to the hospital where I was admitted the evening prior to my surgery. After I was placed in a big white metal crib, Momma left without ever saying a word to me. I screamed and cried, begging her to come back until I eventually cried myself to sleep that night, all alone.

Momma finally returned after the tonsillectomy, only to take me home.

I bounced around from household to household early in my life, living with Beulah, in Madison, my Uncle Levi in Philadelphia and even Granny's nephew, Johnnie Beeler, in Indiana. Uncle Levi loved me like his own daughter and wanted to adopt me, but Momma wouldn't hear of it. Eventually moving back in with Momma and Gordon, this would become the darkest period in my life.

Gordon's drinking became a problem and often preceded some serious physical fights between himself and Momma. Hearing a commotion in the bedroom upstairs, on one occasion, I rushed up to see what was going on. Stopping just outside the partially open bedroom door and peering through the crack, I saw Momma hit Gordon with a right cross. He staggered backward into the door, slamming it shut on my finger. The severed tip fell to the floor as I stood immediately outside the room, screaming at the top of my lungs as blood pulsated all over the door, the wall and the floor.

A dazed Gordon sat on the floor, his back against the door. Momma rushed to the door and pushed him aside. Opening the door, she grabbed me, and carried me down the stairs. As the blood continued to gush from my tiny finger, I went into shock before we reached the front door. Gordon had now regained his faculties and wasn't far behind, carrying my severed fingertip. After rushing me to the hospital Gordon was not happy to hear the doctor say that my finger couldn't be saved. Refusing to accept that prognosis, he and Momma took me to a second hospital. Much to his dismay, they were again told the same thing. Because it was my wedding ring finger, Gordon insisted that the finger be saved. A Chinese doctor in a third hospital gave them a glimmer of hope when he told them that he would sew it back on but couldn't guarantee that it would be successful. While my fingertip was saved, it has remained especially sensitive over the years.

I was only four years old when Momma became pregnant with her third child. A wolf in sheep's clothing, Gordon began to focus his predatory attention on me. The man who was supposed to be my father, my protector, one day reached out and offered me his hand. I gave him mine and he walked me downstairs to the unfinished basement. The emitting stench of liquor and cigarettes gagged me as I haplessly followed him. Once in the basement, he lifted me up and placed me on a bar stool. Placing his large hand on my leg, he slowly eased it up and under my dress. Too young to understand what was going on, my body nonetheless, began to tremble as I sensed that what he was doing wasn't right.

Softly touching the top of my panties, he closed his hands with his fingers now inside them. Sliding my panties down my legs, he discarded them to the floor. I was now exposed from my waist down. Gordon knelt on his knees, leaned forward, and put his face between my legs. Glancing up from time to time, he looked at me long enough to catch his breath and say repeatedly, "It's okay, I'm not going to hurt you." He then reached into his pocket, pulled out a stick of butter and removed it from its wax paper wrapping. Placing the butter between my legs, he rubbed it all over my now trembling body. Fear began to build as he again told me that he wasn't going to hurt me. Nothing he could say or do, at this point, could put me at ease. I knew it wasn't right and I was terrified even though I had no idea of what was about to happen next.

Reaching down, he proceeded to open his pants, now revealing himself to me. He looked larger than life as the terror completely overwhelmed me. He rubbed himself over the entire area that was now covered with butter. I began to whimper as he reached his arm around me so I couldn't pull away. Forcing himself upon me, he ripped me apart. The pain was so intense that I blacked out while he continued his assault.

After cleaning me up, he picked up my ravished, limp body and put my panties back on me before carrying me upstairs. He laid me down on the couch and quickly returned to the basement to clean up and dispose of all the evidence before Momma came home.

When I awoke, I was confused. My body felt as though it was on fire. My trust forever violated and sweet innocence destroyed. The monster responsible for it all sat nearby, staring at me as I shivered in unbearable pain. With an evil stare, he repeated, "You better not ever tell anybody." He continued talking, but I heard little more as I drifted in and out of consciousness. For days, I couldn't think. I could hardly speak and time seemed to stand still. Subsequently, when Momma left the house, Gordon would once again take me back downstairs to the unfinished basement, where an old mattress on the floor had now replaced the bar stool. As he painfully violated me, the stench of cigarettes and alcohol that made me sick to my stomach, became forever imbedded in my senses. It was there, in that unfinished basement that he continued his reign of terror on me for well over a year.

Nearly a year after Momma gave birth to Dinah, she was working at The Occidental, one of the area's premiere restaurants in Washington DC, checking coats and hats. One day, she greeted President Eisenhower and Vice President Nixon. Noticing her condition, Vice President Nixon struck up a conversation with her and eventually asked her if she would name her baby Darlene provided it turned out to be a girl. Not sure if he was serious, she was nevertheless flattered that someone as important as the Vice President of the United States would even strike up a casual conversation with her. He proceeded to write the name on a menu and autographed it before giving it to her. Momma not only kept that menu, she named her daughter Darlene the following July.

No longer living on Berry Mountain, Granny and Granddaddy had moved down into the hollow. The big white house, as we referred to it, was two stories and had plenty of room for the few remaining children and then some. This property was owned by Thornton Berry, who also owned and operated The Grill located on Madison's Main Street. Granddaddy bartered with Thornton by maintaining his property and mending fences for him instead of paying rent. Like the cabin, it too was well off the beaten path and very secluded.

After getting liquored up on his own shine, Granddaddy and his nephew, Roger, made their way into town where they decided to pay Thornton a visit at The Grill. Walking in as they joked and laughed, they bellied up to the counter where Thornton was working on the other side. I reckon Granddaddy had worked up quite an appetite. When he asked Thornton to fix him something to eat, Thornton asked him what he wanted. Granddaddy paused while looking the place over. He'd never been to a grill before and was a bit confused. Shrugging his shoulders, he said, "It don't matter. Just fix me som'm good to eat." Before Thornton could respond, Granddaddy said, "How 'bout fixin' me one of dem hamburgers?" When asked if he wanted lettuce and tomato on it, Granddaddy replied, "Yeah, fix it up like dat."

Thornton slapped a meat patty on the hot grill. As it sizzled, he sliced a tomato, and put some lettuce on the bread before serving it up nice and hot. Granddaddy ate it so fast that Thornton wasn't sure if he even tasted it. After the last bite, he slapped his big hands on his stomach. Rubbing them in a circular motion he said slowly, "Gray - ate day, Thornton! Dat's some kinda good eatin'. Fix me 'nuther one uh dem hamburgers and put me 'nuther hunk o'dat cabbage on it." With a snicker, Thornton began frying another hamburger just the way he'd fixed the first one.

Thornton (middle) talking with two regular customers at his lunch counter inside The Grill. Eddie DeJarnette (left) and Bill Hall (right). Photograph courtesy of Nan Coppedge.

The next time that we visited Granny in the hollow, she noticed something different about me, but couldn't quite put her finger on it. When Granddaddy called me a little whore, I noticed a difference in the way he looked at me. No longer was he just neglecting me. He was now offensive. I was too young to even understand what a whore was, but he usually only said such things whenever he was drunk. It wasn't until I became a teenager that

I would know the meaning of that word. From then on, I always believed that Granddaddy knew what Gordon had done to me and I believed that he blamed me for his violations.

It would be another year before we returned to the hollow again. I was 6 years old. Dinah and Darlene were much younger and still in diapers. By now, only four of Granny's children remained at home. Aunt Suzie, the oldest, was 16. Aunt Poke was the youngest at just 9 years of age. Between them, of course, were Aunt Ruby Lee and Aunt Butter Roll respectively.

When Momma asked Granny to watch us girls while she went to look for a bigger apartment for us to live in, Granny took us in with the understanding that it would be temporary. Even with only four of their own children still at home, Granny knew they couldn't support more than that on a long-term basis. Momma assured Granny that it wouldn't be more than a couple weeks before she'd be back for us. Momma then went back to Washington D.C. Two weeks came and went without any word from her. Weeks became months and still Momma hadn't returned or sent word.

We gradually began to feel more and more at home with Granny and Granddaddy. Having chores and responsibilities helped take my mind off of the fact that Momma hadn't come back for us. When Dinah and Darlene were old enough, they too became part of the family work force. No one just sat around doing nothing. Everyone got up early every day. It didn't matter if it was Monday or Sunday. If you were a Jackson, living in the Jackson household, you were up and at 'em first thing every morning.

Right after breakfast, Granddaddy plowed his garden. The rows of corn were extremely long and after plowing a row or two, he'd pull out a drawstring bag and sit down in the middle of the field for his cigarette break. He pulled his paper out, rolled a cigarette, and smoked it before continuing onto the next row. After the corn fields were done, Granddaddy's mule-driven plow split the earth, turning over potatoes on both sides along each row. The chore of picking the potatoes up, was ours. With buckets in hand, we followed closely behind, picking up the overturned potatoes and placing them into our buckets. The full buckets were then dumped into a wagon. If one of us missed picking up a potato, without ever turning around, he shouted out, "What'd you leave that one for?" Baffled, we always asked ourselves, "How did he know?" We actually believed that Granddaddy had eyes in the back of his head. The potatoes were stored in large bins, in the meat house, piled half way up the walls.

As time went by, Granddaddy began to demonstrate a tender and loving side. Something I had never seen before. Unfortunately, I was not the object of his affections. From the shadows across the room and behind the door, I stood unnoticed while watching the playful, loving ways that he exchanged with my two younger sisters. In the early morning hours, he rubbed their tiny feet before taking the two small pairs of socks from atop the wood stove and pulling them one at a time up over their feet as Dinah and Darlene played and giggled on Granddaddy's lap. I've wondered over the years if it was their blonde hair and cute little faces that he favored over my dark hair and protruding overbite that I thought made me less attractive in his eyes or maybe it was because he blamed me for Gordon's trespasses. All I really know for sure is that the only emotion I ever received from Granddaddy was contempt. I wanted -- yearned to feel the love from him that they got.

Because she didn't drive, someone always took Granny into Madison once a month to buy the staples, sugar and flour. What we couldn't eat fresh, Granny canned. She made soups that she jarred and stored in the closets. Aside from soups, she also made jams and jellies from bushels of peaches. Chickens provided eggs and, of course, when the chickens got to be about three pounds, they were perfect young fryers.

Whether it was preparing the food we ate, working in the garden, or milking the cows, we each had a chore that we were responsible for. The three of us girls hauled buckets of water to the house from the spring in the early morning hours, before going to school. I reckon we hauled so much water, that some days it seemed like all we ever did was haul water. After school, we pitched in by working in the garden.

Playtime was nearly nonexistent, unless it was after church on Sunday. We had to be very creative when entertaining ourselves. We dressed the chickens and pretended they were our baby dolls. During the fall, when the corn shocks decorated the fields, we always anticipated and enjoyed playing house in them before they were rounded up and stored to feed the cows during the winter months.

Being the tomboy, Dinah could be found much of the time climbing and jumping out of trees. She often played alone, spending hours playing in the dirt. Pretending that the small rocks were cars, she pushed them over the mounds of dirt that she had carefully molded into hills and roads for her rock cars to travel on.

At supper time we all sat down together. No one started eating before Granny said grace. Socializing at the table was forbidden. Granddaddy would pop any one of us girls on the forehead with his middle finger or the handle of his knife if we ever spoke while eating. Rare was the occasion that he didn't follow the thump on the head with a crude remark. At the end of each day, Granny always read stories from the Bible to us. After reading the stories, she made sure we said our prayers before tucking us in each and every night. After kissing us goodnight, she'd say, "I love you," making sure that each of us felt loved. As we began to feel like this was our home and Granny and Granddaddy had become our primary caregivers, it just seemed natural that we often referred to Granny as Mama.

After Gordon and Momma divorced, he would sometimes come down into the hollow to spend a few days visiting his daughters. During one of those visits, he tried unsuccessfully to get me alone with him. Later on when Granny needed some wood for the fire, she sent me to fetch some from the wood shed. Gordon heedlessly followed and attempted to grab me in the wood shed, where no one could see him. Throwing the wood down, I pulled away and ran as fast as I could back to the house. Running into the kitchen, I was short of breath and empty handed. Granny once again recognized that something was wrong, but she was no match for Gordon. It wasn't until years later however, when I confessed to her what he had done to me that she would know for sure what had happened. Granny assured me that some day, he would in fact be brought to his knees.

Ruby Lee was Granny's tenth child. A fragile little girl with the face of an angel, her hair was blonde and her eyes were as blue as the skies. She had but two passions; life and school. Because of her delicate condition, she received a great deal more attention than the rest of us children, which made me jealous. I was too young to understand how serious her condition truly was. I did, however, take turns with Aunt Poke, carrying Ruby Lee piggyback down the near-cut trail, to the road where we caught the school bus every morning.

Granny used home remedies to treat Ruby Lee's discomfort in the evenings. Granddaddy cut up an old army blanket and made a pouch to fill with onions that Granny cooked. They placed it on Ruby Lee's chest to help ease her painful and labored breathing. When it was no longer avoidable, she was driven to the doctor, in town. Thornton Berry always volunteered one of his employees, a very young man named Dan Simms, to drive Ruby Lee to town. Thornton was a very generous man who thought the world of the Jacksons. Always electing to ride in the back seat, Ruby Lee never felt comfortable around Dan. He was the only black person she had ever seen and she didn't know what to think about him. Dan couldn't have been more trustworthy and reliable. He started working for Thornton at a very young age and was driving for him as young as fourteen and continued working for Thornton most of his life.

One day, feeling a bit mischievous, Ruby Lee and I sneaked down to the outhouse and latched ourselves inside. We thought it would be fun to see how many cusswords we could count. Ruby Lee said the words while

I kept count. The list grew to more than one hundred as we began to feel rather comfortable and safe. Growing boisterous, we began to let our guard down, giggling and poking each other, as the count grew higher.

Suddenly, the door swung open and much to our surprise, there stood Granny with switch in hand. Larger than life, she stood and without saying a single word, she motioned us back to the house. With heads bowed, we stepped out of the outhouse and marched slowly back to the house as if it were our final mile. Granny followed immediately behind, every step of the way. Once inside, we stopped in the middle of the room where Granny proceeded to whip us both, where we stood, smacking our bottoms and legs with that keen switch of hers.

When Ruby Lee's health began to take a turn for the worse, her leukemia began to control every facet of her life as well as those around her. Thornton directed Dan to drive her, once again, to the hospital where she could be treated.

Whoever was first to spot a visitor coming up to the house, through the hollow, he or she was expected to let everyone else know that someone was coming. It was in June of 1960 when Thornton slowly made another journey back to the big white house. Spotting him first, I ran to let Granny know that he was on his way. She began to cry as she saw his silhouette slowly easing up the pathway to the house. This wasn't going to be a joyous visit by any means. It was with a heavy heart that he brought some very dreaded news. Clinching her fist, tears trickled down Granny's face as she cried out, "He's coming to tell us my baby's dead." Leukemia had taken Ruby Lee's life. She was only eleven years old.

Understanding how strapped Granny and Granddaddy were for money, Thornton and his wife, Nancy came to their rescue as they had so many times before, insisting on paying all of Ruby Lee's funeral expenses. Thornton also made sure that she had a beautiful new blue dress to be buried in. Granny took the death hardest of all. During the funeral service, she broke down and tried to crawl into the casket with her baby girl, only to be restrained by friends and family around her.

Standing in the back are Suzie, Vince, and Butter Roll. In the front, are Poke, myself, and Ruby Lee with Granddaddy standing in the foreground.

❖　❖　❖　❖

Momma

As a little girl, I had always looked up to Momma. I thought that she was the most beautiful woman I'd ever seen. Her clothes were always stylish and fit flawlessly on her perfect frame. With never a hair out of place, she was always freshly manicured and pedicured. When I told Granny how I admired her, she grimaced but never said a dispiriting word about her. A rift had occurred between Granny and Momma sometime during their lives and it was never forgotten by either of them. Momma didn't forgive easily. Granny loved all her children the same and did everything she could for Momma and all three of us girls, but Momma was hard and never expressed any gratitude or did anything to help Granny and Granddaddy financially, especially where we girls were concerned.

When Momma came by to visit, she always came by unannounced and never stayed more than a few hours at a time. I was always thrilled to see her even if it was just once a year. Sometimes, she would come alone but many times she would bring her friends Grace and her husband Vince. They loved Granny and Granddaddy and even came all the way from their home in Maryland without Momma just to visit. It was during that time that Momma met Clyde Farley, a man who worked for the Washington Post as a printer. Preferring to be called CB, he and Momma eventually married. She was never completely honest with him as she kept the three of us girls a secret from him right from the beginning while living many miles away from us.

We had been living with Granny and Granddaddy in the hollow for three years when Grace came with news about Momma. Waiting until she thought I wasn't around, she told Granny that Momma was pregnant. Within hearing distance, in the next room, I heard what she said and became so upset that I blurted out that she didn't know what she was talking about because my Momma was *not* pregnant! Knowing nothing about CB at the time, I was sure Momma would never get pregnant out of wedlock.

left to right: Dinah, Jeanette, and Darlene

❖ ❖ ❖ ❖

I remember feeling ashamed for the way we lived even though I have no doubt that Granddaddy did the best he could for all of us. I reckon that some of that shame was due much to the way we were treated by some of the kids at school who were better off than we were. Our clothes were always homemade and hand-me-downs. We had to do the best we could with what we had. Rainy days made things even more embarrassing because we didn't have rain gear. When the weather was forbidding, I would leave the house wearing plastic window curtains to keep dry until arriving at the bus stop. Before the bus arrived, I removed the plastic curtain and stuffed it into a hollowed out log to avoid being teased.

Our neighbor, Alice made us wraparound skirts and although they often looked nicer than the hand-me-downs, I was still embarrassed at school where all the other kids wore stylish, store-bought clothes. The day I wore a dress cut above the knees, the school principal pulled me from one of my classes. Taking me home, she proceeded to tell Granny and Granddaddy that my dress was too short for school activities.

Her words and attitude didn't set well with Granddaddy. He cut her off and probably would have jumped down her throat if he could. "If you don't approve of what she's wearing," he said, "then, by gawd, you shouldn't have any problems buying her some suitable damned clothes. Until then, she'll be wearing the clothes she has." Turning around, the principal took me back to school. I don't recall her saying another word, but I reckon she had plenty running through her mind. I couldn't help but laugh about it later as these visuals of this very large woman with hips large enough, I swear, to set a 5-gallon bucket of water on, rolled and waddled over the near-cut path, cursing under her breath the entire way, ran through my mind for a long time after.

While visiting Alice and her husband, Stewart one day, I was browsing through their Sears-Roebuck catalogue when I saw a seven dollar dress that I really liked. I had never bought a dress before, so this came with an extra shot of pride and independence as I was able to do so with my own hard earned money I had earned from berries I had picked and sold.

Each of us girls received just one pair of shoes that had to last us throughout the school year. That wasn't always easy considering all the walking we did. When I showed Granny where the soles of my shoes had separated from the upper leathers one Thursday evening after school, Granddaddy had me go to the wood shed and bring him the pig pliers and pig rings. When I returned with his tools, he said, "Now, give me that damn shoe!" and proceeded to clamp the pig rings all the way around it. Handing it back with a quirky smile, he said, "Now you'll go to that damned school or I'll beat you every damned inch of the way."

The next morning, looking silly in my pig ring shoes, humiliated and on the verge of tears, I hugged Granny and said good-bye. She whispered in my ear, "Go to Alice's and ask her if you can stay with her the rest of the day."

"There *is* a merciful God!" I thought to myself. With the biggest smile on my face, I thanked her and turned around and went on my merry way, thrilled that I didn't have to face another embarrassing day at school trying to explain those ridiculous pig rings in my shoes.

The following day was even better as Stewart walked me across the mountain to buy me a new pair of shoes. On our way back, he bought a half gallon of ice cream. Stopping on top of the mountain, we both sat and ate every last drop before continuing home.

Darlene, one year younger than Dinah, was the curious and cantankerous sister. One day, when Granny had to kill one of the chickens for supper, she decided to step up and volunteer for the duty. After catching the chicken, she took it to the henhouse, stuck its head between the door and the door jamb, and slammed it shut, killing the chicken.

Granny often kept a pot of boiling water in the kitchen that was used primarily for washing the white clothes. One day, while her favorite rooster was strutting about in the yard, without provocation, it jumped up and attacked Darlene. After fending it off, she marched into the house, got that pot of boiling water from the stove, went back out into the yard and doused the rooster. While she survived the rooster's attack, the rooster wasn't as fortunate and even though Granny got very upset, Darlene managed to escape her wrath and the rooster was consequently served for supper that evening.

While Granny loved all us girls equally, just as though we were her own children, I reckon Granddaddy was most abusive after he'd been drinking. He never treated me the same loving way he treated Dinah and Darlene, drinking or not. Always trying to make up for his shortcomings, Granny tried her best to be my guardian angel when he overindulged in his shine. He showered Dinah and Darlene with his love and affection while I got nothing but neglect and sometimes abuse from him. I never knew why I was the one he mistreated and abused, but Granny believed that it was because of who he thought my father was. He never believed that Gordon was my biological father.

His verbal abuse would eventually become physical, treating me much the same way he had treated Momma as a child I reckon. For instance, the time I was helping Granddaddy in the barn, he snapped at me because I didn't do something exactly the way he told me to do it. I sassed him and he picked up a horse bridal and swung it at me without regard as to where it struck. With my abdomen slashed wide open, I frantically ran out of the barn and up to the house, terrified and bleeding profusely from the gaping wound. Nearly scared to death,

I showed Granny my wound. She told me, "Honey, run to the hen house and get me a handful of cobwebs." Bewildered, there wasn't time for questions and answers so I immediately ran to the hen house as fast as my feet would carry me. Grabbing a handful of cobwebs, I ran back to the house, and handed it to Granny. She stuffed them into my wound, stopping the bleeding within seconds. Go figure! Today we use sterile bandages and band aids.

Another time when I was sitting on the mill chest in the kitchen and sassed Granddaddy once again. Without warning, he leaned over, picked up a piece of firewood from the pile next to the kitchen stove. Rearing back, he swung it around like a tennis racket, hitting me on the side of my head. Hearing the cracking sound at the opposite end of the house, an alarmed Granny came running into the room and asked Granddaddy what happened. He said, "That little whore will never talk to me or anyone else like that ever again." The damaging effects of that blow would last a lifetime as I lost the hearing on that side.

Granddaddy was very prudent when he went to market to bid on hogs. Before the auction began, he would look them all over very closely, keeping track of the less desirable hogs. He knew he could get them for less than the other hogs. As soon as he brought them home, he began marking the boars. It wasn't an easy task, and he always relied on us girls for help. Even though Dinah was older than Darlene, Granddaddy knew he could depend on Darlene to be the biggest help when it came to that particular chore. Looking for Darlene, Granddaddy found her behind the barn cutting up bugs and picking them apart. Asking her why she was doing that, Darlene said that she wanted to know what they looked like on the inside. He told her to never mind that, he needed her help marking some hogs. Dropping everything, she nearly beat him there.

Instructing Darlene to grab the pig by the mouth, Granddaddy demonstrated with his fist as he held it up to his own mouth as if to blow into it. As she grabbed the pig by the snout, the pig clamped down on her three little fingers. A startled Darlene screamed out, "He's biting me, he's biting me!"

Growling back, he said, "That pig ain't biting you!" Almost as fast as he said it, he noticed that the pig did in fact, have her fingers locked in its mouth. Reaching for the first thing available, he grabbed a nearby hammer and swung it down onto the pig's snout. As soon as the pig collapsed, Darlene jerked away, freeing her fingers. Standing defiantly and rubbing her throbbing hand, she never shed a tear. After all, her injuries were minor compared to the ones suffered by the pig. Granny came out and took over for Darlene while she nursed her wounds until all the hogs had been marked that day.

While Thanksgiving in the hollow was an annual tradition, we celebrated a bit differently in the hollow. There was no turkey, no dressing, no cranberries, and no mashed potatoes and gravy. We didn't have pumpkin pie or anything else that resembled the typical Thanksgiving feast, except for the gathering of family, I reckon. In the hollow, we spent that day and the entire weekend slaughtering hogs. All the aunts and uncles came to chip in. The cool and often brisk temperatures of the season made it ideal for such an occasion.

Dinah, Darlene, and I got up bright and early on Thanksgiving mornings. Making several trips, we hauled buckets of water from the spring to a large metal tub where Granddaddy boiled the water over an open fire. When the water was scalding hot, someone would shoot the pig in the head. Granddaddy cut its throat, and bled it out before placing it in the scalding hot water. Mason jar lids were then used to scrape off the hair before the pig was hung up by its rear feet on a horizontal pole.

These poles were strong enough to support three or four 350-pound hogs. At this point, the belly was cut open and the hog was then gutted out. One particular year, Granddaddy brought out a pig, and I don't recollect who it was, but someone said, "Not that one, that sow's with pigs."

Rolling his eyes, Granddaddy said, "No, it ain't! That sow's not with pigs," at which point, he pulled the trigger on his .22 and shot the pig, point blank. When they split it open, out fell the sack, containing eight baby pigs. It was hard to tell if Granddaddy was more embarrassed or saddened by the fact that he hadn't listened, but there was nothing he could do about it now. The sack of baby pigs was thrown over a hill and everyone continued butchering the sow. Everyone, that is, except for Darlene. She scrambled over the hill and proceeded to cut the unborn piglets from the sack and cut them apart as if they were a science project.

The entire process of butchering hogs grieved Dinah right from the pull of the trigger. She always ran into the house and hid and it was Darlene who usually went looking for her. It didn't take much detective work as Dinah usually hid under her bed. After pulling her out from her hiding place, Darlene would comment on how she thought that Dinah was such a chicken and they would then return to help the rest of the family. I reckon that it was easier on Dinah if she didn't have to witness the initial killing of the hogs. While the men spent the entire day butchering hogs, Granny spent the day cooking tenderloin, liver, and batter cakes for everyone to eat as they got hungry.

After the hogs were butchered, the three of us girls carried as much as we could tote back to the house, where we helped Granny make the hog pudding, sausage, and lard. One year, Coleman Clore decided to bring his Coleman lantern to use for light after it got dark. When he hung it from the ceiling, everyone was amazed at how much brighter the entire room got. Providing a great deal more light than the oil lamps did, we no longer had to strain our eyes to see what we were doing as we all worked late into the night, making sausage and hog pudding and trimming the fat from the chitterlings.

Granny always kept a small batch of strings nearby for this chore in case one of the chitterlings was accidentally punctured. Occasionally, a knife would slip and puncture an intestine. As the contents would begin to escape, she would tie it off with one of the strings she had set aside.

Cousin Kevin, Aunt Butter Roll's son, was your average curious ten year old little boy. Picking up a stick, he began poking at one of the pig bladders. Granddaddy told him not to be playing around with that thing, but he paid his granddaddy little mind. Continuing to poke and prod at the bladder, he jabbed it one too many times causing it to burst, spraying its contents all over himself. Granddaddy looked over at Kevin who was standing there soaked and stinking to high heaven from pig urine. Shaking his head, Granddaddy said, "I tole you not to be playing 'round with that thang."

The day after the hogs were butchered, we girls would take the chitterlings down to the stream where we cut them open and cleaned them out. Totally exhausted by this point, we didn't bother to recover any that slipped away and drifted downstream. Back at the house, we helped with cutting up the fat and putting it in a large cast-iron pot, where it was boiled until liquefied then used for lard and lye soap to wash our clothes and dishes. This was Dinah's favorite part of the day. She loved grinding up the solid internal organs including the liver and heart in the meat grinder to make hog pudding. After all the work was done, we collapsed. Granddaddy celebrated by getting drunk, of course.

The following spring, Granddaddy put on a shooting match. The winners received pork shoulders and hams that were left over from the autumn slaughter. After the shooting match was over, the men gathered in the corn crib, drinking liquor and playing poker until dawn. Dinah, Darlene, and I crawled under the floor before it got dark and waited to catch any money that fell through the cracks of the floor.

I reckon that Dinah was probably Granddaddy's favorite of the three of us granddaughters. She was the one he took with him to do his logging, but only when it was convenient. It gave her something to do when she wasn't in school and she loved going because she got to ride bareback with Granddaddy into the woods. Before she was big enough to help, Granddaddy always made her stand back in a safe area and watch while he felled the trees. Too young to understand that her granddaddy was a seasoned logger, she always feared for his safety, believing that he wouldn't know which way the tree was going to fall and that it might come down and kill him.

Before making his first cut, he walked around the tree, sizing it up and estimating its length and determining where it would fall, causing the least amount of damage. When she was old enough, Dinah began helping Granddaddy split the logs. At the end of the day, they loaded the wood and hauled it back home. When they got back home, it was her responsibility to remove the harnesses from the horse and feed it. Darlene, of course, always stayed home with Granny and helped her with the domestic chores that included cooking and canning.

I don't have many memories of the time when Granny didn't have problems with her left foot. The one vivid memory I do have is from one morning when she woke me up because she couldn't walk on her foot any longer. She asked me to make breakfast for Dinah and Darlene because she could no longer walk on her foot because it hurt so badly. She walked on the ball of her foot all those years, limping until she couldn't go any more. It was then that the doctor inserted a 2 inch plastic leader into her heal that eliminated the need for the built up shoe she wore. It was now replaced by a brace that kept her foot straight.

Nothing kept her from working in the garden, not even that brace on her leg. She worked for hours at a time in her garden and when anyone came to visit, they never left without receiving a generous helping of her garden-fresh vegetables to take home with them. Of course, no visit was complete without a glass of cold lemonade and a healthy sum of ministry. She always shared her faith with everyone -- family, friends, and strangers alike.

Granny's was a total faith in the Lord and his teachings. One of the first things you'd notice upon entering her home was the presence of religious posters throughout the house as well as religious booklets that she insisted everyone take and study.

I reckon that if Granddaddy had a religion, it would have been his liquor and there was usually plenty on hand. When he started drinking, we girls knew to steer clear. Granddaddy could go weeks without a drop, but when he did drink, it wasn't unusual for him to go on a binge, staying drunk for days and sometimes weeks at a time. In a drunken stupor, he'd sometimes lie on the floor for days, never getting up, not even to use the bathroom. Being the angel that she was, Granny always did whatever was necessary to take care of him, including cleaning him up whenever he messed on himself. He'd sometimes stumble around in his birthday suit and she'd fuss at him. "Cover up your nakedness with those dear little grandbabies around," she'd say. But Granddaddy was stubborn and no one was going to tell him what to do.

Sometimes he'd yell to her from a different room in the house, "Ev'lyn, I gotta piss! Ev'lyn, you gonna breng me that bucket?" Rarely did she deny him. Doing whatever she had to do, you might hear her say something like,

"Oh, good golly!" knowing if she didn't do as he demanded, he'd do exactly what he threatened to do.

Granddaddy's drinking binges terrified us girls. I reckon they seemed more terrifying to us than to Granny, or maybe she was just better at concealing her fears. I don't rightly know. There were always telltale signs in his appearance that alerted us of an impending drinking binge. His eyebrows would stand straight up on his forehead, giving him a maddened look. When those physical changes began to show, we knew that it wouldn't be long before he'd disappear and return drunk and often violent. If he returned to find us working in the fields, he'd often hide and throw rocks at us until we took off running, at which point, he'd chase us until he could run no more. I reckon once the chase was over, it wasn't fun for him anymore and he just stopped.

We always ended up hiding either in the barn or in the woods. The weather was usually the determining factor. Never knowing when or where he might strike, we sometimes slept with our clothes on and shoes next to the bed in case it happened in the middle of the night. It was always the same scenario. He'd run us out of the house and into the snow, laughing madly all the way as Granddaddy seemed to take a vicious pleasure in carrying on in a menacing manner.

I reckon the most terrifying time in the hollow was the first time I witnessed, as a little girl, Granddaddy going out of his mind after getting drunk on his own liquor. His condition lasted several days and nights. Granny made sure we went to bed with our clothes on and our shoes right handy in case we had to run from the house during the night. Still in a drunken daze, Granddaddy began to hallucinate, envisioning snakes slithering all over the floors and ceiling, rats crawling in and around jars on the counters and in the cabinets. Out of his mind, he grabbed a broom and beat the stove pipe, shouting at the top of his lungs, "I'm gonna kill that nigger!"

The noise woke me up and I went looking for Granny, knowing something terrible was about to happen. Shouting at the top of his lungs, he began searching the house for Granny. Finding her with me in the living room, he ordered her to sit in the chair near the window. "Don't move until I come back from the wood shed," he demanded.

She was prepared to stand up against him this time, or so she thought. I felt that I had to get her out of there. I told her that Granddaddy was going to hurt her if she was still there when he came back. Crying and pleading with Granny, I said, "I just know he's going to hurt you. Please, let's leave."

With a sigh, Granny said, "Okay, maybe it's time." Looking out the window, I saw Granddaddy returning to the house with both hands inside his bib overalls as if he were hiding something. Granny, Dinah, and Darlene ran out of the house and into the barn. I stayed behind.

Granddaddy stormed back into the house. Not far away, I was hiding under the kitchen table. He was close enough that I could smell that strong stench of cigarettes and alcohol that reminded me of Gordon and made me feel sick to my stomach. Lifting his hand upward, he pulled a large, rusty crowbar from his bib overalls. Raising it high above his head, he paused to focus on the now empty chair, realizing that Granny was no longer there. Now, even more enraged, cussing and threatening to kill her, he began once again to search the house for her. When I was sure that it was safe, I ran from the house to the barn where I told Granny what I had seen.

Holding me in her arms, Granny admitted, "Well, it's time we get help." Picking up the lantern, she took the three of us on a trek to safety. As it started to get dark, we arrived at Alice's house. Granny, still strong, told her what had happened. Volunteering to keep Dinah and Darlene with her, Alice closed the door and locked it from the inside before turning the lights off throughout the house.

Granny and I continued walking for miles, past the old school house and over the mountain to Aunt Suzie and Uncle Ralph's place. The sounds of the animals and the night's darkness frightened me as we journeyed into the darkness. Granny prayed out loud every step of the way. "Lord, give me the strength to get there," she said. It was a miracle that Granny walked all that way with her braced, crippled leg. Not quite ten years old, I was petrified and made the trek with my eyes closed, stumbling over rocks and twigs while tightly holding onto Granny's hand the entire way.

Hearing a commotion, Aunt Suzie and Uncle Ralph opened the door and stepped out onto the porch. There they saw Granny and I coming up the path. Aunt Suzie asked Granny, "What in the world is going on?" After Granny explained what Granddaddy had done, we all got into Uncle Ralph's car and we were on our way to get Uncle Bullpuncher before going to get the Madison police.

The Sheriff and three deputies followed us back into the dark woods, to the house in the hollow, only to find it vacated. By that time, Granddaddy had made his way to Alice's place. I reckon he thought no one was home because how dark it was inside so he wandered farther down the road until he got to Dot and Fred's place. Describing a horrific scene, "There's blood everywhere," he said, "call the sheriff 'cause somebody slaughtered all of Thornton's cows." Recognizing that Granddaddy was drunk, they were also alarmed by what he had shared. Granddaddy turned away and continued back out into the darkness as Dot and Fred went back into the house.

In the woods, Uncle Bullpuncher, Uncle Ralph, and the police eventually caught up with Granddaddy who was carrying a fence rail and shouting that he was going to kill Granny. It took everything that those six men could muster to restrain him. His eyes were radiant green as he fought back with the strength of a mule. Finally restraining him, they took him to the sanitarium in Staunton where he was kept for observation before being committed for several months.

When Granny, Dinah, Darlene and I returned to the house in the light of day, we found many of the windows had been broken out. The house was cold throughout and the four of us had no way of fixing the heavy damages left by Granddaddy's fit of rage. Upon learning what had happened, the church helped by bringing us warm clothes, quilts, and food. We stuffed the quilts into the windows to keep the cold air out. While the essentials had been provided by the church, we were on our own to perform all the work that needed to be done around the house.

As the oldest sister, I assumed Granddaddy's chores. Getting up early every morning, I plowed the garden and did the other jobs that Dinah and Darlene were too small and young to do. I reckon that of all the chores I took on, having to buckle the strap underneath the horse is the one thing that terrified me most. I never knew what that horse might do. Granny always reassured me by saying, "Don't worry, honey. Just do the best you can."

The doctors told Granny that Granddaddy might relapse after only a single drink or he could drink the rest of his life without incident. I reckon that the possibility of Granddaddy relapsing after only a single drink, worried me to no end. As it turned out, Granddaddy remained alcohol free for a couple of years before giving in to the overwhelming desire. I became hysterical, remembering the horrific night of years before. Granny uncharacteristically slapped me to try and bring me out of it. After she got me calmed down, she promised me that everything was going to be fine.

As time passed, we sisters began to grow up and figure things out. Dinah began to realize that Momma had left us high and dry with Granny and Granddaddy in the hollow. She also recognized the increased hardship that we all had to endure because of Momma. Dinah began to speak out, expressing her feelings pretty freely until one day Granny pulled her aside and told her that Momma was her mother and she needed to love her no matter what. Dinah tried to explain why she thought the way she did, but Granny wouldn't hear of it, demanding, "She's still your mother. You love her no matter what!"

Granny never judged anyone, regardless of the circumstances, even when Granddaddy got into some trouble with another woman. Having no place to go, that pregnant woman was taken in by Granny. She gave her a place to stay until she had Granddaddy's baby. Knowing what had happened, Granny's heart was larger than life. After the baby was born, the woman thanked Granny for her kindness before leaving and I don't reckon she ever heard from her again.

The house in the hollow as it stands in 2009.

One day, down by the mailbox, Alice and I were talking when she said, "You know that Gordon is not your daddy, don't you?" You could have knocked me over with a feather as she continued, "He couldn't be. Your mamma didn't know him long enough to be your daddy."

Needing to know more, I asked her, "Well, who is?"

"I just know that Gordon's not your daddy," Alice replied. I had never done the math before and if what she said was true, there now was more than the age difference that separated me from Dinah and Darlene. Even though we shared the same last name, my paternity was now in doubt.

The sixties was a decade of an escalating war in Southeast Asia, social revolution, and counterculture in the United States. Civil rights and communism were the primary concerns that affected the day-to-day lives of the average American. The decade was further darkened by political assassinations but brightened by what became known as the greatest decade for popular music.

I remember receiving a toy piano for Christmas one year. Granny taught me how to play it with just one finger. I learned two songs, hymns that were often sang in church. It wouldn't be until years later that I would truly develop an interest in music, but it wouldn't be as a musician.

Granny and Granddaddy had a transistor radio that they used primarily for listening to the weather reports and sometimes the obituaries. He didn't allow it to be used for anything else. That didn't stop me, however when one night I decided to sneak the radio upstairs at bedtime. Once in bed, I turned it on and turned the small dial on the face of the radio. After dialing through a number of radio stations, I found one that was playing music that caught my ear. Even though the sound coming out of the small speaker was tinny at best, I wasn't distracted or discourage in the least. As the moving rhythm began to overcome me, I started to feel an energy that I had never felt before. Moving from head to toe, my feet started tapping to the beat and before I knew it, I was dancing to the soulful sounds of singers like Mary Wells and Marvin Gaye. I reckon Junior Walker became one of my favorites. It wasn't long before Dinah and Darlene had joined me, out of our bed and dancing directly above Granny and Granddaddy.

Hearing the commotion overhead and having no idea that we had Granny's transistor radio, Granddaddy started hollering from the bottom of the stairs, "How 'bout I come up thar and whip yo little asses with mah stick?" Jumping immediately back into the bed, we snickered for a while, knowing that we had pulled one over Granddaddy before settling down and eventually falling to sleep.

When we returned to school after summer vacation, everyone was talking about a new television show called *The Beverly Hillbillies*. I had no idea what they were talking about. It did, however, pique my interest and upon learning more about the show's characters, I began to relate the Granny character to my own Granny. She seemed to be so much like my Granny that I began calling her Granny from that point on. It seemed to fit and it caught on until everyone was calling her Granny.

At the age of twelve and riding the school bus home one day, Dot's much younger brother, Billy, sat down next to me. I reckon he was pretty anxious because when he was no longer able to contain himself, he told me that I had a brother out there somewhere. Now, really! I brushed him off, believing that he was just spewing nonsense and making up some kind of silly joke at my expense.

When the school bus arrived at the mailbox, I stepped out and onto the side of the road. Pausing as the school bus door closed behind me, I watched as it drove away and stood there pondering what Billy had said. A few minutes later, I shrugged my shoulders and began my one mile hike through the hollow. Billy's words continued to work on me. The closer I got to the house, the more my curiosity grew. When I finally reached home, I told Granny what Billy had said. I knew that she would tell me the truth if I asked her about it.

I reckon she knew that this day would eventually come. As she drew a deep breath, Granny released a long sigh. With a tear in her eye, she told me that I did indeed have a younger brother. She also said that Momma had given him away to strangers when he was less than two weeks old, "and that's all I know about it," she said.

Satisfied, if only for the moment, I went about my chores. As time passed, however, I began to think more about him. I wondered where he was and what he looked like. As I began to dwell on it, it created a dissatisfaction and void that would trouble me for years to come. I often found myself wondering if he was alright and whether or not he needed me. No matter how many times I tried to put those thoughts aside, they always managed to return and press on my mind.

As a young teenager, I began to spend some of my weekends at my Aunt Eliza's house with my cousins Joan, Polly and their younger brother, Buzz. They didn't have running water in the house either, but they did have a well on the porch and electricity. I reckon that the biggest attraction for me was the fact that they had a television. Like so many other teenagers at the time, our favorite television show was *American Bandstand*. Dick Clark played current hit records as the teenage studio audience danced to the music and Joan, and I joined in at home. When the program was over, we were still so excited that we would teach each other the dance steps we saw those kids on TV doing. The Mashed Potato quickly became our all-time favorite dance step.

One day, Granddaddy and a friend had been drinking. Too drunk to walk back home, his friend gave him a ride to the mailbox where he was dropped off and left there to make his own way back into the hollow. Stumbling all along the way, he managed to get most of the way back to the house before tripping and falling one final time. Unable to get back up, he remained there next to the creek while hollering up to the house. Hearing his cries for help, Granny asked me to go down and figure out a way to get him back so he wouldn't freeze to death. As a young teenager, I resented having to take care of him. After all, he had never done anything for me. Unable to say no to Granny, I stewed about it all the way down to the creek, near Alice's house.

Standing over Granddaddy, I wondered how I was going to get this big hulking man back to the house when all of sudden it occurred to me. This was the perfect opportunity to make him pay for all he'd done to me in the past. Turning him face down, I grabbed a' hold to his arm and dragged him all the way back to the house. I blissfully pulled him through every obstacle on the way including water, ice, rocks, and sticks I could find. While it took every last bit of strength I had, Granddaddy got pretty beat up. Every muscle in my body ached the following morning, but it was Granddaddy who seemed to be suffering the worst. As he tended to his bruises and wounds, I heard him say, "Gre-at day, I'd like to git my hands on that som'bitch that beat me up so bad last night." My pain seemed to melt away as a newly found sense of vengeance calmed me. Sitting quietly, I laughed to myself at the thought of my big, bad, granddaddy thinking it was a man who had beaten him. The icing on the cake was the fact that Granny stood quietly, smiling and never let on that she knew who was responsible.

After recovering, Granddaddy got drunk again and cornered Granny in the kitchen, behind the stove. Bracing himself against the wood box, he started kicking her crippled leg. I couldn't just stand by and let her take such a beating. Intervening, I tried to pull him off of her. Throwing his arm up into the air, Granddaddy bounced me to the floor like a ball in a pinball machine. I reckon I may have had the upper hand when he was passed out, but I was definitely no match for his strength otherwise.

There was a time, I recall, when Momma got the best of him. After kicking Granny back into the corner of the kitchen, he grabbed her by the neck and began choking her. Momma grabbed a piece of wood from the wood box and struck him on the back of his head, knocking him unconscious and saving Granny from what might have been a much worse fate.

Granny's life evolved around the church, scripture, and her family, but not necessarily in that order. It's hard to tell which she held higher. Images of the Lord were always prominently displayed throughout the house. She read the Bible to us every day and we loved hearing the stories much to the dismay of our granddaddy, who wasn't shy about voicing his objections. One day, he demanded that she stop reading to us from the Bible and discontinue her church activities. I reckon his demands fell upon deaf ears as Granny never curtailed her church activities or Bible studies, not even for the likes of Granddaddy. I reckon he thought he'd get even with her by hiding her Bible from her. It remained hidden for two weeks until Dinah or Darlene found it in an old iron pot hanging on the side of the meat house.

Granny also loved taking us to church every Sunday morning. Walking down the near cut path until we reached the mailbox, we waited there until the preacher picked us up in a van-like vehicle. Upon boarding the tiny bus, the preacher put it in gear and drove us to the worship services. Revivals were also an important part of Granny's life. She not only attended the week-long events when they came to town, she actively participated in the service by playing her harmonica whenever song broke out.

After each daily session ended, Granny walked us through the rough terrain of the hollow, back up to the house in the dark with just a kerosene lantern in hand easily taking thirty minutes or more to walk from the mailbox back to the house. Uncle Delmar sometimes gave us a ride back in his car, but the road was so rough beyond the mailbox, he would have to park it and walk us the rest of the way.

One night, a bull saw the lantern and began to charge it. Uncle Delmar got between us and the bull and when the bull got close enough, he kicked it as hard as he could. That not only threw the bull off track, but discouraged him from ever charging again. This trek at night was rather scary even though we knew the route as well as we knew the backs of our hands. An undeterred Granny always assured us that the good Lord would take care of us all.

One day while CB was at work, Momma told a five-year-old Cheryl that she was taking her to visit her sisters. Looking at Momma like she had two heads, Cheryl thought to herself, "Are you crazy? Susan's in the crib. We're all here. Who would we be going to see?" Until then, she knew nothing about her extended family. They left the house and boarded a Virginia-bound bus. It was a long journey for little Cheryl, but she was about to learn exactly what Momma meant. Taking a taxi from the bus station to as far back into the hollow as it could go, they all got out and walked the remainder of the way. This was all new to Cheryl, but once we all met each other, we all grew to know and love each other. I reckon we didn't always get along, but we did stick together when the chips were down.

It was during the summer of 1964, while I visiting Momma for a couple of weeks and the phone rang. Answering it, I heard the voice of what sounded like an intoxicated man—a voice that I hadn't heard for years. Much to my dismay, it was one that I knew all too well. In the background, I could hear a woman. I reckon that it was when he realized who he was talking to, the conversation took a very ugly turn. Sexual in nature, he proceeded to say things that he wanted to do to me. The woman in the background laughed as his conversation grew increasingly vulgar. She obviously didn't know that her friend was talking to his teenage daughter.

I threatened to hang up the phone and told him that if he called back, I would tell Momma everything he did to me. I reckon he thought that this was all fun and games, but I slammed the phone down on the receiver. Nearly as soon as the line was disconnected, it rang again. Nearly in tears, I reluctantly picked it back up. He wasted no time resuming right where he had been cut off, this time describing what he wanted to do to me with his tongue. Now in tears, I slammed the phone down again. Hearing the commotion, Momma rushed into the room saying, "I want to know who the hell that was on the phone and what the hell is going on!"

Trying to pull myself together, I told her that it was Gordon on the phone. "He's saying horrible things to me," I said. Taking a deep breath, I then told Momma that he had raped me when I was little and that he continued raping me for years afterward. Acting like she had no idea, Momma said that she didn't believe me and appeared to go into shock. It was about that time that CB came into the room and noticed that Momma had been shaken. Without asking any questions, he coddled Momma and took her into the kitchen. Sitting her down at the table, he proceeded to fix her a mixed drink and tried to calm her down. I was left behind to deal with my own fragile, violated state, crying and trying to figure out what I had done that was so wrong.

A couple of days later, Momma went to see a friend of hers who was also a judge. She told him what Gordon had done to me. Much to their dismay, he explained that there was nothing that could be done because too much time had passed since Gordon's violations. After leaving his office, Momma got a' hold to a gun and went directly to the Charlottesville grocery store where Gordon was working. Confronting him with the gun, she threatened to kill him if he didn't leave town. He had no doubt in his mind that she meant what she said. He subsequently quit his job, packed his belongings, and left the state.

I reckon Momma continued to have loving feelings for Gordon throughout her life with little or no regard to my own feelings. After several years had passed, she would still sometimes ask me to drive her to Florida to visit him. It wasn't until I blurted out to her, "I don't want to go see that child molester," that she never asked again. Fourteen years passed before he once again came back into our lives.

Once again I began to spend more time thinking about my half-brother. I spent many nights crying over Momma's decision to sacrifice a child so that her husband wouldn't find out that she had been unfaithful. I never understood how she could do such a thing without experiencing the least bit of remorse. Often wondering what kind of life he had, I also wondered if he was okay. Most of all, I wondered if he needed me. I knew absolutely nothing about him -- not even his name. All I could do was remain on the lookout for a boy not much younger than myself, with similar features.

Granny also grieved over the loss of her first grandson. There were several times I heard her say, "I pray to the Lord that I will someday get to see his dear little face just one more time before I leave this earth." How could a mother do such a thing? After all, Granddaddy and Granny took care of me, Dinah, and Darlene. Why not one more? How much harder could that have been? Those were just some of the questions that constantly weighed heavily on my mind for many years.

I often wondered what it would have been like to have a sibling so close in age to share things with. Dinah and Darlene, only a year apart themselves, were too much younger than me to have such a relationship with. The older I got, the more time I spent thinking about it. There were years of tears, questions, and unanswered prayers.

In high school, I realized a talent for playing basketball, but I knew that Granddaddy would never tolerate my being involved in sports. I asked Uncle Bullpuncher if I could go live with him and Aunt Shirley during the school year so I could try out for the varsity basketball team. In return, I promised to clean the house, cook the meals, and take care of their son. I had just turned sixteen when they welcomed me into their home with open arms. Aunt Shirley immediately bought me a new floor-length housecoat to wear around the house. I reckon that anything shorter would not have been appropriate where she was concerned.

Uncle Bullpuncher and Aunt Shirley usually spent Saturday nights at the Fire Hall dance. After moving in with them, I too began to go along. As I opened the car door to get in, there, in the back seat, quietly sat a handsome young man with coal black hair, sporting a red sweater. Uncle Bullpuncher said, "Oh yeah, I forgot to tell you. Michael is your date for tonight." Excited by the prospect, I hopped right in and sat at his side in the back seat. Uncle Bullpuncher used to bring Mike up in the hollow when he'd visit Granny and Granddaddy. Back then, I would just hide behind the kitchen stove and peep out at him from time to time. When I got older and began to take notice of boys, naturally, Mike was at the top of my list.

Unfortunately, I had made other plans with another young man that evening and I told Mike that I couldn't let him pay my way into the dance. He didn't take that lightly and said, "I'll tell you one damned thing! If you won't let me pay your way in and you sit with me, don't you ever speak to me again."

"Well, fine," I said, "if that's the way you want it, that's the way it'll have to be." I was really thinking *Just who does he think he is?* When we got to the hall, I walked over to Wayne, my date, and danced with him throughout the night. Sitting with Uncle Bullpuncher and Aunt Shirley all evening, Mike never got up to dance. When the dance was over, Mike decided not to ride back home with us, choosing instead to hitch a ride with someone else.

As I looked out through the kitchen window the next day, I noticed Mike standing alone, across the street at the gas station. I scampered back to my room where I put on a short purple dress and pranced across the street as if I was going to buy a loaf of bread. I tried to strike up a conversation with him, but he was still upset over the way things turned out the night before. "You bitch!" he said, "Don't you ever speak to me again."

Remaining upbeat and unwilling to allow him to bring me down, I turned and walked away, saying, "Okay, if that's the way you want it." I reckon it was over before anything had a chance to get started. From then on, whenever we saw each other at the dances, we didn't dance with each other and, of course, we didn't even speak to one another.

The homecoming dance was coming up and I so wanted to go. Since all the school dances had chaperones, I saw no reason why I wouldn't be allowed. Having no objections, Uncle Bullpuncher did suggest that I discuss the matter with Aunt Shirley as well. Aunt Shirley said that she would only allow me to go if she could go too. Well, that didn't suit me at all and I told her, "Well, I just won't go if I have to take my thirty-year-old aunt with me."

She and Uncle Bullpuncher began arguing over her insistence. When all was said and done, I reckon Aunt Shirley decided to see how far she could take it. "Bullpuncher! If she's not out of here...," pausing for a minute before continuing, she said, in no uncertain terms, "in two weeks, that's going to be the end of our marriage." A sudden silence fell over the room. Uncle Bullpuncher looked from her to me. With a frown, he shook his head before dropping it in defeat. Not wanting to come between them, I returned to my room, closing the door behind me. I packed my few possessions into a grocery bag and left.

I walked to the bus stop at a nearby gas station with no more than the grocery bag and my meager allowance. After buying a one-way ticket to Washington DC, I sat quietly, waiting for the bus while fighting to conceal the overwhelming hurt and fear that had overcome me. I'd never struck out on my own before, and I had no idea what I was going to do. It seemed like an eternity before the bus finally arrived. Boarding the bus, I claimed a seat, and was soon on my way with only one thought on my mind. How was Momma going to react when I just showed up at her front door unannounced?

After arriving in DC, I got off the bus and walked over to a cab. Handing the driver a slip of paper with an address on it, I asked him if he could take me there. I must have been quite the sight, standing there with only a grocery bag and no luggage. He looked me over before saying, "Sure, hop in!" When the cab pulled up in front of Momma's apartment, I paid the driver and began to walk what seemed like a mile from the curb to the door. Now standing at the door and nearly in tears, I took a deep breath. I knocked and anxiously waited.

A few moments later, the door opened and there stood Momma, very surprised to say the least. Fighting to hold back my tears, I just blurted out, "Here I am. Give me a place to live or I'll go somewhere else." At the end of my rope, with no idea where somewhere else might be, I had nothing left to lose at that point.

"Come on in here she said, "what the hell is going on?" Entering her apartment, I told her everything that led up to my being there. Assuring me that together, we'd work something out, she proceeded to ask how I got there. When I told her that I took a cab from the bus station, she asked how much it cost. I told her and she flippantly said, "Well, he must have drove you all around DC."

She never made me feel welcomed. In fact, she seemed to delight in humiliating me in front of CB, Cheryl and Susan. Mocking my country ways, she also constantly made fun of the way I talked. Unlike the spacious rooms of the house in the hollow, the rooms in the apartment were small and cramped. Like a bull in a china closet, I reckon I bumped into things quite often. Momma would say things like, "You're so clumsy! You're the clumsiest person I've ever seen in my life."

At night, out of habit, I would sometimes slip up and say, "Blow out the light" as I went to bed. Momma seemed relentless with her demeaning remarks about my ways. In contrast, however, CB was much more caring and understanding. A good man, always the dedicated and loving husband and father, he now added peacekeeper to his credits.

While Momma was having a procedure done that required a short stay in the hospital, CB called me to the balcony of the apartment and told me that he wanted to know how my sisters were living back in the hollow. Deciding not to hold back, I said, "They have no electricity and no running water," adding "They walk a mile each way to and from school. They have to work sunup to sundown, and they aren't allowed to do anything else."

Distraught, he lowered his head and cupped his face with his hands and wept. Standing immediately in front of him, I couldn't help but share his pain while at the same time I was hoping that he might be able to reunite us so they wouldn't have to continue living in poverty. Lifting his head, and looking up at me with determination, he said, "I'll tell you what. I promise you that they'll be here, with us, within two weeks." Inside,

I was jumping with joy, but knowing how Momma was, I contained my excitement while managing little more than a smile of gratitude.

When Momma came home from the hospital, CB told her that she was to get a bigger apartment right away and then bring Dinah and Darlene to live with us. No sooner had he said it, Momma bolted into action. Beaming with joy, I thought I had done the right thing for Dinah and Darlene. Little did I know that unlike myself, they loved their lives in the hollow. Darlene admitted years later that she didn't want to leave her home in the hollow. "You mean to tell me you're the one who's responsible for that?" she had said to me, "For taking me away from Granny? I ought to kill your ass!" It was only then that I realized that their lives with Momma were as close to hell as it could have been.

About a month before school was scheduled to begin, Granny received a letter from Momma requesting that she not enroll Dinah and Darlene in school for the fall semester because she was coming to get them. Granny told them to pack all their things because their mother and her new husband were coming for them. It was about that same time that Darlene had been playing in Granny's pots and pans and broke Granny's crock pot. To keep from getting in trouble, she hid the broken pieces, hoping that Granny wouldn't find them until after she left.

They gathered their few belongings and put them in a small cardboard box. Granddaddy hitched a sled to his horse and towed the box filled with their hand-me-down clothes and what few other possessions they had from the house down to the mailbox where they met CB and Momma. The last thing Granddaddy told them before they left was "No matter what happens, don't let your mother cut your hair off." The first thing Momma did after getting them home was to take us all to a salon and proceeded to have our hair cut to a very short length. I guess Momma didn't want to have to spend much time brushing and caring for long hair. We were devastated, and Dinah may have taken it a little harder than Darlene as she felt guilty for letting their Granddaddy down.

It wasn't long after their arrival that things started to go awry. Momma never had a kind word for either of them. Dinah, in particular, couldn't do anything right in Momma's eyes. Frequently getting smacked and punished for one thing or another, she rarely knew what she'd done wrong. Homework was to be done as soon as we got home. Momma always made us sit at the dining table until we finished it, regardless of how late it got. Sundays were now spent ironing clothes. Church was no longer a part of our lives.

CB, on the other hand, was wonderful to all of us. The three of us were just as much his daughters as were Cheryl and Susan in his eyes. "They're all my daughters," he'd proudly boast. When he heard me refer to Momma as Sugarloaf instead of Momma, he said to me, "Jeanette, honey, please don't call your mother Sugarloaf. She is your mother and she is the only mother you have and the only mother you will ever have." Granny and Granddaddy had always been Mamma and Daddy to me, but feeling the sincerity in his plea and recognizing how it upset him, I respectfully began calling her "Momma" in his presence.

Darlene was taken by the modern amenities and conveniences in the Farley household, but that was short-lived. There were many nights that she cried herself to sleep. Then one day, she got the crazy notion to burn the place down. She thought that if it did burn down, we'd have no place else to live, and would be returned to the hollow. She says that she thought about that every night after going to bed, but she never actually acted upon it.

Becoming Cheryl and Susan's primary caregiver, she let go of such thoughts. As Momma began to spend less time at home, Darlene took it upon herself to make sure that the girls' homework got done and their baths were taken in the evenings. Momma had other plans for me.

It was Christmas Eve when I learned that Momma had arranged a date for me that very evening. Excited by the prospect of meeting a man, I went to my room and prepared for my date. A short while later, there came a knock at the door. Knowing who it was, Momma told me, "You get it." When I opened the door, there stood a short, much-older man. Deeply disappointed, I quietly turned around and dashed back to the kitchen, leaving the door wide open. Momma was right on my heels, demanding, "What the hell is your problem?"

Nearly in tears, I replied, "I'm not going anywhere with that old man." He was nine years older than me. Quite an age difference, especially to a girl who was only sixteen.

Angrily shaking her finger in my face, Momma shouted, "You're not only going to go out with him, but you better be good to him, too!" Fearing what might happen, I reluctantly went out with Jimmy. I don't rightly know what Momma meant, but I reckon she was warning me that I better do whatever was necessary if I wanted a place to stay.

Momma told Jimmy that he could take me anywhere, anytime, for however long he wanted without worry, as long as he had me back in time to go to school on Monday morning. That evening, we went to a party at a house owned by one of his friends. Entering the smoke-filled living room, I noticed that the air was thick with a peculiar and unfamiliar smell, and there was enough alcohol flowing to sedate a mule. Wearing a pair of slacks, a top and trench coat, I immediately felt underdressed as everyone else was dressed in semiformal attire. I don't rightly think that anyone besides me noticed as no one seemed to mind. Before I could take a second step into the room, I was offered a drink, at which time Jimmy reached out, placing his hand between the drink and myself as he said, "Oh no. She doesn't drink."

By the time I began to overcome my initial embarrassment, Jimmy decided it was time to leave. As we drove through town, I took special notice of the Christmas-themed store windows that lined the streets. The lights were beautiful and we didn't have anything like that back in the hollow. Our weekend-long dates became routine as Jimmy picked me up every Friday evening and no matter where we went or what we did, he was sure to have me back in time for school on Monday morning.

In the spring, when the weather began to warm, we started going to a beach in Delaware on Friday nights. By now, Momma believed that we were sleeping together, but she didn't know me well enough to know that I would never do anything like that. Spending our entire weekends on the beach, I went swimming and did some shopping when time allowed. Jimmy was a perfect gentleman the entire time, never once trying to take advantage of me or any situation.

When I met a boy named Frank in school, I immediately took a liking to him. We started seeing each other behind Momma's back. She would never have approved of our relationship, not because I was already seeing Jimmy, but because Frank was a dark-skinned Puerto Rican boy. When he asked me to the prom, I knew I wouldn't be able to keep him a secret any longer. When I told Momma about him, she acted exactly as I expected, saying that she wouldn't allow me to go with "that nigger!"

Hoping Jimmy would be more understanding, I approached him about going to the prom with Frank. Much to my surprise, he had no objections. In fact, he encouraged the date. He was so supportive that he bought me a gown, gloves, new shoes, and whatever else I needed. He even sent me to a beauty salon to have my hair done professionally.

Frank and I went to the prom before a private party afterward. There was good chemistry between the two of us. We had the time of our lives that night and he still managed to have me back home by 2:00 a.m. When Momma got wind of my date with Frank, she told me that she would not allow me to see him again, demanding, "You will not go anyplace else with that nigger!"

Undeterred, I continued to find ways to see Frank. The swimming pool became our favorite place to meet. There, he taught me how to swim. We'd go to the bottom of the pool where I'd sit on his lap for as long as we could hold our breath. On the way home, we frequently stopped at a little drugstore to have a soda. There, we could sit next to each other, in our own little world as we talked and laughed together while sneaking in a quick kiss and hug whenever the opportunity presented itself.

On another occasion, after I had been babysitting for one of Momma's friends, Frank showed up to walk me home. Unbeknownst to either of us, Jimmy was also waiting to take me home in his car. As I began to walk away with Frank, Jimmy rolled his car window down to let me know that he was there to drive me home. When I told him that I had already told Frank that he could walk me home, he rolled the window back up and quietly drove away. He later called me and explained how disappointed he was that I wouldn't ride with him before demanding to know what I was up to. Laughing now, I said, "Oh, I'm sorry to hear that. It doesn't really bother me one bit."

Frank eventually revealed to me that his parents had a house in Puerto Rico where we could live rent free and proceeded to propose to me. Only sixteen, I knew I wasn't ready for that. Laughing nervously, I acted as if he were only joking. Upon arriving home later that evening, I was so elated that I couldn't help but share the news with Momma, who in turn, forbade me from seeing Frank again, reiterating, "You're not going anywhere with that nigger!" I reckon that this whole situation weighed heavily on Frank after he found out what happened between Momma and me. Not long after that, he was involved in a car accident that totaled his father's car. Thank God, he wasn't seriously hurt. I never saw him again, but not because of Momma or Jimmy. This time it was Frank's father who forbade him from ever seeing me again.

III

OUT OF THE HOLLOW

Left to right: Darlene, Dinah, and Jeanette

Once again, back with Jimmy, I came home after an evening out when Momma called me to her room. Still full of surprises, she told me that Jimmy was going to ask me to marry him. I couldn't believe my ears. "Do what?" I replied.

"Jimmy's going to ask you to marry him," she said. "He's got plenty of money, and he can take good care of you." Before I could get another word out, Momma gave me a final ultimatum. "You'd better say yes OR ELSE!" I didn't rightly understand Momma's attitude, and I felt like I had once again been betrayed by her. I could almost feel my life becoming a perpetual downward spiral. Turning around, I stormed out of her bedroom and ran to my room where I cried myself to sleep.

Feeling trapped, I figured my only option at that point was to go ahead and marry Jimmy if only to get away from Momma. A few days later, Jimmy asked me to marry him just like Momma said he would. Accepting his proposal, we married without my ever challenging Momma's ultimatum. I never found out what Momma meant when she said "or else." I only knew that I wasn't needed anymore and that there was no other way out for me.

If I wasn't ready to marry the one I thought I was in love with, I certainly wasn't ready for someone who was nine years older than I was. That age difference seemed like generations to me and Jimmy was certainly not what I had envisioned for a husband. Returning to the hollow wasn't a realistic option. Transportation was my first obstacle. Even if I returned on the bus, without transportation, I couldn't get a job and then I'd once again become stuck in a lifestyle that I didn't want -- no electricity and no running water. On the other hand, I figured that I would marry Jimmy, live with him for a month or so then get out of the marriage with a new found freedom and independence.

I took Jimmy up to the hollow to meet Granny and Granddaddy. The mountain road was so rough, we had to abandon his car and continue on foot. Not far from the house, we passed a very inebriated Granddaddy laying helplessly on a bank, a short distance from the house. We passed unnoticed as he muttered profanities in a drunken state. Humiliated, I tucked my chin to my chest and prayed for the ground to open up and swallow me whole. Jimmy said nothing. I reckon he must have felt my embarrassment as we continued on our way, back into the hollow.

Extending us a very warm welcome when we arrived, Granny hugged and kissed us both before inviting us in, and offering us something to eat. "You hungry?" she asked. "I got some hot batter cakes I just cooked on the stove and I got a pot of brown beans on." I told Granny that Granddaddy was lying on a bank against the hill, drunk. Granny replied, "Well, I wasn't sure where he was at, but he has been drinking again." I confessed that he had said some terrible things that really embarrassed me in front of Jimmy. "Well, Jeanette, honey," Granny explained, "that's the liquor talking."

Then Jimmy chimed in by saying, "Don't pay it no mind, you didn't do it. He did it," as he tried to put us at ease.

Granddaddy eventually sobered up enough to come up to the house while we were still sitting around, talking. When Jimmy asked him for my hand in marriage, I reckon he told Jimmy what many fathers might tell a man who was seeing his daughter. "By gawd, I'll tell you one thing! You better not mistreat her." Somebody pinch me. Was this the same Granddaddy I grew up with in the hollow?

With just two weeks remaining before our wedding day, Jimmy and I were sitting on the couch when he began to come on to me. Visions of Gordon's violations immediately began to run through my head and one thing led to another. When I began to cry, a concerned Jimmy asked if he had hurt me. Embarrassed as I was, I assured him that he hadn't. "Well then, what's wrong?"

he asked. When I finally got myself composed, I told him that I was pregnant.

His concern quickly turned to anger as he blurted out, "You're pregnant? How the hell do you know you're pregnant?"

Frightened now, I thought that Jimmy was making fun of me. I said to him, "I know I'm pregnant because you put it in me." He began laughing out loud and told me that he didn't finish, so I couldn't be pregnant. Confused, I asked him what he meant. It was only then that he began to realize that I was much more innocent than he could ever have imagined. He sat down and patiently explained to me how it happens. Sitting quietly, I was beginning to feel a bit foolish. Jimmy started laughing as I began to cry once again. Here I was, sixteen years old, nearly a woman, and clueless about the facts of life. Granny had always led me to believe that once a man penetrated a woman, she became pregnant. I've had mixed emotions about that since then. Sometimes I get mad that I didn't know the details, but then I'm thankful that I believed the way I did.

As the manager of a successful car rental business, his work demanded a lot of his time. There were a lot of conventions, after hours business dinners, and other social events. He enrolled me in charm school before he'd allow me to accompany him to any of these affairs. There, I learned how to set a formal table for guests, sit and eat like a lady, how to dress, apply and wear makeup, and even how to make a bed, but not how to deal with being violated as a little girl.

The grand convention in the Bahamas usually lasted one week. I was excited about going until he told me that I didn't have the proper clothes and there wasn't enough money in the budget to buy them. I reckon it was spent on charm school. Of course, I was very disappointed, but not as disappointed as I was when I learned that he decided to extend his stay an extra week after the convention ended.

No marriage is ever problem free. Ours certainly was not. I reckon that the demands of Jimmy's job and my inability to overcome what Gordon had done to me as a little girl didn't help matters. To his credit, though, Jimmy continued to give me ample latitude.

Not having felt well for a while, I went to the doctor. Following a quick examination, the doctor said, "Well, it's blue."

I didn't rightly know what he meant. This too was new territory for me so I asked, "What's blue?" then he explained that it meant I was pregnant. "Pregnant!" I shouted out, nearly falling off the table. That spelled real trouble. I didn't want the marriage, and I certainly didn't need a pregnancy to complicate matters.

Jimmy was none too happy about the news as he told me that he didn't want children. Unfortunately, it was too late to do anything about that now. Morning sickness continued to plague me, making it increasingly difficult to remain in school. No matter how hard I tried, I began to miss more classes and fell so far behind that I eventually had to quit.

After telling Cheryl about the three of us older sisters being abandoned at Granny and Granddaddy's for what was supposed to be only two weeks, she mentioned it to Momma. Cheryl told her that she didn't understand why her older sisters had been left with Granny and Granddaddy. She said to Cheryl, "Well, Gordon, who was supposed to be Jeanette's, Dinah's, and Darlene's daddy, got into something he shouldn't have and I went after him with a gun at his work. I figured they would be safer with Granny and Granddaddy during that time."

A young and impressionable Cheryl accepted Momma's explanation.

She certainly didn't let it keep her from enjoying her visits with Granny and Granddaddy on the weekends, although she did sometimes wonder, "Will this be the time that mom doesn't come back for me and Susan?" Granny loved Cheryl and Susan and always did everything she could for them including reading the Bible to them. Like all the others before them, they too loved hearing the stories, especially when they could snack on the cottage cheese, blackberry jelly or jam, and cheese and crackers that Granny put out for them. At bedtime, she always tucked them in and kissed them before saying, "Good night" and "I love you."

One day while Dinah and Darlene were in school, Momma showed up unannounced and told them, "Come on, we're leaving. Get all your things, we're going home." It all happened so fast that they only had time to clear out their school lockers. Uncle Bullpuncher was waiting back at the apartment with a rental truck. All the furniture had already been packed. After the two girls made sure that none of their things were left behind, and before they had a chance to say good-bye to any of their friends, they were on their way to Madison. Momma had already rented a house in Brightwood. Keeping his job at the *Washington Post* in DC, CB commuted by bus on the weekends. I don't rightly know why Momma decided to leave DC so suddenly, but things like that weren't out of character for her.

Things were different for Dinah and Darlene when they returned to the Madison school district. Their social status had improved since the last time they were there. They were no longer the poor girls they were known as before, and their clothes were the first indication to their classmates. As Dinah walked the halls between classes, she overheard comments that I don't reckon were meant for her ears. "Oh my gawd! Those are the Williams girls," the other girls were saying, "What happened to them?" Of course, Dinah hadn't gone unnoticed by boys either. There was even a wager on whether or not the popular boy in school could get a date with her. Not only did he succeed in getting that date, he became Dinah's first sweetheart.

Now in the eighth grade, Dinah was living with Aunt Suzie and Uncle Ralph for a short while. Aunt Suzie had been working for a local ham-curing business in

Madison County when her boss mentioned that he and his wife were in need of a babysitter. Aunt Suzie thought that Dinah might be just what they were looking for. As it turned out, Mrs. Kite, a school teacher, already knew Dinah from school and was very fond of her. Dinah was offered the job, which she gleefully accepted. She worked for them throughout the summer and they both fell in love with her and eventually asked her to move in with them. She didn't have to give it a lot of thought, as one of the main attractions for her was that she knew she would be allowed to play sports in school. After all, if anyone knew how important sports were, it was Mr. Kite, a former pitcher for the New York Yankees.

She brought her few belongings in a couple paper bags and moved in with them just before Thanksgiving. But the most important reason Dinah wanted to go live with the Kites was to get away from Momma's physical and emotional abuse. Dinah was given her own room in the basement which also included a bathroom of her own. Aside from accompanying them to church on a regular basis, she helped in the preparation of the meals and went to the country club in the evenings with Mom Kite where she played golf and their two younger daughters took swimming lessons. She lived with the Kite family through high school. They loved her like their own and even offered to put her through college, but she gracefully declined. I reckon she had other plans that included her then boyfriend.

Still living with Momma, Darlene got a job working evenings at the nearby truck stop. When not at work, she took care of Cheryl and Susan. Whenever Darlene went anywhere, she usually took ten year old Cheryl along, except on one occasion. Also working at the truck stop was another girl named Doris who Darlene became pretty close to. One day, they decided to take their paychecks and go Christmas shopping. Cheryl was devastated when she wasn't allowed to go along. Little did she know that she was about to have one of the best and most memorable Christmases of her childhood.

On Christmas morning, Cheryl and Susan woke up to an entire room full of presents purchased by Darlene just for them. Gifts ranging from clothes to pocketbooks filled the room and Cheryl couldn't believe her eyes. It was a Christmas she would never forget, with a treasure trove of gifts that included a pair of pants with a 7Up hip pocket, a red shirt with black stripes and a gold buckle, pocketbooks, everything a little girl could want.

This was very different from the Christmases that Darlene, Dinah, and I had grown up knowing in the hollow with Granny and Granddaddy. Back then we all went out and cut down our own cedar tree. Placing it in a five gallon bucket, we packed it with rocks and dirt to make it stand upright. We decorated it with some old silver garland that Granny wrapped around the tree and some homemade ornaments that we made in school. Using a cotton thread, we threaded popcorn, making popcorn garland to compliment the paper cutout angels and snowflakes we had also made. Typical Christmas gifts were modest and usually included a hairbrush and comb. As a special treat, Granny bought bags of candy and fruit as Christmas gifts. All these things were purchased with the money that Granny earned from cracking and selling black walnuts by the pound. Without weighing scales, she substituted canning jars to measure the walnuts. I reckon that each full jar was more than a pound, but that was the gain of each lucky customer.

It was in December when Cheryl and Susan's paternal grandfather died. They went to stay with Granny and Granddaddy. Granddaddy picked them up at the mailbox.

The ground was covered with snow following a recent storm. The girls were so excited that they jumped onto Granddaddy's big sled and sang Christmas carols all the way up to the house. Getting off the sled, they each grabbed a piece of wood from the wood pile and filed into the house. Smiling from ear to ear, they placed the wood on the stack inside, before going to the table where Granny had dinner waiting for them.

Cheryl and Aunt Butter Roll's daughter, Cheryl Suzette, would play for hours upstairs from an old trunk that contained a variety of old, long dresses and other clothes. It was a treasure trove for little girls who loved to play dress-up. Cheryl's favorite dress was navy blue with a white collar and red trim. She loved wearing that and pretending she was British royalty. Granny's saucers were perfect for such occasions. As a special treat, Granny made pies for them as they played and always gave Cheryl a piece of raw dough as a very special treat. Granny would say, "It's not good for you, but a little piece won't hurt."

In the summer months, on the weekends, everyone showed up at Granny's for fun and a game of softball. Using whatever was handy for the bases, not all of us had gloves, but it was very competitive while the emphasis was always on having loads of fun. Granddaddy always sat the games out, on the porch, rolling and smoking an occasional cigarette while watching. Momma was an exceptional athlete and she loved the competition. I reckon one of her best plays was one that everyone talked about for many years afterward. She caught a game-ending, bare-handed line drive at first base that surprised everyone -- maybe even herself as well, but she would never admit that it was luck. Following the game, they all went up to the house and had a big dinner before sitting around with bellies full, laughing and talking into the evening.

This was Granddaddy's time to entertain the kids. While barrels filled with water were now more than he could lift at his age, he managed to show off how strong he still was by lifting heavy wood chairs with high backs by one leg with only one hand and raise it above his head while everyone looked on in amazement. When the kids began to shout and beg for more, he'd get down on his hands and do push ups. Not just your plain old everyday pushups either. Pushing his body up and away from the floor, he would push with enough force to clap his hands together and bring them back down before his body could hit the floor. For an encore, he'd make sure all the kids were gathered around, directly in front of him. Once completely assembled and with their complete attention on their granddaddy, he picked up a deck of cards and proceeded to rip it in half.

Jimmy never expressed any objections to me going to the dances without him. I reckon it was all just innocent fun as far as he was concerned, and it was a chance for him to spend the evening in the bars. I didn't drink, and the bar scene wasn't where I wanted to be. Dancing much of the night away, I rarely stopped to rest. It was a passion that I discovered that night, years ago, back in the hollow. Ever since then, I felt a need to get out and cut a rug from time to time. One night, a man who'd been watching me said that he really liked the way I danced and asked if I'd be interested in a job dancing with his band. Flattered and excited, I accepted and it wasn't long before I was dancing professionally at the Sugar Shack.

When Jimmy and I stopped by Uncle Bullpuncher's house, we discovered that Momma was also visiting. Getting ready to go to a dance, she invited me to go along. I accepted her invitation and Jimmy decided to stay behind. Arriving at the club, Momma took me to a table where two men were seated with drinks in hand.

She proceeded to assign me to one of the two men as my date for the evening. I knew right away that I had been set up. Adamantly, I said, "No, I'm not."

Momma sounded like she was ready to battle when she came back with, "Oh, yes, you are, and you'll be nice to him."

Knowing what that meant by now, I firmly stood my ground as I reassured her that I was not going to play along. The tension remained high as the four of us did little more than just sit at the table for the remainder of the evening. Refusing to dance, I hardly even spoke another word. The three of them just carried on as if I wasn't there. The ride home was so tense you could cut the air with a chainsaw. Momma was obviously very upset over the fact that she couldn't make me do as she wanted. Walking through the door, I told Jimmy what had happened. He smiled and burst out laughing, further humiliating me.

Spending more time at work and staying late, Jimmy began to work weekends, traveling to DC on Friday nights, and staying until Sunday evening. While he attended his business convention in the Bahamas, Granny came to stay with Pam and I for the week. I was thrilled to have her. It didn't take much to entertain her. We had a wonderful time just talking and laughing together. Not much of a cook, I insisted on preparing a steak dinner for the two of us. Even though I prefer my meat well done, I still ended up overcooking it to the point where it was so tough that neither of us could eat it. I reckon we must have thought it pretty funny as we both broke out in laughter and opted to go out for a couple of hamburgers instead.

Feeling the need for a change, I applied for a job with a small, local airline company. In the middle of my interview, I was asked how I felt about flying to Philadelphia right then. The interview was going very well and the invitation sounded promising. Within ninety minutes of accepting the invitation, I boarded a plane and flew to Philadelphia to meet Mr. Simmons. We both connected instantly, and before I returned home to Richmond, he told me that the job was mine.

With a new job that could possibly become a career for me, I felt that things were looking up until I received a disturbing phone call. The voice on the other end asked if she was talking to Jimmy's wife. "Yes," I said "Who is this?"

"I want you to listen to what I have to say to you." the anonymous voice insisted before continuing, "The problem with your marriage is Gloria Whitman."

Taken aback, I said, "What? I didn't know I had a problem with my marriage."

The anonymous caller reiterated, "The problem with your marriage is Gloria Whitman." A clicking sound ended the call before I could learn any more. When I called Jimmy at work, the receptionist told me that he was in a meeting and couldn't be disturbed.

"Get him out of that meeting," I demanded, "and on the phone now!" Within a couple of minutes, I was speaking to Jimmy. Upset, himself, he demanded to know what was so important. I told him that he needed to come home right away. Sensing the urgency in my voice, he put everything on hold and drove straight home where I told him about the distressing phone call.

Trying his best to calm me down, he said, "You know, when couples are getting along, there's always somebody that wants to make trouble. There is no one else," He finished by saying how unfortunate it is that it always seems like there is somebody trying to make problems for others.

I never planned on being married to Jimmy as long as we had been at this point, but the birth of Pam had changed things. I certainly never saw this coming. When I came home from work one evening, there was Jimmy standing at the door. "I'm leaving," he said. Thinking that he meant he was going out for drinks with the guys, I asked him where he was going. "I don't think you understand," he continued, "I'm not coming back." Turning around, he went up the steps to the bedroom. When he came back down, he was carrying a suitcase that had obviously already been packed.

Visibly upset, I said, "Jimmy, this is nothing to kid about."

"Jeanette," he replied, "I'm not kidding. I won't be back." He continued to walk out the door and get in the only car we had. I asked him to take Pam and me to Granny's before leaving.

Needing someone to talk to, I knew that Momma wouldn't give me the support that I needed. The ride was a quiet one as Jimmy took both Pam and I to the hollow. Stopping at the mailbox, we got out of the car. Never even offering to help, he instead drove away without saying a single word to either Pam or myself.

Trying to remain strong for Pam and almost in tears, I lifted the suitcase in one hand, and with Pam in my other arm, we began the long trek up the hollow. Before we got to the front door, a pleasantly surprised Granny was there to greet us. I told her what had happened and that we needed a place to stay for the time being. As I began to cry, Granny assured me that they would do the best they could to help us.

Still an infant, Pam slept with me in the side room. I cried myself to sleep for many nights, trying to figure out what I was going to do. I knew I couldn't just live there and not work, especially since I had a child to support. Making matters worse was the fact that I now had no transportation, so I couldn't continue working at my current job. Except for our clothes, I left everything I owned for Jimmy to keep, hoping that he'd eventually feel guilty and want us back. That never happened.

Now, not only a single mom, I was still a teenager which made things a lot harder on us. A couple of weeks later, Momma dropped by for a visit. I asked her if Pam and I could come live with her long enough to get back on my feet again. She welcomed us and even helped me get a job at the truck stop where she was working. Setting conditions on our living arrangements, she insisted that I help pay the rent. I worked the night shift so Pam would sleep while I was at work. In addition to the rent, Momma insisted that she be paid for babysitting during the nights while I worked. I was in need of my own transportation and when Momma decided to put her 1964 Ford up for sale, I told her that I wanted to buy it. We agreed on terms and I made payments to Momma until my debt was paid in full.

In the 1970's, the United States pulled out of Viet Nam. The Watergate scandal led to the resignation of the U.S Vice President followed by President Nixon. The first test tube baby was born and the Peoples Temple cult leader, Jim Jones, instructed his 900 followers to commit revolutionary suicide in Jonestown, Guyana. Citizen Band radios were all the rage and I joined in on the fun. My handle became "Lady Geno."

When I began making enough money, Pam and I moved from the low income apartment, into a trailer I found. Not long after, Cheryl came to visit. We were talking about Momma when I warned her, "You'd better be careful or she might give you away like she did our brother." She got real quiet as she tried to process what I had just said. I reckon that was the first time anyone had ever mentioned a brother to her. When she went back home, she decided to ask Momma about it. Cheryl sat down on the commode where Momma was just finishing her shower. Recognizing that something was on her mind, Momma asked Cheryl what was wrong. She told her what I said and Momma became enraged and she said to her, "Well, she's a damned liar. Don't believe anything she says."

Attending a local dance, I ran into Big C, Mike's brother. He told me that my friend was back in town. It had been three years since Mike joined the Marines and the news that he was back really excited me. Not letting on, I asked, "Who would that be?"

"Don't act dumb," he said, "you know exactly who I'm talking about." I wanted to hear him say it. He only said that if he didn't show up that night, he'd definitely be there the following night. Not in a relationship at the time, I truly was excited at the prospect of seeing him again. I watched the door the entire night. Much to my dismay, he never showed up.

When I arrived at the dance hall the following night, I saw Mike sitting at a table. I melted at the sight of the drop-dead gorgeous man. Looking in my direction, he motioned for me to come over. As I stood in front of him, he took me by the hand and pulled me down on my knee and began talking. The music started playing and we went out to the dance floor, embraced, and began swaying to the rhythm. Holding me tightly, he whispered in my ear, "I love you." Tears began to trickle down my cheek. He then added that he had always loved me and was sorry for the way that he treated me before. I reckon that it wasn't what he said as much as it was the loving way he was with Pam that made me fall in love with him. Pam wasn't quite two years old when he'd put her on his lap and read to her and treat her like she was his own little girl.

As things began to look up for me, they began to deteriorate between CB and Momma. They had their disagreements from time to time, but as he began to drink more, the tension grew and they would engage in some pretty fierce fighting. Momma could be rather vicious when she got mad and as CB attempted to grab her during one of their altercations, Momma thought he was attempting to choke her. She bit his thumb nearly off and when the dust settled, she fixed him a drink. No ordinary drink, it was strong enough to knock him out. Once she was sure that he was unconscious, she left the house.

While working the night shift at the truck stop, Momma served a stranger who had stopped in for a bite to eat. She felt an immediate attraction to him. A wolf in sheep's clothing, he presented himself as a man with money and that's all she needed to know. He introduced himself to her as Josh and he became a regular customer at the truck stop from then on.

One Saturday morning while Pam and I were living with Momma, CB came home from work and Pam lit up as soon as he walked through the door. Running up to him, she leaped into his arms. Lifting her up, he placed Pam on his lap. As he bounced her on his knee, she said indifferently, "Papa Josh slept in Grandma Sugarloaf's bed last night."

The bouncing stopped. CB paused, bewildered by what she had said. Too young to understand, Pam looked at him curiously, wondering why he stopped playing. A nervous hush blanketed the room. CB's joy suddenly turned to deep concern. His tone grew very serious as he called for Momma. Rounding the corner, Momma walked into the room shouting, "What the hell do you want now?" Calmly, he asked Pam to tell Grandma Sugarloaf what she had just told him. Sensing the friction, Pam hung her head and began to fidget.

CB assured her that she wasn't in trouble. "Go ahead and tell Grandma Sugarloaf what you just told me," he said. Pam looked up and softly repeated what she had said. As the tension ratcheted up a few notches, CB stood up and left the room. Not long afterwards, he walked out of the house with his bag in hand. Walking to the bus station, he boarded the next bus to Washington DC, where he resigned his job as a printer and went to Beckley, West Virginia. He lived with his brother and sister-in-law and took whatever jobs he could find. He washed dishes, scrubbed toilets and never returned to Momma. I don't rightly think she even cared. She had finally found herself a man with money and seemed determined that she was going to live out her life on easy street.

Approximately ten years old when her dad left, Cheryl didn't see him much after that day. Whenever she did see him, however, he always asked her how her mom was doing. She filled him in and he would always finish by saying, "Well, you tell her that I love her," which always brought a tear to her eye. Even though Momma had betrayed him, his love remained unconditional and never waned.

Upon learning that her mother was going to marry Josh, Cheryl asked her if she loved him. Momma simply said, "I ain't marrying for love. I'm marrying for money." She didn't know it yet, but Momma had not only lost the best man she ever had, but she lost the best man she would ever have.

Years later, CB was placed in a convalescent home after suffering a stroke. While he was recovering, I drove up to visit him. He was thrilled to see me. While we talked about things in general, he asked why I ever married Jimmy. When I told him that Momma told me I had to, he choked up a little bit and asked me why I didn't come to him at the time. He continued to tell me that he wouldn't have let it happen if he knew that in the beginning. CB didn't take the news very well when I confided that I was very afraid of Momma. I could see the pain in his eyes as he slowly shook his head and fought to hold back his tears. I loved CB like my own father and wanted to bring him back to Virginia, close to Cheryl and Susan. They both thought it was a good idea and I moved him back to Madison where he lived in a local convalescent home near all five of his daughters until his death following cancer surgery.

Josh was a snake-in-the-grass, but like the finely polished brass buttons on the army sergeant, Momma never saw what the man was truly made of. Her life began to spiral downward, out of control when she brought him into it. I reckon Momma was the only one who couldn't see through him.

Josh and a friend paid a visit to Granddaddy one day in the hollow. As soon as they arrived, he noticed Granddaddy mistreating his mule in the field. Acting the big man, Josh yelled down at Granddaddy, "How would you like it if I gave you some of that same treatment?"

He had no idea what he was in for now. Granddaddy wasn't in the mood and shouted back, "Well, if you thenk you're man enough, breng yourself on down here." Josh wasn't a big man by any means and he was certainly no match for Granddaddy. He grabbed Granddaddy by his collar and before he knew what was going on, Granddaddy hauled off and let him have it. A swift right cross put Josh down for the count. Cousin Kevin wasn't far away. He took off like a bolt of lightening and ran toward the house yelling all the way, "Granny! Granddaddy just killed Josh. Granddaddy just killed Josh!"

Meanwhile Granddaddy told Josh's friend, "I don't know who he thenks he is, comin' 'round here and tryin' to tell me my business, but you best pick him up and git him outta here. Now!" He did exactly that and I don't reckon Josh ever came back around.

Every bit as cunning as Momma was, some swore that Josh was the devil himself, if not his brother. One time, he told Momma that he'd received a phone call from me inviting him to the trailer where Mike and I were living. "I went over there," he said, "she opened the door and stood there completely naked and tried to get me in bed with her." True to form, Momma confronted me. I told her that it just wasn't true, but she chose to believe Josh over her own flesh and blood. We didn't speak to each other for a very long time after that.

Wanting nothing to do with Momma's new husband, friends and relatives eventually stopped coming around. No one trusted him, especially Susan, now a teenager, who began to keep things next to her bed -- bats, broken bottles, anything to protect herself.

When Josh tried to assault Cheryl, she managed to fend him off before he could harm her. Quick thinking gave her the upper hand and he found himself cowering in a corner. When she threatened to tell Momma, he just shrugged his shoulders and said, "Go ahead. She won't believe you," which further infuriated her.

When Momma came home, she could tell something wasn't right. She asked Cheryl what was wrong. "Nothing," she said, giving Josh his victory.

The following morning, as Cheryl prepared for school, she was going to make sure that things were going to be different from that day on. She left school early to go see her doctor. Once in his office, she explained to him what Josh had done and asked for his help. Helplessly shaking his head, he confessed that there was nothing he could do until Josh actually violated her.

In desperation, Cheryl decided to tell Momma. Still in denial, Momma said, "You're a damn liar!" Calling Darlene on the phone, Cheryl told her what had happened. She and Big C were there that weekend and took Cheryl away, tearfully leaving Susan behind. She never went back home.

Things continued to deteriorate for Momma. Coming home late one evening, she found Josh in the hallway. Standing just a few feet away, he pointed his pistol at her and discharged it, narrowly missing her. Trying to remain calm, she asked him if he was trying to shoot her.

He said "If I wanted to shoot you I would have hit you." I reckon Momma didn't believe him this time. She called the police and had him arrested. As they took him away, she yelled out that she was going to have him committed. Shouting back, he boasted that nobody would ever put him in Staunton. "I'll kill myself first!"

After promising to appear in court on the following Thursday, he was released on bail. Later, when he failed to appear, a search party was sent out to find him. Nowhere to be found, Josh seemed to have disappeared into thin air. That is, until Momma later found him in his truck behind the trailer park they lived in. He'd died of asphyxiation and because so much time had passed, his body was decomposed beyond recognition. He could only be identified by his watch and boots that he was wearing when he disappeared.

Upon learning that Gordon was going to be back in the area, Dinah and Darlene grew very excited with the anticipation of seeing him again. Dinah, Darlene, Big C, Mike and I all went to the bus station to greet him. Naturally, I wasn't as enthusiastic as my two younger sisters. I went along, however, to support them more than anything else. At the bus station, none of us could believe our eyes. The big, strong, and handsome young man we once knew, was now less than half the man we remembered. No longer was he the hulking figure and clean cut man that he was when he left. His frame was slight, his hair, long and greasy.

Mike and I now had two children of our own. Speaking first, I made sure that Gordon understood that under no condition would he be staying with me, Mike, or our children. Expressing a desire to baby-sit them occasionally, I assured him that there was no way I would allow him to be alone with them -- not even for a moment. When he asked why, I remained steady and firm. "You act like you've forgotten what you've done to me," I said.

With a grin of a child who had just been caught with his hand in the cookie jar, he said, "Well, I hoped that you either forgot or at least put it behind you."

Without hesitation, I said, "No! That won't ever happen." Taking a deep breath, he smiled at the others and said that he had married a woman named Jeanette. That news gave me an immediate sick feeling in the pit of my stomach. Rolling my eyes, I thought to myself, "What a very sick sense of humor he has." I had already had more than I could stomach from him.

Gordon ended up staying with Darlene and Big C until he got a job working at a chicken plant, at which time he got a place of his own across the mountain in Stewart's Draft. Unable to conquer his own addiction, it wasn't long before he started drinking again. He never could hold his liquor and he quickly found himself in trouble, calling me in the early hours of the morning. "What are you doing?" I asked.

"I'm in jail," he said. He had been arrested for being drunk in public and was calling to ask me to come get him out.

"No," I said, "you're right where you should be," and hung up on him.

Dinah and Darlene continued trying to rebuild their lives with him until the day Dinah got fed up with giving him money every time he asked. After talking it over with Darlene, they both bought him a one-way ticket out of the state and insisted that he never come back or call them again. Driving him to the bus station, Dinah and Darlene remained there, making sure that he got on the bus before it left with him on it. While we had seen the last of Gordon, he continued to harass me with phone calls in the wee hours of the morning, only when intoxicated, of course. When I told Mike what he was doing and that I wanted to change our phone number, he wouldn't agree.

The calls eventually stopped and none of us ever heard from him again.

Cluster, another one of Aunt Paige's sons, was talking to his Uncle Ohmer after learning that Granddaddy had cancer. With pain deep in his hip, he said, "Gawdamit! They ain't no bone in there. It's gawn!" believing that it had been eaten away.

Trying to ease the situation, Cluster replied, "Ya got it all wrong! I know exactly what's ailin' ya."

Hoping that Cluster might be onto something, Granddaddy asked, "By gawd, whatta ya thank it is?"

Playing it like a poker hand, Cluster said with his stern poker face, "Ohmer, what ya got is the gout. Plain and simple!"

Back then, people thought that gout was a lazy person's disease and I don't reckon Granddaddy appreciated anyone insinuating that he was lazy. He adamantly snapped back at his nephew, "I ain't got no dammed gout. I know damn well I got cancer!"

Cluster got a kick out of Granddaddy's reaction and said with the biggest grin, "No, indeedy!" Granddaddy's cousin, WM, pulled up in his car as he was turning to go up the steps. Giving WM a wink, Cluster told him to holler at Uncle Ohmer before he gets in the house. "Tell 'em that ya know exactly what's wrong with him is the gout!"

With a snicker, WM yelled to Granddaddy, "Hey Ohmer!" Stopping in he tracks, Granddaddy turned to see what he wanted. WM continued in a serious tone, "Ohmer, I want to talk to you."

Granddaddy asked, "What is it, M?"

"Ohmer," he continued, "come on down here." Granddaddy walked right into their fun, making his way back to the top of the stairs. WM asked him, "How ya feelin' today, Ohmer?"

Rubbing his hip, Granddaddy said, "Dammed if muh hip ain't killin' me!"

Hardly able to contain himself now, WM said, "Well I know exactly what's wrong."

Still unaware of where WM was going with this, he asked, "Well, by gawd, you do, M?"

Easing up the steps, closer to Granddaddy, he finally let loose. "Yeah, Ohmer," he said, "you got the gout."

As both the boys began to laugh out loud, Granddaddy spewed back at them, "Gawd-dam. I ain't got no gout! There ain't a lazy bone in my body." Turning around, he walked back into the house, rubbing his hip. Granddaddy was in a lot of pain and felt he might be close to death, but wouldn't go to the doctor.

Soon after, Granddaddy expressed a desire to go to church with Granny the next time she went. She wasn't sure why he'd make such a request, but when Sunday arrived, Granddaddy accompanied her to church and became a different man that Sunday. While everyone in the congregation had their heads bowed and eyes closed, the minister asked if there was anyone who wanted to be saved. "Raise your hand," he said, "to indicate yes." Granddaddy's hand went up into the air as deliberate as could be. After his sermon, the minister asked Granddaddy if he understood what he had done that morning by raising his hand. After a few more questions with a few close friends at his side, the minister was convinced that Granddaddy had indeed accepted Jesus Christ as his savior. He continued going to church every Sunday after that.

Much to my surprise, while I was visiting Granny, Granddaddy spoke up and said, "Jeanette, come over here and sit on Granddaddy's lap."

Never in my life did I ever expect to hear such words from him. I was speechless. My body language said no while I kept my distance from him. Granny placed her hand on my shoulder and said, "Jeanette, go ahead and do it." Untrusting of Granddaddy, I knew Granny wouldn't betray me. Reluctantly, I walked over and stood next to him.

Reaching out to me, he took a' hold to my hand and gently brought me to his lap, where I sat rather uncomfortably, not knowing what he was up to. Putting his arm around me, he said, "Jeanette, honey, you don't think Granddaddy loves you." He paused, giving me time to respond.

Slowly nodding, I cautiously said, "Yes, that's right."

Granddaddy looked directly into my eyes and told me that he did love me. "I love you just as much as I love my own babies, but I have never been able to show you." Tears began to run down his cheek as both he and Granny began to cry. He was finally reaching out to me after all those years of neglect and abuse. I gave my heart to him that day and we all had a good cry together. Not much longer, Granddaddy's health became visibly worse.

I reckon that Aunt Suzie was probably the one who celebrated her father's new start on life more than anyone. She accompanied both Granddaddy and Granny to church, and when he had grown so weak that he could no longer walk, Aunt Suzie carried him from the house to her car then from her car, into the church each Sunday morning.

One Sunday night, Granny called Aunt Suzie to tell her that Granddaddy was near his end and asked her to come and stay the night with her. She did, and he died on Monday. When the people from the funeral home came and attempted to pick up his body, Aunt Suzie stopped them. "I will do it" she said. "It's the least I can do for Daddy." The once colossal man was now less than one hundred pounds. Aunt Suzie picked up her father's body and laid it on the gurney before it was taken away.

At the funeral parlor, Charles stood next to his Uncle Ohmer's casket. He noticed that Granddaddy's hands were folded together on his stomach, but his index finger pointed straight up into the air. Several people had tried to make it lay flat, but nothing seemed to work. Afraid of breaking it, no one forced it. Seeing his Uncle Ohmer's finger like that really upset Charles. Feeling like he was pointing at him, Charles reached inside the casket and as he passed his hand smoothly over his Uncle's hand, it revealed the finger lying flat against the other hand just like he thought it should. Giving Granddaddy a big smile, Charles said "you're welcome, Uncle Ohmer," before turning and walking away one final time.

I suffered from the same recurring nightmares for many years. The scenario was always the same. Granddaddy chased me with a big stick or some other large object in his hand. As I ran away, I always tripped and fell. Defenseless, on my back, I was pinned down by that object and struggled desperately to get away. I'm not strong enough and I begin to feel my life slip away. Jumping up in bed, I'd scream, holler, and cry out loud, helplessly frightened to the bone.

During the 1980s, a new transcontinental plague identified as AIDS was causing widespread fear and discrimination. President Reagan announced a new defense plan called Star Wars just prior to an assassination attempt on his life.

Now working as a setup machinist at Crouse-Hinds during the day, I began selling Home Interiors during the evenings and on weekends. Mike took care of the kids while I tended to my Home Interiors duties. It was during that time that I bought a two-acre parcel. Mike built our home on it and I continued working at Crouse-Hinds and selling Home Interiors for the next 25 years, becoming quite successful and using the extra money to help pay the bills.

Momma was also working for Crouse-Hinds during that same period. One day, a coworker came to me and said that Momma was quite upset and had asked for me. I found her sitting alone, crying. She asked me to take her home. Once in the car, Momma again began to cry uncontrollably. This uncharacteristic side of Momma was one that I had never seen before. "Momma, what in the world is wrong?" I asked.

She agonizingly confided, "Jeanette, sometimes I feel like I'm going to lose my mind." She continued to admit to having done a number of things in her life that she wasn't particularly proud of. Trying to comfort her as best I could at the moment, I told her that no matter what it was, I would never hold it against her, and no matter what she had done, whether it was right or wrong, I believed that she did what was best at the time. Right or wrong!

With chin on chest and tears rolling down her cheek, Momma's face was tormented and twisted as she painfully confessed that she had given birth to a baby boy, ended its life moments later, and disposed of its body in a plastic garbage bag. I reckon I had heard so many lies from her that I didn't know whether to believe her now or not. I wondered if she was even speaking clearly from memory or talking out of her mind. I just didn't know. What I was sure of was that she could spin a tale as well as anyone. I wondered if she could be confusing the facts and talking about the son she had given away so many years earlier. Regardless of whether or not this was a fabrication, I knew that her condition was serious, and she certainly needed help that was beyond anything I was qualified to give her. Arriving home, I made sure that Momma was comfortable and that she would be all right before I returned to work.

No matter how busy my life ever got, I always managed to find time for Granny and made sure that she didn't go without. I took her places to give her a change of scenery, especially when she wanted to go visit her friends who were in convalescent homes. When Granny noticed that her friends weren't being treated as well as she thought they should be, she always made it a point to tell me that she never wanted to end up in a nursing home. I always promised her that I would never allow that to happen.

Unfortunately, not too much later, in 1987, Granny's health deteriorated to the point that she was no longer able to care for herself. Diagnosed with FTD -- Pick's Disease, as we called it, robbed her of the ability to speak and write. When she required around the clock care, the doctor consulted with Aunt Suzie, Aunt Butter Roll, and Uncle Bullpuncher, suggesting that Granny be put into a nursing home where she could get the professional help that she so desperately needed. All three of them were holding down jobs and realized that even though they could probably take care of her for a while, they wouldn't be able to maintain the constant care that she would require for as long as one year.

None of us wanted to see her go to a nursing home. I reckon they all struggled with the decision of placing Granny, their mother who was always there for them in their times of need, into a convelescant home. They did what they believed had to be done. At ease with her decision, Aunt Suzie told me that Granny had told her that she was looking forward to living in the Madison nursing home, the nursing home that she watched being constructed. She was the one who broke the news to Granny, telling her that she was going to go to the home she had so wanted to go to. Unable to move any part of her body except her eyes and the muscles in her face, Granny looked at her daughter and smiled approvingly.

I reckon what upset me most was the fact that they were making decisions for her without allowing me to have a voice. When I learned that they had placed my Granny in a convalescent home, I contacted each of them and requested that I be allowed to care for her in my home. Uncle Bullpuncher explained, "I know Mama loved you as much as she loved any one of us and that you did as much for her as any of us did, if not more, but the fact remains, you are only the grandchild and you don't have a damned thing to say about what we do with Mama."

Devastated, I called Aunt Butter Role and asked her if I could take Granny and keep her. "That would be like me asking one of my children what we should do with Mama." she said, "I agree with Bullpuncher that what we do with Mama is none of your business." Still not satisfied, I called Aunt Poke who told me that she had had this conversation with Mama several times. She said that if it ever came to a point where it was necessary to put her in a nursing home, Granny had no problem with it. As a last resort, I called Momma who told me that she thought it would be a good thing if I took her. However, her one voice wasn't enough to change the other siblings' minds.

I found each and every visit especially painful from then on. Granny yelled and hollered whenever I was there. I played sermons that she had recorded on her tape recorder to try and calm her. It seemed to be the only thing that soothed her tormented spirit. Seeing Granny like that was heartbreaking. I knew that she didn't want to live her final days like that and I felt an extreme amount of guilt after having promised her that I wouldn't let that happen. Unfortunately, there was absolutely nothing I could do to change it.

Aunt Suzie confided in me that while she and Granny were out driving one time, she noticed construction on a new nursing home in Madison. Granny told her that she liked what she saw and that if and when the time ever came when she would need to go to a nursing home, that was the one she wanted to go to. I reckon Granny had told her on more than one occasion that she felt it was being built just for her.

The doctor kept us all informed on what and when to expect from her illness before any changes developed. The pastor from Granny's church visited her from time to time and during one of his final visits, he said, "Miss Jackson, I am envious of you." She silently gazed back at him as he continued, "Do you know why I'm envious of you, Miss Jackson?" Knowing that she couldn't respond, he still allowed her enough time for a response before continuing. "I'm envious of you because you are going to get to meet Jesus before I am," he said with a smile on his face. Returning his smile with an even bigger smile, he reached over and grabbed a' hold to her hand firmly in assurance.

Granny's health continued to deteriorate until she was pronounced dead within minutes of my twenty-eighth birthday. It continues to trouble me that I wasn't allowed to care for her the way I had promised her so many times.

Still working at the Crouse-Hinds plant, I was told that I had to return to school for additional instruction in order to keep my job as a set up machinist. That wasn't the case as I learned not long after completing the required classes, the plant shut down. After 19 years with the company that I thought I would spend my life working for, I found myself unemployed. When I learned of an opening at the Coors Brewing Company in Elkton, I became certified as a forklift driver and was hired in just two weeks. The hours were long, my workweek short, and the money was good.

One day, while trying to close a rail car door, I felt a popping sensation in my lower back. It was so painful that I could hardly stand upright. Leaving work early, I went directly to see my doctor who rushed me into surgery to repair two herniated discs in my lower back. I never reported the injury and while I did keep my job, I did give up selling Home Interiors after 25 years.

Granny's absence created a formidable void in my life. Now recovering from back surgery, I had more time to think about the void of my missing half-brother. I asked all my aunts what they knew. Each of them denied knowing anything about Momma having a baby boy, not to mention giving him away. It was infuriating, knowing that Granny and Uncle Bullpuncher had both admitted knowing it, but everyone else in the family denied it. After having approached every one of Momma's siblings, there was only one other family member who I had not confronted.

It had taken a long time, but I finally worked up the courage to face up to Momma. I wanted to know more about my half-brother, including where he was and who had him. This wasn't going to be easy. Scared to death, I had no idea how she was going to react. Showing up at

Momma's apartment, I found her standing at the stove, preparing supper. "Momma," I asked with my heart in my throat, "is it true that you adopted my brother out?" A wild look came over her as she stood silently, as if in a trance. The ice had finally been broken, and I was beginning to feel a bit more empowered, however still quite anxious. "Don't stand there and deny it because Granny told me, and I know that Granny would never lie to me," I said. Still, she said nothing. Was she collecting her thoughts and selecting her words wisely for a change? I was now in uncharted territory.

Suddenly, as if the giant had been awakened from a deep sleep, she shouted, "Hell yeah, I adopted him out and if I had it to do over again, I would have adopted every damn one of you out!" Momma's reaction managed to take me by surprise. I certainly never expected to hear her say that. As we both stood there, in the kitchen, face to face, it was Momma who now began to feel more empowered as I trembled. She trumped the exchange by threatening, "And if you don't get the hell out of my kitchen, I'll throw this damn boiling water right in your damned face." A sense of fear set in and I just turned around and left immediately. It was well over a year before we spoke to one another again. I reckon that exchange weighed heavily on Momma, too. When we did begin talking again, she told me that if I ever decided to look for my brother, she wanted to be the first to know, explaining, "I don't want to be around if and when you find him."

With questions still unanswered, I continued to wonder why and what if? Night after night, I continued to cry myself to sleep, wondering for years. I don't reckon Mike ever understood my pain. He never was an empathetic person and certainly not where my heartache was concerned. He only thought that I was foolish for wasting my time on something I had no control over and said things like, "You think of the dumbest shit!" and, "I don't know why you just don't let that go!" Not once did he ever attempt to console me during my times of need and despair.

In the 1990s, the Hubble Space Telescope was launched during a Space Shuttle Discovery mission. Later in the decade, the world wide web was publicly introduced as an internet service, while the cold war ended with the dissolution of the USSR after they were financially unable to successfully counter President Reagan's' Star Wars plan.

When I learned of Alice's passing, I attended her funeral. Her brother, Haywood, was also in attendance. Now a widower, with no children of his own, he came over and began talking with me. As he walked me to my car, I asked him if he knew anything about my half-brother. "A brother?" He asked, "I never knew you had a brother." I told him that I was trying to find him but everyone I talked to denied knowing anything.

Changing the subject, he said that he knew one thing for sure -- when I was born. I reckon I was just as surprised by his revelation as he was by mine. "You were born on October 30, 1950," he said. When I asked him how he knew, he told me that Momma had written him while he was in Korea and told him in her letter.

Now in my late forties, I thought it would be fun to see what a psychic at the Green County fair might be able to tell me even though I believed that their words are the work of the devil. As the psychic examined my palm before looking back up into my eyes, she said, "I see that you have a brother." Pausing, she then glanced back down at my hand and continued, "Yet, you don't have a brother. Does that make sense to you?" With tears now trickling down my face, I confirmed her visions. After our session ended, I had become so rejuvenated that I decided to once again renew my search for him.

Upon sharing what I'd learned from the psychic with a coworker, she told me of an Indian psychic whom she, herself had seen and highly recommended. Starved and wanting to learn more, I looked her up and scheduled an appointment. When we sat down together, she asked me if there was anything I didn't want to know. "I want to know it all," I replied ecstatically. I could hardly sit still as my anxiety mounted higher and higher. As the eighty-year-old woman took my hand in her own, palm up, she examined it carefully as her finger traced the lines in my hand. She said that she saw I had a brother who was now absent in my life. "You know not where he is," she added. Smiling ear to ear, I nodded. The psychic leaned closer into the table that separated us. Continuing, she said, "You can find him in one of the C-states." She also told me to quit worrying about who I thought my father was. "I'm 99 percent sure that the man who you think is your father, is indeed your father!" adding, "And I can take it a step further, this man paid your mother off to keep her quiet when she became pregnant with you."

I asked her why my mother wouldn't tell me who my father was. She replied, "She doesn't know who he is. She has slept with so many men that she does not know."

The Indian psychic proceeded to shuffle and deal the tarot cards. One by one, they all came up red. "Oh, me!" she exclaimed, which alarmed me. Not understanding what it all meant, I asked if it was good or bad. "This is as good as it gets," she said, "health, love, and money." After our session was over, I again, left very pleased by what I had learned. I felt sure that I could focus my search for my half-brother in the states that begin with the letter C, but I wasn't sure what she meant about the older man who was going to come into my life.

During a subsequent telephone conversation, Haywood informed me that there had been something on his mind and he needed to talk to me about it. Asking me if I was sitting down, I said "No, Do I need to?"

Well, I was about to get the shock of my life as he proceeded to say, "I'm 95 percent sure that I'm your daddy." My mouth was now hanging wide open as Haywood continued, "I can name the place. I can name the time, and I can tell you how." Stopping him there, I said that I didn't want to know all those things. He was so sure of his feelings that he didn't feel a DNA test was necessary. After all, he thought there was an obvious family resemblance. The calendar was certainly on his side. He had been with Momma at the right time, just before he left for Korea. After a year of pleading with him, Haywood finally agreed to a DNA test. I ordered the test kit, we swabbed each others mouths and I mailed the samples to the lab.

When the results came back, Haywood had been redeemed. The numbers confirmed that he was indeed my biological father. Closing another chapter in my life, no longer would I have to wonder who my father was. We were both just as pleased as we were relieved to finally know the truth. Deciding to break the news to Momma first, we went to the convalescent home where she was now living.

Referring to Haywood's last name, a proud Sugarloaf boasted, "She's all Berry, isn't she?"

Haywood smiled and said, "She's 50 percent Berry and 50 percent Jackson." Momma motioned for him to sit next to her on the bed. They were both very happy about the outcome even though Momma and Haywood were second cousins.

Telling him that she loved him, she added, "I always have and always will."

Momma's siblings didn't take the news as well. Aunt Poke didn't believe it one bit, adamantly stating that she knew for a fact that Haywood wasn't my daddy, even though she would never say how she knew, choosing only to say, "Because your daddy is dead!"

Darlene, now a nurse, felt that she could better explain what the DNA numbers meant and tried explaining them in simpler terms for everyone's benefit. Aunt Poke still didn't understand and continued to insist that she knew who my real daddy was, still without divulging any details.

None of the negative feedback bothered either of us and it certainly didn't deter us. I was as satisfied as I was happy to finally know who my biological father was and I wasn't going to be denied any longer. We spent as much time as we could together, becoming a great support system for each other for years to come. I even accompanied him on his annual POW reunions. They were a real eye opener for me as I learned so much about how they were mistreated by the Chinese and all they had to endure while they were prisoners. We were both very happy, and I was even more encouraged now to find my half-brother. If only I knew the names of the couple who had him, I was confident that I could find him and complete my family circle once and for all.

Hoping that Dot's sister, Francis, would be able to tell me something about the couple Momma gave my half-brother to, I decided to pay her a visit. She said that she only knew what she had been told. "It was my sister who made the arrangements with that couple," she said. Giving me Dot's phone number, Francis assured me that her sister would tell me anything I wanted to know.

When I finally got to talk with Dot, she regretfully admitted that there wasn't much she could remember after all those years, further explaining that it was actually her brother, Tom, who knew the couple. Unfortunately, he was deceased now. "He was in the Navy with the man that he brought home on weekends with his wife. I do recall that their name was Hawkins, Hopkins, Haskins, or something like that," but she couldn't remember exactly what it was. This was so much more than I already knew, I finally felt like I was making progress and continued to press forward. Dot told me that she would let me know if she remembered anything and asked me to keep in touch with her regarding my progress.

After contacting my sisters to see if they would aid me in my search, they either said that they couldn't help or they wanted no part of finding their brother, believing that it might upset Momma. Deciding to let it go, I felt that it was best to postpone my search for the time being.

Sometime later, I decided to continue without the help of my sisters. After hiring a private investigator, I felt like I just threw my money away. Several months and hundreds of dollars later, he had learned nothing more than I already knew. Once again, I postponed my search.

Now living in Michigan, Dot had been going through some old boxes in the attic and found an old Christmas card from Orange, Texas. The postmark was dated December 29, 1953. The original three-cent stamp was still affixed to the upper right corner. Inside, was a personalized Christmas card that pictured a baby propped up at the end of a couch next to a teddy bear. The caption read: "*Seasons Greetings from our house to yours,*" It was signed Bobbie, Leslie, and Teddy. On the back side was written Teddy Haskins 3 1/2 months old. Dot made a copy of the card and sent it to me with the following handwritten note:

> *Jeanette*
>
> *Found this in the attic yest. Hope it is of some use to you. Had states mixed up.*
>
> *Good luck, Dot*

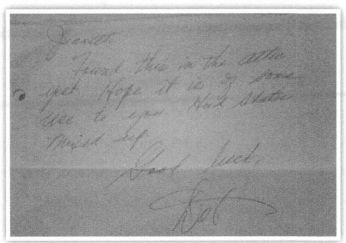

Receiving her letter gave me renewed hope. Now I knew his name. I had always hoped and believed that he might still be someplace nearby. I believed I was on the right track now, especially since I had been told that he was in one of the *C* states, and now that I had a name to aid in my search.

I started with a phone call to the long-distance operator in Orange County, California only to learn that there was no Bobbie, Leslie, or Teddy Haskins in the area. On the positive side, the list of people named Haskins was quite extensive. After she told me that I would have to pay for each additional phone number after the first, I explained why I needed all of them. She was so touched that she gave them all to me without any additional charges.

I came up empty after making my initial calls. Becoming discouraged, I decided to call one more number before giving up for the day. A very annoyed man answered his ringing telephone. I reckon that I was interrupting something because when I told him that I was looking for a Haskins that had been adopted his indignant response was, "I'll have you know that I'm one of fifteen brothers and sisters, and I can assure you that not one of us is adopted!" I never got to say another word before he slammed the phone down on me.

Hoping that someone might take notice and talk to me, I ordered personalized license plates for my car. Wanting the closest thing to "looking for Teddy" I came up with LKN4TDY. I desperately hoped that anyone named Teddy would stop me after seeing the plates. It did receive some attention, but most were curious about what it meant. Much to my dismay, no one I spoke to was named Teddy or even knew a "Teddy."

Not long after my fifty-seventh birthday, I believed my chances were significantly greater now that I had those names. When my son, David, told me about a local investigator that a friend of his worked for, he assured me that this guy was very good at what he did and was every bit as reliable as he was talented. I decided to call him solely based on what David said. After a brief phone conversation, the investigator agreed to come out to the house and talk to me. During the interview, Mike made it clear that he wanted nothing to do with it, explaining that he didn't want me to get hurt anymore. He'd seen me cry night after night from my anguish and pray at church for years without results. "I don't want to see her hurt again," he said.

Realizing I wasn't going to get any support from him, I told the investigator that I was going to do it anyway, with my own money if I had to. Investigator Tonker said he would do it if I could pay him four hundred dollars in advance. Asking him if he'd accept payment in rolled quarters that I had saved up, he, paused for a moment and said that quarters will spend as well as any other form of cash and accepted the job. I gave him four hundred dollars in quarters and a copy of the Christmas card with the baby picture and names on it. Explaining that he wouldn't work on it every day, but he would do what he could as time allowed. He also said that if he exhausted the four hundred dollars and needed more to continue his search, he would let me know. I agreed to his terms and in January of 2008, he began his search.

His first objective was to find out about the couple identified on the Christmas card, if in fact they were the couple in the car at the base of the mountain whom Momma had given the baby to. Making a number of phone calls, he started getting some leads. After a month had passed, he called to report his progress and requested additional money to continue. Satisfied with his progress, I made a second payment in rolled quarters.

On Christmas Eve, Mr. Tonker called to say that he was 99 percent sure that he had found my half-brother, but needed more time to be positive. I was so excited that I told Dinah that our next Christmas was going to be a whole lot different and a whole lot better. Dinah looked at me like I was crazy. Laughing it off, she figured that I must have thought that I was going to win the lottery or something like that. She truly had no idea what I was talking about.

IV

THE SEARCH

Jeanette

Investigator Tonker went on to learn that Bobbie was indeed the name of the woman in the car. Born in 1916 Alaska, she grew up the daughter of a Norwegian immigrant and an Alaskan native with a Christian upbringing. Her father, Tommy, came to America at the young age of twenty accompanied by his brother. The allure of the Alaskan frontier proved to be more than either brother could resist. After arriving on Ellis Island, they continued their journey across the country, settling in Alaska. Making his living on the sea, Tommy met a pretty Alaskan native named Bertha and they eventually married. When he and his brother had a disagreement of sorts, they parted ways and never spoke or saw one another again. Tommy and Bertha went on to have two children, Inga and Teddy.

Inga and Teddy

With a love for the outdoors, Teddy became an exceptional swimmer and trapper. It wasn't unusual for him to spend days at a time in the wilderness. Early one morning, he went out to check his traps. When night began to fall, he made camp. After establishing camp, he started to settle in and get comfortable when a stranger came in from the dark. Welcoming the man, Teddy offered him some hot food. The stranger thanked him for his hospitality and stayed the evening. Days passed and Teddy hadn't returned home. No one had seen him or knew of his whereabouts. After several weeks without any information, it became apparent that Teddy wasn't going to return.

One afternoon, as Tommy was sitting in the house reading his Bible, he heard someone knock at the door. Marking his place in the scripture, Tommy laid it down, and got up to see who was there. Opening the door, he could hardly believe his eyes. There stood Teddy, smiling and looking as fresh as he could be. With a broad smile and a sigh of relief, Tommy welcomed his son in. Teddy didn't come any closer and told him that he was fine and there was no more need to worry, before turning and walking away. Motionlessly standing in the doorway, Tommy watched as his younger child, his one and only son, dissolved into the bright daylight from which he came. Feeling a sense of calm, Tommy went to the other room where

Bertha sat sewing on her foot-pedal sewing machine. She turned her attention to her husband as he sat down next to her. Taking a deep breath, he calmly told her that Teddy had just visited him. He continued to say that their son was fine and didn't want them to worry any longer. Quietly gazing into each other's eyes, Bertha nodded her head with a sense of calm that seemed to put them both at ease.

Years passed before the town drunk confessed to killing Teddy and burying his remains in the wilderness. He'd been sitting in wait for him, determined to kill the man whom his wife had been having an affair with. The Sheriff went to talk to Tommy and Bertha. Explaining the turn of events to them both, he asked if they wanted the man to be prosecuted. Tommy, the good Christian that he was, shook his head as he wrapped his arm around Bertha. Feeling that the man had suffered enough, they both felt no ill will against the man.

After high school, Inga moved to San Francisco where she met and married a man named Harrison. The marriage didn't last long. After realizing that the man she married had a problem with alcohol, she divorced him. She had been working for the telephone company as a telephone operator when she befriended two other women, Lucille and Barb. They became inseparable, going everywhere and doing everything together.

One day, they decided to create unisexual nicknames for themselves. Inga became Bobbie and that nickname stayed with her for the rest of her life.

Born in Wisconsin, Les would eventually grow up on a farm in Southern California, one of fifteen brothers and sisters. As a young man, he worked in the movie industry as a studio messenger. One day, while in a hurry, he nearly ran a red light and came within inches of hitting a man walking in the crosswalk. The pedestrian was a rather portly man and looked like he could have been a lot of trouble if he wanted to be. Les's adrenaline raced as the near-victim approached him. Standing at the driver's door and appearing larger than life, film star Oliver Hardy of the famous Laurel and Hardy comedy team, said, "It's a good thing you didn't hit me."

Realizing how much trouble he would have been in and feeling very nervous, Les replied, "Yes, I know."

When asked if he knew why it was a good thing he didn't hit him, Les shook his head, figuring that Mr. Hardy was really going to let him have it now. Asking him why, Les braced himself for whatever might be coming his way. Mr. Hardy only smiled and said, "Because you would have wrecked your car." The tension began to ease as they both started laughing, however, Les's laugh was a nervous one. Mr. Hardy assured him that all was well and said, "Drive a little slower and be safe." Les thanked him and apologized as Mr. Hardy brushed it off and walked merrily on his way to the studio.

When the United States joined the rest of the world in World War II, Les enlisted in the Navy. Ready to ship out to the pacific, he found himself in San Francisco, an inebriated sailor celebrating his final days stateside when he met a telephone operator. This new relationship was as passionate as it was brief. Three days later, they ran off to Reno and got married. After returning to San Francisco, Bobbie continued working for the telephone company and Les shipped out, figuring never to return alive.

Surviving the war, Les's first stateside port of call was Los Angeles. Anxious to see his parents and brothers and sisters again, he went directly to his mother's house first. Seeing him, she became hysterical and jumped into his arms with a grip that he had never felt from her before. Tears streamed down her face as she thanked God for answering her prayers. A bit embarrassed by what he thought was her overreaction, he asked her what it was all about. As she calmed down and caught her breath, she explained to him that they had been told that he was killed in the war.

When the time came, Les reenlisted and became a career sailor in Uncle Sam's Navy. Bobbie followed him as he was transferred from one location to another before ending up at the naval base in Norfolk, Virginia. Nine passionate years had passed since they met and married. They were enjoying life and the many friends they made over the years, but there was a painful void. They loved children, but they had been unable to conceive their own. After many years of trying, they had all but given up on their dream of having children, when one day a shipmate told them that his sister's neighbor was going to have a baby that she couldn't keep.

Shortly there after, they left the navy base and drove about two hundred miles, out into the country. Waiting in the car, they spotted two women walking down the rural dirt mountain road. One of them was carrying what appeared to be a baby wrapped in a blue blanket. Bobbie and Les remained in the car as the woman carrying the baby walked up to the car's passenger door. Putting out her cigarette in the ashtray, Bobbie rolled the window down, and the woman handed me through the open window to my mom, in the car. No words were exchanged. Mom lovingly accepted and held me tightly in her arms as the woman stepped back, away from the car. As the window rolled back up, we drove away. Eventually, a birth certificate was issued stating that I, Teddy Haskins, was indeed born to Les and Inga Haskins in Albemarle County, Virginia.

Now the Haskins family, Mom and Dad were no longer the childless couple. They were in love with being parents and having a baby they could call their own. The nine year void had finally been replaced by a miraculous gift orchestrated by a few angels here on earth. I have no doubt that Mom thanked the good Lord for that gift each and every day afterwards.

They shared that experience with the Taylor family. Joe Taylor was another shipmate of Dad's. He and his wife Edith were the proud parents of a three month old baby girl, Inga Jo, named after Mom and Mr. Taylor. Edith and Mom vowed that their babies would grow up to be close and very good friends as well. That wasn't to be, however, as the United States Navy had other plans. It wasn't long before we were being sent to Texas and preparing for our first Christmas as a complete family.

Left to right: Dad, Teddy, and Joe Taylor with Inga Jo.

Now living in Orange, Texas and getting ready for Christmas, Mom and Dad showered me with gifts. Christmas was different now and it would always be more meaningful from now on. Mom and Dad had a personalized greeting card made from a picture they had taken of me sitting on the couch, propped up by a teddy bear. They mailed it to Tommy's sister, Dot, since she was the one who had made it all possible. The inscription was simple, *"Seasons Greetings from our house to your house."* Below, Mom signed it, *Leslie, Bobbie, and Teddy.* On the back, she wrote, *Teddy 3 1/2 months.*

❖　❖　❖　❖

Teddy and Suzie in Texas

It was in Texas that they were reminded how quickly life can be taken. Mom and I were outside in the front yard. It was a warm sunny day. The moment Mom became distracted, I crawled away. A car came speeding in my direction, when

Suzie, our little black dog, dashed into harm's way. With her head down, she rammed into me, knocking me to the other side of the street as the car continued on its way without ever slowing down. Hitting the curb hard, I began crying. Hearing the commotion, Mom ran to my aid, grabbed me up, and took me into the house where she dressed my wounds that included a long deep gash along my backbone. Unscathed, Suzie may very well have saved my life on that day.

Before they could establish themselves in Texas, Dad got orders to go to California. Mom and Dad fell in love with the San Francisco bay area and bought a home in Vallejo, located in the North Bay area. Of course, the military life never let anyone stay in one place for a very long time, and after a couple of years there, Dad received transfer papers to Japan for a three and one-half year assignment. Mom decided that we would all go since it was for such an extended length of time. I was nearly four years old when they leased the house out, and before we knew it, the three of us were on our way to Japan. Traveling by ship, Mom got seasick and I ended up taking care of her much of the way. Hearing some of the other passengers talking about the flying fish that could be seen from the deck, I pleaded with Mom to take me out to see the ocean's waters and the flying fish. When she felt better, she took me out on the deck a couple times to satisfy my curiosity, but the motion of the waves only made Mom's condition worse. We quickly returned to our room, where for the most part, we remained for the duration.

Teddy and his Japanese friends, circa 1958

❖   ❖   ❖   ❖

I was a shy little boy, but I managed to make friends pretty quickly in Sasebo, Japan. We lived on the base in the beginning, but only long enough to find an apartment off base. It was small and directly above a mom-and-pop's store. The proprietor was a very friendly, frail little man with a gray beard whom everyone lovingly called Papa San. I would get up in the mornings and wander downstairs into the store where he was always cooking on an iron skillet over a wood fire. He loved sharing with me whatever he was cooking. Much of the time it was one of my favorites, taco balls—a milky batter with chunks of seafood, including octopus. Papa San poured the milky batter mix into each of the little round, concaved pockets of the iron skillet until it was brown on the outside. With a small scooper, he scooped it out and turned it over, forming a round ball when completely cooked. He placed the taco balls into a paper bag from which I ate the delicious treat while it was still steaming hot. Sloshing it around in my mouth, I sucked air to cool it off while chewing it. That's the way I saw all of my Japanese friends eating the delectable treat. One day, I decided to take this tasty treat upstairs to share with Mom and Dad. Opening the bag, I offered Mom the first bite. She put her face near the top of the opened bag and turned her nose up. I convinced her to at least taste one and with an approving shrug, said that she liked it, but she didn't eat any more. Dad, on the other hand, turned to our Japanese maid and asked her if it was safe to eat. Smiling at me and giving me a wink, she assured my dad that it was fine. The Navy had warned all personnel and their dependents to be very careful when consuming the native food because much of it was grown in pastures and farmland that was fertilized with human waste. It never seemed to do me any harm and I loved it all.

Our tiny apartment had a small ice box in the corner in which Mom kept the perishables. It was also furnished with a porcelain hibachi pot that we used for cooking. Back in the

States, we had an electric refrigerator and gas stove, making these things in Japan seem so primitive to me. Undaunted, I loved living like it was "the olden days," as I called it. Mom brought home an electric deep fryer to make donuts as a treat one day. She always encouraged me to experience new things and when she made the batter for the donuts, I joined right in. Of course, safety was always a priority and she didn't allow me near the hot grease. As she poured the batter into the small vat, I watched with big round eyes as the batter turned brown on the submerged side and then watched as Mom turned them over to brown on the other side. Before eating them, I got to sprinkle the sugar over them while they were still hot. That's when they were best, and I absolutely loved them.

As an enlisted man, Dad didn't make much money and he didn't want Mom to work outside the home. That was the agreement they made when they decided to become a family. There were times that they went without so I wouldn't have to. There were even a few times that they didn't eat so that I could. When they needed a little extra cash, Mom ironed other people's clothes late into the night. One night, after having gone to bed while she was ironing, I woke up not long after having gone to sleep. Noticing that the light in the other room was still on, I wandered out to find Mom still ironing clothes. I couldn't yet tell time and had no concept of how long I'd been sleeping, but I thought she had been ironing all night long, without any sleep. I asked her why she was still ironing clothes and she explained that it was still quite early in the evening. Taking me by the hand, she walked me back to bed.

Teddy sitting next to Papa San in front of his store. Our apartment was directly above.

At Christmas time, there were lavish decorations with Santa Claus figures everywhere we went. Some were life-sized hollow plastic figures that glowed from a light within. I was aware of the prevalent Japanese religion, Buddhism, and it surprised me to see Christmas being celebrated there. It was a very magical time for me and when Mom asked me what I wanted for Christmas, I surprised her by saying, "I want brothers and sisters." Brushing it off as a passing phase, she said that she couldn't have any more children, so I would have to decide on something else. It would be the first of many times that she would hear that same response from me throughout the early years of my life. I didn't like the loneliness that being an only child would often bring.

Mom taught me the story of Jesus when I was very young. She and Dad even found a manger with Mary, Joseph and the baby Jesus figurines with all the animals and three wise men that a local Japanese carpenter had built. They bought it and it became the focus under the Christmas tree, front and center every year from then on. There was even a hole drilled in the back of the manger for a Christmas tree light to fit through it. I spent many hours every year arranging and rearranging the figurines as I played out the story of Christ's birth in the manger. Dad was always passive and never said much about religion, choosing to always support Mom in her faith. She rarely ever wore jewelry, but the one thing she always wore, as long as I can remember, was a small gold cross on a gold chain around her neck. It didn't occur to me until I was an adult that Dad was probably agnostic and let Mom teach and share her faith with me.

I always received a plethora of gifts at Christmas. Maybe it was intended to take my mind off of wanting siblings, but no matter how many gifts I got, I always ended up wishing that I could have a brother or sister to share with. Receiving a bicycle for Christmas that year, I learned to ride it in the park across the street. Dad tried patiently to teach me how to ride it. He instructed me to push the pedals with my feet to make it go and squeeze the hand brakes to make it stop. Terrified, I tried not to let on. I didn't think that it was natural for someone to ride something with just two wheels, one in front of the other no less, without falling. Even though I had seen many others riding bikes successfully, I thought that the rickety training wheels on the back tire were too small and unstable to keep me from falling over and getting hurt.

Dad steadied the bicycle as he pushed it to get me started. When he thought that I was ready to safely ride it on my own, he let it go. Panic struck as fast as it struck deep. I became petrified at the thought of the bike falling over and my face driving fast and hard into the gravel pathway, leaving me looking like a jack-o-lantern. Dad repeatedly shouted at me to turn, but it was useless. Whenever I turned the handlebars, the bike would lean, bringing me closer to the ground. I was in no hurry to pick myself up from the graveled trail. My legs weren't long enough to put my foot down on the ground and come to a safe stop, so I did the only thing I could do. I continued to coast straight ahead until the bicycle ran into a tree. Over I went, face first into the graveled path like steel to a magnet. Trying to push myself back up, my face felt like it was on fire. It was all scraped up, with tiny pieces of gravel imbedded in my skin. Dad lost his patience and was mad at me for not listening to his instructions. I cried all the way home. Mom assumed the motherly role and did what mothers do—she lovingly tended to her baby's wounds, both physical and emotional.

Teddy on his new bicycle in Japan

Teddy and his Christmas manger, California

I never forgot what my mom said about not being able to have any more children, but I didn't like the loneliness of being an only child. Trying another approach, I asked her why we couldn't adopt children. She said that if I had siblings, it would mean that I would have to share everything with them, including all my toys. Well, I understood and accepted that. Having brothers and sisters to share things with was what I had always wanted. I was persistent and kept bringing it up for many years, but the answer was always the same. While I enjoyed having my own toys, I became very lonely and grew up hating that feeling. I always felt like something was missing. I never really understood why my desire to have siblings was so intense but there was no doubt that it existed. My parents gave me nearly everything I wanted except for the one thing I wanted most—brothers and sisters.

It didn't take me long to pick up the Japanese language, and I was soon speaking it fluently. When the Japanese puppeteers brought their traveling shows to the neighborhood, all us kids delighted in the enchantment, fun, and yummy snacks like the taffy that they brought with them to sell before the show began. Loving the puppet shows, they were very much a part of the magic of my youth. I loved being entertained and transported to a different place and time when the hand puppet show began.

One of my favorite snacks was the delicious napkin-wrapped baked sweet potatoes sold from the pushcart vendors on the streets. I was mystified by the wooden carts never caught on fire from the hot coals within that cooked the potatoes.

I was so intrigued by the puppeteers and their puppets that Mom decided to show me how to make sock puppets. She taught me how to sew the button eyes and stitched noses on the end of a sock to create a face. Initially, I was embarrassed at the thought of being a boy who was learning to sew, thinking it was something that only girls did. She always had a way of explaining things to me and she explained how she thought that all men should know how to sew. She said that all the men she knew, growing up in Alaska, knew how to sew. They were men who made a living on the sea and had to know how to stitch a sail when repairs were needed. She also began teaching me how to cook during that time, explaining that she wanted to know that I could take care of myself in case anything should happen to her and Dad.

I loved watching television and going to the movies. Those two activities occupied a lot of my time growing up. The Japanese were huge fans of the American westerns and baseball. Westerns, of course, were always a favorite of mine too. Tarzan was a very close second when selecting a movie to go see at the theater. Many of my Saturdays were spent at the movie theater as a child. Either Mom or Kazico, our maid took me to the Saturday matinees.

One particular Saturday, Kazico took me to the theater located just a few blocks from where we lived. Back then, you always got to see a double feature for one price. That particular Saturday was western day -- two matinee westerns. After the first western was over, I couldn't believe my eyes as a lavishly produced, live stage performance took place during the intermission. Dancing women came out onto the stage, beautifully dressed as caterpillars. They disrobed for their metamorphosis. Of course, my eyes became fixated on them when that happened. They were actually nude on the stage and Kazico frantically tried feeding me ice cream in order to distract me. I wasn't having any of that, preferring what was on the stage rather than what was in my hand. The melting ice cream made quite a mess as it ran all over my hand and down to my elbow. All her attempts to clean the melting ice cream were well intended but futile as there was much more ice cream than there were napkins. When we got back home, a very embarrassed and apologetic Kazico told Mom and Dad what had happened. Much to her surprise, neither of them got upset. They could only laugh after hearing about the ice cream and how big a mess it made.

On yet another occasion, Kazico wanted to go to the movie and Mom and Dad tried talking me into going with her. The movie was *House On Haunted Hill*. I was only five years old and even though I couldn't tell you what the word haunted meant, I did associate it with the word scary. I told them that I didn't want to go. When Dad asked why, I said it sounded like a scary movie and I didn't like them. He asked why I thought it was scary and I said, "Haunted Hill. That means it's scary." I never knew why, but he tried to associate it with Boot Hill and said it sounded like a western to him. I didn't win my case and ended up going to the Vincent Price movie. I didn't know who he was at that time, but I learned to associate his name with scary movies. It was only one hour and fifteen minutes long, but I spent much of that time with my hands over my eyes. It was the longest seventy-five minutes I ever spent in a movie theater. It wouldn't be until the mid 1960's that I would become a fan of Vincent Price movies when he starred in a series of films based on a number of Edgar Allan Poe stories. I loved reading Poe as a teen.

While at the movies one day with Mom, I noticed a little girl being held by her mother. Standing in her mother's lap with her head over her mother's shoulder, and her hand in her mouth. I pointed out to Mom that the little girl had no fingers.

She explained that no matter how bad you think you may have it, there is always someone else who is not as well off as you are. She added that I should never single out someone like that or ever make fun of those things that couldn't be helped. She seemed so wise to me and I promised her then that I would never do anything like that.

As a special treat, we went to the beach. Papa San took us out on his boat where he dropped us off to spend the entire day on an island with a private beach located safely inside a small cove. I was usually the only kid, but there were almost always a bunch of Dad's buddies from the ship who went with us. There was always plenty of beer for the adults and plenty of soda for me. Food was always bountiful on such occasions which they cooked over an open fire on the beach. I didn't know how to swim, but I spent a lot of time at the shallow water's edge, catching hermit crabs and entertaining myself.

Teddy playing at the beach in Japan, circa 1958

Dad played organized softball for the ship's team. Mom and I were always there to support him. He was an exceptional ballplayer and usually played shortstop. During one of the games, I wandered away from the bleachers and got between a pitcher and catcher who were warming up. One of the pitches hit and knocked the wind out of me, giving everyone quite a scare. Thank goodness, the ball hit me in the stomach and not the head, which undoubtedly would have had a very different outcome. When I got bored with the games, I would play in the creek behind the bleachers, catching bullfrogs and tadpoles. One time, I caught a bullfrog that had a broken leg, and brought it home to take care of it while it mended. When it healed, Mom and I took it back to the creek and released it. Reluctant to let it go, Mom explained how much happier the frog would be if he could return to his family. Saddened by losing my frog, I was happy that I was able to help its leg mend. As I stood on the edge of the water, I crouched down and released the frog. Jumping from the shore into the water, he quickly swam away as I stood there feeling that sense of loneliness once again, but happy for the frog who was now returning to its home and family.

I enjoyed playing outdoors with my friends. We liked exploring and would often walk up to the Japanese cemetery and look at all the headstones and the Buddha statues with offerings of food and incense left by surviving family members for the deceased. Always respectful, we never disturbed a thing. One day, we journeyed beyond the cemetery and came upon an older Japanese house. Our curiosity got the best of us as we peered through the slightly opened sliding door into a room where an old man with a shaved head was wearing nothing more than a white loincloth. Incense burned as he sat cross legged on the tatami mat, facing a Buddha statue. He looked to be praying or meditating. We watched for a short while, became bored and left without ever being detected.

When school started, I watched all my friends leave for the day. Too young to go to school, I wanted to go anyway. Once again, I was alone and couldn't wait for the day when I would be old enough to go to school. When that day came, Mom and Dad enrolled me at Cherry Blossom Elementary School, a Catholic school. It was the only local school where English was spoken and taught. The nuns were a very new experience for me. Sister Mary John was a regimented authoritarian with a masculine appearance and ruled with an iron fist and wood paddle. She was always by the book and never deviated when it came to discipline.

Always wanting to do well and make Mom proud, my curiosity often got me into more trouble than I was actually guilty of. That's not to say that I never did anything wrong, however, I did get the ruler across the back of my hand more often for things they suspected I had done rather than what I was actually guilty of. When I spoke out in my own defense, the sisters seemed to turn a deaf ear as they took a sadistic pleasure in smacking my hand with that ruler. It terrified me. I always thought it was going to break the tiny bones in my little hand. The sting certainly felt as though the bones should break even though the worse that ever happened was some minor swelling and redness.

One of the things I enjoyed about going to the Catholic school was learning some of the lessons from the bible and the stories of Jesus. Every morning, the day at school started with a visit to the church, where we prayed. It was not only a sacred place, but a magical place to me. With all the marble statues of Jesus and Mary, I felt like I was truly in the house of God. I was a good little boy and even said a prayer on my knees at the side of my bed every night. One day I asked Mom why I never saw her pray and she told me that she prays silently, in her mind every day.

Sister Mary Elizabeth was always so kind and patient with me. I thought she was the most beautiful person I'd ever seen and I was quite taken by her Australian accent. Her blue eyes were as beautiful as the sky, but it was her habit that made me most curious. One day, I told Mom how curious I was about what was under those black and white hoods they wore, but she didn't seem to pay much attention.

At the end of a school day, while standing in line to get on the school bus, I was pulled to the side by Sister Mary Elizabeth, away from the sight of all the others. Much to my surprise, she lifted her hood to reveal her short blonde hair that was hidden under the garment. My curiosity was now satisfied, but unbeknownst to Sister Mary Elizabeth, it was on that day that she stole my six-year-old heart.

Most of the staff and other students treated me like I was special. I didn't understand that, but I did enjoyed it just the same. Mom and Dad always told me that it was because I was the only kid at school with blonde hair. When the time came for us to return to the States, the teachers and all my classmates threw a going away party for me, complete with cake and ice cream. Little did I know then, but that was never done for anyone else before me and I didn't give it much thought until many years later when I was the best man at my best friend's wedding.

V

CALIFORNIA

Left to right: Geno and Ted on Mt. Tamalpais

Upon returning to the States, we stayed with Barb and Fred in San Bruno, just south of San Francisco, until things could be worked out with the people who leased our house in Vallejo. They were Auntie Barb and Uncle Fred to me. Auntie Barb had serious respiratory problems, and she would sometimes lie in her bedroom with an oxygen mask on her face and oxygen tank next to the bed.

Except for their Cocker Spaniel, Auntie Barb and Uncle Fred were a childless couple. Flasher, their cocker spaniel, was their baby. Uncle Fred and I often played together. One of my favorite things to do was to dress Flasher up in Uncle Fred's pajamas. Flasher had an adopted sister, Suzie, the little black terrier mix that had saved my life in Texas. Mom and Dad had given her to Uncle Fred and Auntie Barb before we went to Japan. As Mom and Dad explained it to me when we returned from Japan, Auntie Barb and Uncle Fred had become attached and Suzie had a companion in Flasher. They didn't feel right, taking her away from that so Suzie stayed.

Mom and Dad made several trips from San Bruno to Vallejo, where our house was being leased by a family who didn't want to give it up. After some legal actions were taken, they moved out and we finally moved back to the old neighborhood.

Once again, Johnny and I were playmates along with his older brother, Tommy. I didn't remember many of the other kids in the neighborhood from before, but many of them seemed to remember me. Mom came to the rescue and helped fill in the cracks. Tommy and Johnny became my good pals before I left to go to Japan. Our friendship was quickly rekindled until a couple years later when I learned that Johnny and his family were moving away. I was about to lose my best friend and once again, I had to get used to being alone. After Johnny moved away, we lost contact. He would return several years later. I never knew why, but he told me that he was dropping out of school. I could tell that he was having problems at home and he seemed very unhappy. His visit lasted only an hour or so. He left and that was the last time I ever saw or heard from him.

As was the situation in Japan, I once again spent a lot of time watching TV after we returned to the States. The *Lone Ranger* was one of my favorites. And while many of the other kids were coming home to watch Mayor Art and Popeye cartoons, the *Three Stooges* quickly became the after-school favorite of mine. Becoming a real knucklehead, I had fun imitating Curly. Maybe a little too much fun for Mom's liking. One day, I got the scissors, went into the bathroom and proceeded to cut my hair off at the scalp in front of the mirror. I didn't get very far when Mom walked in on me. I'd only cut a small patch in the front when she immediately took the scissors from me. Sending me to my room, she said that I could deal with my dad when he got home.

I thought that I was really going to get it. Having absolutely nothing to base that on, I just t thought that Mom knew those things better than anyone. Much to my surprise, Dad wasn't as upset as Mom was, but he gave me a good talking to nonetheless. Afterward, there was little else to do but to sit me down in the kitchen where he usually gave me a haircut. He got the hair clippers out and finished the job that I had started in the bathroom, cutting it down to the scalp just the way I had wanted it to begin with.

One afternoon, while Dad was at work, I was watching a TV show about a professional rodeo rider. I began to rhyme words after hearing the rodeo announcer say, "Look at that bronco buck!" Working in the kitchen, Mom was within hearing distance. Little did I know, she was listening to my every word. After the first few words, I spouted out a word that catapulted her from the kitchen, to my immediate side. Like a mad woman, her eyes looked like they were on fire. However new this reaction was, I knew it wasn't going to end up being a good one. She stood directly over me as I lay on my back defenseless, trying to figure out what I had done to make her so angry. "What did you say?" she asked. Having no idea what she was about to do, I did know one thing for sure. Trouble was but a single word away—serious trouble judging by the flames in her eyes and the fire she was breathing.

"Mom," I said, "what do you mean? I was only rhyming words." Still hovering directly over me with her arm drawn back like the hammer on a 44 magnum, I felt I was staring directly down the barrel of a cannon. She ordered me to start from the beginning and she would let me know what she was so upset about. Still having no idea what I had said to make her this upset, I did know, however, that an unknown wrath of Mom, if not the devil himself, was about to be unleashed upon me at any moment. Pleading with her once again, I tried to explain that I really didn't know what I had said that was so wrong. I had only been innocently rhyming with the word "buck" on the TV. I might as well have been speaking Greek. She wasn't buying any of it and ordered me to start rhyming all over again. Getting through a few guesses without consequence, I Inhaled deeply before continuing what I could remember saying in the first place. When I said the word she was waiting for, she snapped.

"That's it!" she shouted, as she quickly swung her arm 360 degrees, clocking me so hard she could have unseated Sonny Liston and knocked out Cassius Clay with the one roundhouse that sent me reeling across the room. The next thing I knew, I was sitting on the floor propped up against the wall with my legs extended out in front of me. Looking up at her still standing in the same spot with her hands on her hips, I heard her say in no uncertain terms, "Don't you ever say that word again." It's a wonder that she didn't knock it out of my memory, she hit me so hard.

When I was about ten years old, I was cooking bacon and eggs before going to school one morning. Mom and Dad sat at the dining table, having their morning coffee adjacent to the kitchen. As I was finishing up the bacon, I lifted the pan to remove it from the fire on the gas stove. Moving it away, to place the pan where it could cool a bit, my arm brushed over the open flame, burning the underside of my forearm. Reaching with my free hand to grab the grease filled pan, I rotated it to escape the intense heat of the flame. The hot grease spilled all over my free hand. Dropping the cast-iron skillet, I screamed loudly and instinctively dashed over to the sink to run cold water over the already blistering hand. Mom and Dad jumped out of their seats. Mom grabbed and held me after going back to her chair. Dad ran to the refrigerator where he pulled out a stick of butter and rubbed it over my burn, intensifying the pain. It literally felt like my hand was being basted. While Mom held me tightly, Dad continued to rub it all over the burned area of my hand, not knowing that the butter wasn't helping. Blisters rose quickly as I cried for the longest time. Mom tried her best to comfort her little boy, trying to assure me that everything would be all right.

She must have felt as badly for me as I felt from the pain. They ended up taking me to the Mare Island dispensary where the doctor treated the burn and bandaged it up. I didn't go to school for a few days and when it was time for me to return, I didn't want to go because I was embarrassed by the smell of burned flesh. I didn't want to be bothered by a bunch of embarrassing questions from the other kids. Dad tried to convince me that I was the only one who could smell it, but logic told me that if I could smell it, everyone else could too. A few days later when I was out in the front yard playing with my dog, Lady, a collie-shepherd mix, leapt up and snagged my bandage with her fang, piercing one of the larger blisters and causing it to immediately drain. The burn left a scar from my wrist to the first knuckle on my fingers. A closer look revealed the puncture wound from the dog that day, which is still visible to this day.

Family moments, sitting around the dining room table, talking, would bring up stories, new and old. One of the stories that came up more than once was from a time before I was born. Dad had been leisurely rowing Mom in a boat down a slow moving river in Virginia. All of a sudden, a water moccasin dropped from an overhead tree branch down into the rowboat. As it coiled up, Dad stood up with an oar in his hands, raised above his head and heroically beat it to death, saving Mom. With my mouth wide open, I realized the seriousness of what could have been the consequences had he not acted so quickly. "Wow," I said, "if you didn't kill that snake, I might not have been born."

Mom and Dad looked at each other with a funny smirk and he said, "Well, you might not have been." I always thought that was a strange response, but it would be many years before I understood it.

He got a kick out of telling others about taking me from what would have been a life of poverty and giving me a better chance at life. I guess he had a hard time keeping it to himself so he would sometimes be so bold that he would talk to his friends about it in my presence. He made sure, however, that I didn't know who he was talking about. I overheard bits and pieces of those conversations from time to time, but I never knew that I was the one they were talking about and to be honest, I didn't really care. I just thought that it was the liquor talking much of the time. The only thing I can think of is that the entire turn of events must have been pretty extraordinary when they got me or he wouldn't have been so compelled to talk about it.

Mom always called me her miracle baby. They both even told me that she got pregnant once before and lost the baby, but I was the one that God blessed them with. One of the stories they told me on different occasions was about how I was born. As she neared full term, they decided to take a drive to visit some friends of theirs in the remote Appalachian Mountains, hours from the navy base in Norfolk. On that trip, Mom went into labor, delivering me in the car. Some of the details changed a couple of times, however. One of the versions included a taxi driver who delivered me in the back seat of his cab on that journey. Of course, the discrepancies confused me, but I never pressed the issue.

The story that they told me was very different from the varying versions they told Dad's brothers and sisters, as well as their friends and neighbors. His siblings were sworn to secrecy, but because I resembled him so much, they all believed that Dad fathered a baby with a woman in Virginia and adopted it. Consequently, Mom and Dad told varying versions of that story to many others.

When Dad was between his graveyard shift and his day shift at work, it always happened on a weekend. Those were always four-day weekends for him so he would sometimes make it a point to take me fishing on the banks of the Sacramento River.

He taught me how to bait a hook and cast a line. We didn't have a boat so we always fished from the shore. Cutting up sardines for bait, we fished for Striped Bass. He told me about the minimum size limit, but he said the ones that weren't legal size were perfect as long as they fit the pan that cooked them. Instead of putting them on a stringer and in the water, they were thrown into the bushes in case the law came around. That's the only time I ever recall him being dishonest.

He always preached the importance of being honest and humble to me. We had some pretty good times together. Our father and son moments were always centered around sports. He taught me how to play catch as he really enjoyed sports. I remember going through Mom and Dad's old photo albums. The pictures of them before I was born were the ones that interested me so much. There were lots of pictures of him and Mom together on the beach and dear hunting. I always asked him if he would take me dear hunting some day when I was older and he always said he would. That day never came, though. I think Mom had something to do with that. She didn't want guns in the house and she never explained why, although I always felt that it was a safety issue with her.

Dad used to bowl when he was younger. I mean when he was much younger, working in the movie studios. Oddly enough, his bowling buddies back then were Boris Karloff and Bela Lugosi, best known for their roles as Frankenstein and Dracula in the movies. When I found out that he liked to bowl, I asked him to teach me, but that never happened either even though he said he would. When he told me about almost running over Oliver Hardy, I never believed him even though I was pretty young and impressionable then. I had a hard time believing that my dad ever knew any famous people, not to mention hang out with them. I think that somehow, somewhere along the line, Mom was pretty close to Bela Lugosi since she got so upset by the news of his death. I never understood why she would be upset over the death of someone she didn't know. That just wasn't like her.

Living in the San Francisco Bay Area, we occasionally went to the San Francisco Giants' games. When Dad's brother, Sam and his wife, Blanche would visit from southern California, you could be sure that there was going to be one heck of a party. Sometimes his sister, Donna and her husband Jim would come too. When the Dodgers were in town playing the Giants, we would go to Candlestick Park to cheer the home team and jeer the visiting team. Of course there was always a lot of friendly badgering between us over the game or the players. Like most other kids, I was a big fan of Willie Mays. Always wanting to get his autograph, Dad never would allow me to do that -- explaining that they didn't want to impose on him or any of the other players, but I eventually figured that they just didn't want to spend time waiting around for that opportunity. Nonetheless, they always made sure that I had a great time. During those visits with my aunts and uncles and cousins, there was always a lot of drinking and getting drunk. We kids always entertained ourselves and rarely paid much attention to the adults.

Learning about Abe Lincoln in school was very intriguing to me, especially his early life, growing up in a log cabin. I always thought that it would have been so much fun being born and raised in a log cabin. I loved that rustic lifestyle fantasy and always wished I could have lived like that. I have often felt that I was born much too late in history and would have made a better outdoorsman than a child of the 1960s.

In the fifth grade and still feeling the void of losing Johnny, a girl at school caught my eye. Robin, a petite girl with dark hair and brown eyes, was rather shy and always seemed to be with her friend Jessie. I, too, was shy and insecure. It was quite a struggle to overcome that shyness, but I really wanted to be her friend. Dan Mini Elementary School was within walking distance so I could go home for lunch. After Robin and I had become good friends, I asked Mom if she could come home and have lunch with me some day. She called Robin's mother and set it up. I was so excited to have her come to my house for lunch. After we ate, Mom took us out onto the patio to take our picture. As we stood near the orange tree, Mom told me to put my arm around her. I don't know who was more embarrassed over the fact that I was putting my arm around her for a picture. Robin and I ended up becoming great friends and spent a lot of time together during recess at school and on the phone during the evenings. When her family moved closer to us, I spent much of my time at her house and got to know her parents and sisters rather well.

On November 22, 1963, I came into the school classroom with the rest of my classmates right after the lunch recess was over. I sat in my assigned desk located in the front row near the teacher's desk. We hadn't been too far along with our art projects when the school janitor entered the room through the door located at the back. Walking to the opposite side of the room, around all the desks, he deliberately walked down the far side of the classroom, and right up to the teacher's desk. Leaning over Mrs. Edwards desk, he whispered into her ear. I watched with deep curiosity as it was a very rare occasion when the janitor did anything like this. Usually messages came over the public address system from the office.

As the janitor whispered in her ear, Mrs. Edwards' expression was one that I will never forget. In total shock, her mouth dropped wide open. In total disbelief, she just looked at him. Something very serious had happened. Again, he leaned over and whispering a little louder this time he said, "The President has just been shot." Even I heard him this time and now it was me who was in total disbelief. As I tried to make sense of it all, I reasoned that it must have been the principal who he was talking about. After all, I thought the principal was mean enough to have some enemies even though shootings where we lived were just unheard of.

After the janitor left the room, Mrs. Edwards stood up and tried to share the news with us. There was already a buzz going around the room and Mrs. Edwards asked everyone to quiet down. When she had everyone's complete attention, she said the inconceivable, "The President of the United States has been shot." When one of the kids blurted out that he thought it was a good thing, everyone else spoke out against him making sure he knew that he was alone in his cold opinion.

The entire world went into shock. Many thought that the assassination was the beginning of the end of the world. For weeks, it seemed everyone was filled with doom and gloom. There was nothing on television except the assassination of President John F. Kennedy and then the subsequent murder of his alleged assassin on live television, intensifying everyone's emotions and fears. Even at such a young age, I couldn't believe that security was so lenient that a man could get close enough to shoot and kill the man said to have assassinated President Kennedy. The entire nation watched the funeral of the President on television, but on the other hand, there was nothing else on television to watch. Most people didn't have more than a half dozen channels to choose from back then. I spent much of my time talking to Robin on the phone instead of watching the same old thing on TV. The nation remained in mourning until February 7, 1964.

When a Pan Am jet landed at Kennedy International Airport carrying four long-haired musicians from Liverpool, England, America began to heal. The reception that awaited them was fit for a king. Quite the spectacle, these long-haired musicians were the talk of the nation. Rarely ever missing the *Ed Sullivan Show* on Sunday nights, when Mom and Dad heard that the Beatles were going to be featured on his show, they decided to watch *Wagon Train* instead.

I didn't really know who the Beatles were at that time, but I had heard all the neighborhood girls talking about them. Michelle, one of my playmates who lived across the street, invited me over to watch them on their TV. She and her sisters stood in the middle of the living room, in front of the black and white television set when the Ed Sullivan Show began. I had no idea what I was in for. Michelle and her two sisters became hysterical as soon as Ed Sullivan announced them for their first of two sets of songs. The Beatles were making history that night and would continue on that path for the rest of the decade. Never before had anyone been on his show twice in the same evening. I didn't know what all the excitement was about and still wasn't sure about those four "mop-topped" musicians from England. Being a little slower to catch on, when I eventually did. It was a life changing experience for me.

The Beatles were quite the phenomenon. Not only did they save rock and roll, but they proceeded to change the world. From then on, my life evolved around music. Music was like a drug to me. Whenever anything started to get me down, all I had to do was tune my transistor radio into KYA radio or KFRC. Rock and Roll could always carry me away to a different world -- a euphoric panacea, if you will.

At the airport on the very same day the Beatles arrived in New York was someone else who would come into my life and help shape it forever on a more personal level. Geno and his family were returning to the States after his father, an American soldier, had completed a tour in Germany. They didn't know what all the excitement was about at the airport. They thought that it was possibly the President of the United States passing through.

In the sixth grade, I was taken by another girl at school. In the same grade I was in, I thought that she was about the cutest girl in school. Besides being so cute, she had a great spirit and was a lot of fun to be around. When I learned she lived around the block from me, I started spending more time over there, dividing my time between Robin and this new girl. Playing hide-and-seek with the other kids in the neighborhood, her little sister, Pam joined in. It wasn't long before I began to feel an attraction to her. When the older sister caught us kissing in the kitchen, one door closed, and another door opened.

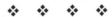

During the summer of 1965, preparing to transition from elementary school to junior high school, I grew rather anxious about the differences between them. I asked as many of the other neighborhood kids who were already in junior high school if they would tell me what to expect. Most were of no help, then someone suggested I go introduce myself to Geno. He had just finished the seventh grade at the junior high school. Geno was a fairly new kid on the block, living in the same house that Johnny had lived in, but I knew nothing about him or his family.

Life took on a new dimension for me on that day. We became best friends and surrogate brothers. We became practically inseparable. Geno and his older brother, Mike were trumpet players. They shared their love for music with me, and we all shared that same appreciation for the music of the Beatles. Mike joined a garage band. I think he was asked to join because they could use his garage to practice in. I thought they sounded pretty awful at first, but they improved until one weekend they decided to compete in the local battle of the bands.

They were very popular not only with the crowd, but the judges, too. They outscored all the competing bands, but didn't win the competition. After the judges deducted points because they had signed up late, the Gremlins ended up in second place. They took it pretty well since they knew they were the better band in the end. That part of the bay area produced some pretty big names in music such as Credence Clearwater Revival and Sly and the Family Stone. Sylvester "Sly" Steward actually attended the same high school as we did - albeit, a few years earlier.

Aside from the Beatles, Geno and I loved the music and energy of Paul Revere and the Raiders. Geno's dad wouldn't allow us to play Beatles records in his house, but his mom had no objections to that so we just never played them while his dad was home. The Beatles were the scum of the earth as far as he was concerned, therefore, it was Paul Revere and the Raiders that we played and listened to for hours on end. Geno's dad wasn't crazy about them either, but he was a bit more tolerant of them. He said on numerous occasions that Mark Lindsay, the band's lead singer, sounded "more black" than any of the black recording artists did. We didn't see anything wrong with that. We loved soul music too.

While the Beatles led the British music invasion of America, it was Paul Revere and the Raiders who tried to stave off this extensive incursion -- this time with guitars and drums rather than muskets and cannons. Every day, after arriving home from school, we would watch *Where the Action Is* on television. It was a pop music variety show that often featured Paul Revere and the Raiders, five zany, mad capped musicians wearing three corner hats and American Revolutionary War military costumes. While appearing to some as nothing more than a novelty band, they were all very serious musicians and recorded hit music throughout the 1960s. Geno and I idolized Mark Lindsay, even when he eventually left the Raiders and went on to have other musical successes including a brief solo career in the 70s.

When it wasn't music that had our attention, we liked watching old Hercules movies. When Geno got a weight set, we began working out in his garage. Neither of us stayed with it long enough to realize any Herculean results. We were, however, satisfied with the results that we did achieve. I returned to bodybuilding from time to time throughout my life, and even pursued it more seriously later on as an adult.

We spent a lot of time outdoors, playing like Tom Sawyer and Huck Finn on the Napa River, not far form our homes. We built rafts that we rode up and down the river while fishing and camping. One time during low tide we decided to have a little fun on the mud flats. Running for a short distance, we jumped and slid for yards having the time of our lives. The mud didn't have a very pleasant smell, but it was so much fun, we paid no attention to how awful we ended up smelling. We thought that we were going to be in big trouble when we got home and our clothes were covered with mud. Mom and Dad were pretty understanding and as I recall, they just threw those clothes away.

We also did our share of hiking up to Hunter's Hill where we would camp out and explore caves, while trying not to get caught by the property owner who didn't like anyone out there. The rocky cliffs and deep, dark caves were pretty dangerous, but very inviting to two eager and adventurous boys who didn't see the dangers. We packed our backpacks with a loaf of bread, a jar of peanut butter and filled our canteens with water in preparation for the five mile hike that sometimes lasted the entire weekend. On one of our initial trips, coming upon an apiary, we thought that if we just quietly passed without physically disturbing anything, everything would be just fine. As we proceeded, however, some of the bees got stirred up and a swarm chased us for about 100 yards. Geno and I were a bit faster than Kevin, another neighborhood kid and third member of our hiking party. He wasn't fast enough to keep up with us and ended up getting stung, but not seriously.

Another time, a different neighbor joined us. As Geno and I were checking out the base of the cliff, Sonny was at the top, chucking off boulders while shouting out over the cliffs below "Konga Kill!" which began a ritual that we repeated each time we returned.

It wasn't unusual for us to be gone for days at a time, and our parents never had to worry about where we were or what we were doing. One weekend, a group of us that included, Geno, his brother Mike, Kevin's older brother Mike Lindke, and myself went fishing at Lake Berryessa in the middle of winter. We didn't plan the trip very well and ran out of food Saturday night. Sunday morning while hungry and on a steep embankment fishing, Geno's brother, Mike found a can of peaches in the car that belonged to Mike Lindke. Feeling a bit devilish, he said, "I'll give this can of peaches to the first guy who jumps in the lake." Mike Lindke spoke up and said that the can of peaches belonged to him. Grinning ear to ear, Geno's brother said, "Yeah, but I have it and possession is 90 percent of the law." The next thing we knew, Mike Lindke actually stripped down to his shorts and jumped into the frigid lake. Before he could get back out, Mike Shepherd had opened the can of peaches and eaten them. Mike Lindke was not only wet and cold, but he was now out of the last bit of food he had brought with him on that trip. Fortunately, we were going back home later that day.

One week, every summer, Mom and Dad always took me camping on Prosser Reservoir, near Truckee. A couple of those early years, my cousin, Mark joined us so I would have someone to pal around with. When he wasn't able to go one year, I asked if Geno could go with us. Mom and Dad had no objections and he went with us every year from then on, camping lakeside. One year, his older brother, Mike came with us. His trip was cut short when he got sick on the first night and went back home the following morning by train.

The early morning and evening hours were filled by fishing. When it warmed up in the afternoon, we swam in the lake. Late at night, we sat around the campfire and tuned the radio to XERB and listened to the very celebrated disc jockey, Wolfman Jack. No matter how late we stayed up at night, we got up before sunrise to go fishing on the lake the next morning. The altitude was about 8,000 feet above sea level and the summer night temperatures could be bitter cold. As cold as it got, it never stopped us or slowed us down when it came to fishing.

One of the best places to catch fish was on an island between two channels of water. The channel between the lakeside shore and the island was about twenty feet wide and five feet deep. The only way we had to get across was to wade or ride an air mattress in the ice cold water. Once across, we walked forty or fifty yards, to the other end to fish the far channel. Sitting on the predawn ground, we shivered and prayed for the sun to quickly rise and warm our cold bodies and dry our wet clothes. As soon as our clothes dried and our bodies were warm, it was time to wade across the channel once again and return to camp. The other campers were always amazed at the size and quantity of the catch we always came back with. Few others had the good luck fishing that we enjoyed there. Sometimes, the fishing was so good that we would reel in our lines with two trout at a time on the same line.

While camping on Prosser Reservoir in 1965, my Uncle Tom Ambrose, his wife, Millie, and their daughter Judy joined us. Tom wasn't really related. He and Dad had known each other during their navy years and became very close. Tom was a great guy and I loved him like an uncle. He loved sports as did my dad. I liked sports but I loved movies. Judy was several years older then Geno and I, but we shared that love for movies. She picked up a newspaper in Truckee and while looking over the listings, she got the idea to go to a movie while we were camping. Going to a movie while roughing it out in the wilderness just didn't seem right, but Geno and I went along with her just the same. Deciding to go to the nearby Squaw Valley theater, we saw *Shenandoah*, a movie about a Virginia widower who was opposed to the civil war.

I felt a peculiar connection to the story. There was a pride that the southerners had that I wanted to be part of. Even the theme song felt special. Nearly everything that had to do with the south seemed special to me. Disappointed, I always felt that my southern connection was by happenstance because my parents happened to be stationed there when I was born. Neither of them were southerners. I always wanted it to be more than that. I was always envious of Geno's southern heritage but I never really said so. Geno, Mike, and their older sister, Barbara often talked about how nice Ohio and Kentucky were and how friendly everyone was back there. I wanted to be part of that, but knew that I really was no more than a southerner by happenstance.

The mid 1960s was a very turbulent time. I was attending Solano Junior High School and the student body reflected the nation's civil instability. In addition to civil unrest, there was the antiwar movement against the U.S. involvement in Vietnam to contend with. Civil rights protests were in the news often, if not daily. Mom and Dad always stressed that no one should ever be judged by their race or religion. I don't know for a fact, but I can only guess that Mom may have felt a degree of racial discrimination some time in her life, being half Indian. Dad personally witnessed discrimination when his sister was shunned by their parents after she married Jim because he was of Spanish descent. I learned to respect others' differences, no matter what they might be.

As I was saying, the junior high school I attended had a very low white student population and very high black student population. The black students were not easily intimidated and the civil rights movement seemed to embolden them. They controlled most, if not everything on campus with a firm grip, particularly the administration.

In their infancy, the Black Panthers, an anti establishment, militia type organization, were gaining ground and becoming widespread around the San Francisco Bay Area and across the nation. Solano County was no exception. They published and distributed free copies of their unique Black Panther newspaper that depicted violence against police in various graphic cartoons in which pigs were being slaughtered by black men dressed in black military style uniforms, very different for the times. Police were synonymous with pigs in the eyes of the Black Panthers and that's how they referred to them in all their literature and speech. The black students emulated the

Black Panthers and intimidated the other students in school with verbal and physical threats.

Martin Luther King's assassination sent shockwaves across the country. Even though he insisted on peaceful demonstrations, his death caused racial rioting everywhere and Solano Junior High School was no exception. While classes were in session, the hallways became filled with black student protestors running through the school, beating lockers, and shouting out, "Remember Martin Luther King!" The teachers must have been on alert as they all locked their doors to prevent spillage from the hallways into their classrooms. The administration closed the campus, called the police before all the student's parents were called and told to come pick up their kids.

I never felt threatened by any of the racial bickering in school until one day while walking in the school hallway, on my way to gym class. Out of nowhere, a black classmate came up from behind. Putting a knife to my side, he whispered an inaudible demand. Trying to keep my cool, I told him that if he stuck me with his knife, he'd better make sure it took me down, but he'd regret ever setting eyes on me if I got back up. There was a nervous pause. I was hoping that he was every bit as uneasy as I was. Pulling back, he folded his knife, and put it away. With a nervous smile and a pat on my shoulder, he told me that he was only kidding. I never let on how frightened I really was even though I always felt sure that I could take care of myself in any one-on-one situation.

One day, while walking home from the junior high school after football practice, I was stopped by three black guys, all of whom I knew from school. As they all stood on the sidewalk, the bigger one of the three spoke up and said that they decided I needed a beating and they were going to give it to me. He was several inches taller and quite a bit bigger than I was. Having no idea what this was all about, I did know that I didn't stand a chance against the three of them. Before I could say or do anything, the big guy hit me in the jaw, knocking me unconscious, to the ground.

Regaining consciousness, I was alone, lying in the street between a couple parked cars. My books were scattered about. I gathered everything up and continued on my way home. My pants were torn at the knees, and I had a few scrapes and bruises, but not from the beating. They were caused by the rough asphalt. Arriving home, my parents asked me what had happened. After explaining everything, they took me back to the school to file a report. One of the women in the administration office told us that there was nothing the school could do because it happened off campus and after hours. Pausing a moment, she looked over her shoulder. Leaning closer, she whispered that her husband was an officer in the Vallejo Police Department and suggested that we go there to file a report.

At the police station, I identified the kids who beat me up by name. They were consequently rounded up and brought in for questioning. Each one of them denied the allegations, and the mother of one of them even covered for her son, saying that he was at home with her when it all happened. Those kids weren't new to that type of thing, and the police officers knew very well who they were. Unfortunately, it was my word against theirs.

While having dinner one evening, we were also watching Perry Mason on the television. I remember telling Mom and Dad that I knew what I wanted to be when I grew up. Well, Dad looked at me and said, "What do you think you want to be?" When I told him that I wanted to be a lawyer, he told me that I wasn't smart enough. "You'll have to do a lot better in school if you want to be a lawyer," he told me. I was crushed. Mom had always told me that I could be whatever I wanted to be, all I had to do was work for it. I knew that my grades could be better. School seemed so hard for me, but now my dream to become a lawyer had been snuffed out by my own dad. Dad pointed out that I should learn a trade and that as long as I had a trade, I would always be able to find work. "Focus on sheet metal shop or wood shop at school," he told me.

I enrolled in the sheet metal shop and wood shop in school. I loved sheet metal shop and did pretty well, but I couldn't envision a career in that line of work.

I was usually a pretty easy going guy. It took a lot to get me fighting mad. Walking down the school hallway, I was having a bad day and my fuse was abnormally short. It wasn't going to be a good day for anyone who was looking for trouble and thought I might be an easy target. One student in particular felt the need for a challenge as I walked by and he said something to me that set me off. He had been mouthing off at me all year long. I had managed to ignore him until this time. This time was different and I wasn't going to turn the other cheek. As I turned and rushed him, he began to retreat. He quickly discovered that there was nowhere to go. His back was truly against the wall. Both of us fell to the floor, as I had him in a hold and I wasn't about to let go. We exchanged a few more words and with my left arm, I held him around the back of his head, while I pounded his face with my other fist repeatedly and uncontrollably.

A crowd quickly gathered. It took several teachers to break it up. When I was pulled off of him, I was unscathed. He wasn't so lucky as he ended up pretty badly beaten and bloodied. We were taken to the vice principal's office where we were both subsequently suspended. Having the most to lose, I was on the track team. Without ever receiving official notice from the coach, I never returned to practice. My victory was bittersweet as the other kid never gave me any trouble after that. In fact, we become friends from then on.

My temper often got the best of me when I was very young. As I matured, I learned to be more disciplined. The beating I gave that kid in junior high school helped me realize how much damage I was capable of doing. I managed to keep it in check most of the time as I got older. I did, however, let it get the best of me that day and just one more time in high school.

Walking across the campus to my car after classes were over at Vallejo Senior High School, a bad day was about to get a lot worse. A classmate, standing outside with his girlfriend, thought he'd show off for her. Like the kid in junior high school, he too had been mouthing off at me throughout the school year. I had always ignored him. This time, I decided to settle the score. Once and for all!

I asked a bystander to hold my books. Sensing a fight, he eagerly accepted them. With my back now turned to the first kid, I removed my jacket. Turning back around to face off with him, I was caught with a hook that I didn't see coming. It was the first and last time he ever hit me -- or anyone else. Enraged by his sucker punch, I grabbed him. It was at that point that I knew I had the upper hand, seeing the obvious fear in his eyes. Feeling a double jolt of adrenalin, I took him to the ground and pinned his arms down with my knees. Grabbing his ears and hair on the sides of his face, I began slamming his head repeatedly into the ground until I was pulled off by several teachers who had pushed their way through the crowd that had quickly gathered.

One week later, that same kid was riding in the back of an open pickup truck on the way home from school. Northbound, they were on a two lane road that ran adjacent to the railroad tracks, lined with eucalyptus trees on the right side. Off to the left side of the road was an open field. Ignoring the double yellow line that divided the two lanes, the driver decided to pass a slower-moving vehicle. Pulling up alongside the slower vehicle, the truck driver found himself facing some oncoming traffic. Losing control of the truck, he cut the wheels hard to the left causing it to flip over. The passenger in the back was ejected onto the asphalt. Both, the driver and passenger in the cab of the truck survived. Unfortunately, the ejected passenger did not.

In junior high school, I made the basketball and track teams. Knowing that I was never going to excel in basketball, I only played to stay in shape at my dad's suggestion. Making the track and field team, I tried my hand at shot put and discus, but it was clear I wasn't going to excel in either of those events. Even though I sat the bench most of the time, I did letter in both sports. Football was reserved for the freshmen at the junior high school level. It was six-man flag football, competing against the other five junior high schools in the county. Exceeding my own expectations, I became a starting halfback on the team. I wasn't a fast runner, and I knew I wasn't ever going to be a star athlete, but I loved competing and ended up lettering in football as well. It was at this time that I had been seeing Pam on a regular basis and we began dating exclusively. We ended up going steady off and on not only through junior high school, but also throughout high school.

At the end of the school year, the Vallejo High School football coaches came to the junior high school to explain their successful program to the athletes interested in playing at the high school level. There were big shoes to fill there. The Vallejo High School Apaches were not only champions, but their winning reputation was known all over Northern California. They had the best football program in the North Bay League. None of that intimidated me, however, and I was sold and excited about trying out and hopefully continuing the Apache legacy as one of the best in the entire state of California. The Vallejo High School Apaches had made quite a reputation as they had been undefeated for three seasons and they weren't just winning, they were obliterating their opponents. When people in other cities would hear any mention of the Vallejo Apaches on the radio, they turned their radios off in disgust. Not only were they one of the best teams in the state, but Vallejo was also ranked in the top five high school football teams nationally. I was nothing more than a mediocre athlete and I worried about how I was going to match up against the others on a team that had such a reputation.

That summer, Kevin invited me to go swimming with him across town. I never felt comfortable swimming at a strangers house, but I accepted his invitation this time. Arriving at Dolly's house, Kevin introduced me. She welcomed me to her house and said that anytime I wanted to come over to swim, I was welcomed. A short elderly woman with very short graying hair, Dolly lived in what looked like a palace to me back then. She loved having kids over during the summer. With no kids of her own, she said the pool would be wasted if friends didn't use it. Not long afterwards, Geno joined us at Dolly's. We spent hours swimming, clowning around and just having a great time.

On the patio, there was something that I really found intriguing. Dolly had an old- fashioned, red Coca Cola machine that actually dispensed the bottled soft drinks. Not knowing anyone with a Coke machine at their house, I thought that was almost as cool as having a jukebox. The best thing about it was that it only cost a nickel for an eight ounce bottle of Coca Cola.

We had many a fun-filled summer days at Dolly's house back then, swimming and learning how to dive off the diving board at the deep end of the pool. Dolly was also in charge of the theatre guild a few blocks away. Taking notice of the way we were playing and clowning around, she invited us to come down and try out for some of the live theater productions. Embarrassed, I just thought she was only trying to be nice. I really didn't think of myself as having much talent, so I didn't take her up on her invitation. Besides, the thought of having to memorize all those lines and go out on a stage in front of a bunch of people was terrifying to me.

The summer of 1968, I got to go with Geno's family on a month-long vacation to meet their relatives in Ohio and Kentucky. I decided to do some odd jobs to earn some extra spending cash. Mr. Lundquist who lived across the street and up a few doors said that the eves of his house needed painting and asked me how much I would charge to do that if he paid for the paint. It looked like at least one day of work and I told him that I would do it for 80 dollars. He thought that was fair and I started the next day. Little did I know that it would take the better part of a week to do all that painting with a brush. I held up my part of the bargain and he did too. Of course after I had finished, I realized it was worth a lot more than what I actually got paid.

When it came time to leave, we made the journey in their white Ford station wagon. The extra row of seats that lifted up from the floor made the trip with six passengers and one driver manageable. Mom Shepherd didn't drive so Dad Shepherd did most of the driving. Barbara, or "Bob" as she preferred to be called, was the oldest of their children, but didn't drive either. Mike was second oldest. He did have his driver's license and shared much of the driving with his dad. Because Geno hadn't had his driver's license very long, he didn't drive much during that trip. Maybe it was because he was driving when we were nearing Denver. We had been on the road since leaving Vallejo. We stopped only to fuel the car and grab something quick to eat, so we were all getting pretty weary by this time. Geno dozed off behind the wheel. Fortunately, Dad Shepherd, caught it before anything serious happened and relieved him of his driving duties. We stopped in Denver to refresh ourselves and get a good night sleep.

I fell in love with Kentucky. The Shepherds had told me a lot about the blue grass that grew naturally, and while I found that intriguing, it was the mountain people there that I so quickly connected with. Finding them to be some of the friendliest people I had ever met and realizing that they were completely opposite of the languid and often feuding hillbillies that the movies and cartoons had so often depicted, I not only fell in love with the country, I had a great admiration for the people as well. Living off the land, they constantly worked the fields, growing the crops that provided all their food. They were some of the hardest-working and God-fearing people I ever met. I treasured the experience of living like they did. When I had to take a bath in a wooden tub of water in the smoke house located a few yards away from the house, I thought that was the best. When Mike, Geno and I went for a walk on one of the dirt country roads, I came across an old abandoned brown hat. It reminded me of the one worn by Jed Clampett of the *Beverly Hillbillies* television show and I quickly grabbed it up and put it on my head and wore it proudly. Absolutely loving it there, I didn't want to leave when it came time for us to begin our journey back to California. Of all the souvenirs I bought, it was the hat that meant the most to me. I made a promise to myself and some of the family there that I would return someday. When we got back home in California, I couldn't wait to share my experiences with Mom and Dad and give them a couple of keepsakes that I had bought for them in Kentucky. When I told them that Kentucky was such a special experience for me and that I felt like I belonged, they turned and looked at one another. With quirky smiles, they remained silent and just played along with my excitement. While thinking their behavior was a bit peculiar, I never gave it a second thought.

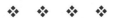

At the young age of fifteen, I applied for a job at the Taco Bell on Sonoma Boulevard where Geno had been working for a while. During my interview, I explained that because I didn't have my own transportation, I would be relying on Geno. She said that she had no problem with scheduling the two of us together and she was more than happy to work around my football schedule. Working one Saturday afternoon, a man came up to the window and asked for a number of items. When he mispronounced frijoles as "free-holes," I could hardly contain myself. After he left, I went to the back of the store where Geno and the manager were working. I told them what that customer said and her reply was, "You should have told him to come to the back door because we don't serve those up front."

One day I was scheduled to work without Geno. When I brought it to the manager's attention, she asked why I couldn't work without him. When I told her that I didn't have my drivers license yet, she said that she wouldn't have hired me had she known that. I was a good worker and she liked having me as an employee. Not only did she keep me as an employee, she worked with my availability until I got my driver's license. She also worked around my football schedule by not scheduling me during football season. After football season ended, however, I was disappointed to learn that there was a change in management. The new manager refused to honor the arrangement and let me go. After my junior year of football ended, I went to work down the street at McDonalds for the next couple years. They were very happy to have me and more than willing to work around my football schedule.

As the end of the summer grew near, I started thinking more about playing football for the high school. I figured that the most difficult thing I was going to face was keeping my grade point average high enough during the season to avoid being cut. Besides having to work harder scholastically, I also knew that making the team was going to require a greater degree of work and talent on the field. Realizing I couldn't do it alone, I sought the help Glen Reid, a neighbor of mine, who was a star football player in his high school years at Vallejo High School. One of his old teammates and still close friend was Mike Sweatfield, who was the current Apaches' head junior varsity football coach.

Making a blocking bag, Glen instructed me on blocking techniques in his front yard. Putting in a lot of hours with me, he taught me how to block and drive, using the homemade blocking bag. We always had fun and he rarely missed an opportunity to jab me with some jovial sarcasm, telling me that I would never make the team. He always followed up by saying that he would make it a point to put in a good word with Mickey. That's what he called his long-time friend, Coach Sweatfield.

Dad helped me train during the summer months before conditioning practices began in August. When we went to Prosser Reservoir I took the opportunity to train in the Sierra Mountains by sprinting up steep grades to get my legs in shape.

I knew that I would be competing against other guys that had played organized football much longer than I and I figured that gave them an advantage over me. I was very insecure and wasn't sure that I was going to make the team. Not knowing how I might react upon learning that I had been cut, I made sure no one else was around before looking at the list of those who made the team. I couldn't bear the thought of someone seeing my disappointment upon discovering my name wasn't on the roster. Figuring that all the other guys would rush to the gym as soon as it was posted, I decided to wait until I was sure to be the only one there. Peeking around the corner of the vacant corridor, the list was posted on the bulletin board, half way down the hallway. Once again, making sure that no one was around, I knew it was now safe. Walking down the hall, I slowly came upon the bulletin board with my heart in my throat. Looking at the list, I nervously scrolled down the names in alphabetical order. There it was. I had not been cut! Breathing a great sigh of relief and hardly able to contain my excitement, I walked away calm on the outside, with a little more confidence than I had enjoyed during the tryouts and conditioning phase of the preseason. That wasn't the end, however as there were going to be two more rounds of cuts before anyone knew who was actually going to make the team that would represent the greatest high school football team in Northern California.

I eventually made the team and became an alternate starter as an offensive right guard. With forty-three players on the junior varsity roster, it was the largest roster they had ever had. The athletic department, unfortunately, wasn't prepared for so many. There weren't enough helmets to go around and some of the players had to wear the old leather style helmets that the school still had from a period long passed when my Uncle Fred played for the team. The players who saw the least amount of playtime had to wear them and were lovingly called "punkin heads." My most embarrassing moment that season came when Coach Sweatfield decided we were going to have a one-on-one contact drill after our blocking and tackling looked sloppy during the previous Friday night game.

After marking out a small square area just small enough for two linemen to line up and face off within, the adjacent center snapped the ball to the coach. He handed it off to the first running back in line, who had to run through the marked area where the two lineman would battle it out without getting tackled. If a lineman with a regular helmet lost to a lineman with a leather helmet, he had to relinquish his and wear the leather helmet for the following week.

As my turn came up, I was matched up against one of the smaller guys whom I was confident that I could beat one on one. I had never lost to him during any of the drills before. Taking the position of the defensive player, we faced off in the small boxed in area. I stared into his eyes as we were now prepared for action. The ball was snapped. Defying the basic rules of engagement, I immediately stood straight up to grab him. Much to my surprise, he hit me at the belt line exactly as he was supposed to. I was immediately at his mercy and he showed me none as he drove me right out of the square and the running back ran through untouched. I was as devastated as I was embarrassed. So overconfident, I did exactly what I wasn't supposed to do. We exchanged helmets and I became a "punkin head" for an entire week. Coach Sweatfield's verbal assault further humiliated me in front of all my teammates who were quietly having a good laugh at my expense. With no place to hide, I just lowered my head and returned to the line where I had plenty of time to think about it before my next turn.

On the eve of my sixteenth birthday, Michelle was helping me celebrate. Dad was sitting at the dining table while Michelle and I had been listening to music in my bedroom. He had been drinking all evening and was rather intoxicated by this time. At the stroke of midnight, September 6, Michelle went into the kitchen and mixed me a stiff drink of bourbon and water. Handing it to me, she dared me to drink it right down. Sensing that some fun was in store, I did exactly as she dared. A few minutes later, she made me another drink. This fifty-fifty combination was a tad stronger than the first. Doing the same thing, it wasn't long before I began to feel the effects of the alcohol. Making a third drink, Michelle mixed this one even stronger. Like the first two drinks, I, again, drank it right down. A few minutes later, I was leaning against the wall trying to stay on my feet. We were both laughing and having a good time when a totally oblivious Dad began to notice and wonder what was going on. When I attempted to walk across the room, he started to get mad when I stumbled and fell down laughing. Michelle decided to go home when Dad made an ugly scene, demanding to know what was going on. I told him that everything was okay and proceeded to go to bed. I had to get some sleep so I could be ready for the first of a double session football practice that was scheduled early the next morning.

Waking up with the sickening after-effects of that little celebration, I rose and went to practice. While we were running through some plays, I had to pause and walk away from the huddle. Softly walking over to the inner edge of the track that circled the practice football field, I lifted my helmet up without removing it from my head, leaned over and left what little remained in my stomach on the dirt track before returning to the practice field.

After the first of two practices ended, Mom and Dad picked me up to take me to the downtown Ford dealership. They were buying me a used car for my birthday. As it turned out, they bought the car that was formerly owned by the football coach of the cross town rivals. They tried to get me to test drive it, but I was so sick, it was all I could do to just sit there without heaving. Seemingly much more intense, I barely made it through the second practice session. To this day, I can't even smell bourbon without feeling like I'm going to be sick.

As a junior on the varsity football team, I wasn't a starting player and didn't see much playtime except for what I did on special teams. We finished the season undefeated with a record of 8-0-1. The varsity's reputation was still intact and that was going to be the major challenge of my senior year—preserving that reputation.

When my senior year began, I was ready to make a name for myself on the football field. During one of the practices, during passing drills, I ran a pass pattern. As I turned to catch a pass, the quarterback known for throwing bullets, threw the ball to me. I laid my hands palm up, directly in front of me but the hard thrown ball hit directly on the end of my fingertips and bounced away. As I went to pick it up with my left hand, I felt a peculiar tugging sensation in my little finger. Picking the ball up from the ground, I placed it in my right hand to have a look at the little finger on my left hand. Much to my surprise, I couldn't move it as it was half closed and pointing in a direction that it was never intended to do. Having no idea what had happened, I went directly over to the coach who said that I should get a shower and then go to the doctor.

Mom took me to the doctor after I got home. They told me to lay flat on the table, where there were going to give me some numbing shots in that finger. The doctor left the room for about 20 minutes. When he returned, he began tugging on it but couldn't reset it. He asked me if I had done anything with it and I assured him that I hadn't. Some how, some way, it had obviously reset itself. The worse news came when he put a cast on my hand which sidelined me for several weeks.

Pam and I had dated off and on throughout high school until late in the football season of my senior year. When I asked her to be my steady girl, she accepted and we once again became a steady couple for the last time. My cast was removed the week before the final game. Not one I wanted to miss, it was the biggest game of the season. I was especially eager to get back on the playing field for that one.

This was the cross town rivalry game between the Vallejo Apaches and the Hogan Spartans. We scored first and maintained the lead throughout the game. I was one of the defensive linemen on the field when the Hogan Spartans had the ball in the final minutes. With only seconds left, we had less than a six-point lead. I felt strongly that they were going to run the ball in my direction. Up for the challenge, I was not going to allow myself to become overconfident. The Spartan's strongest runner was a speedy running back named Thayran Grisby, whom I had known throughout junior high school. As the Hogan offense came out of the huddle, a fellow teammate came running in from the sideline, shouting, "Haskins, Haskins!" I couldn't believe my ears. The coach was pulling me out for a another player! A freshman no less who hadn't played a single play during the game. I sprinted off the playing field then watched in utter disbelief as the play I was expecting, began to develop. The freshman was blocked hard and taken out of the play, creating a hole big enough to drive a big rig through it.

Grisby ran the ball into the end zone, untouched for the game-winning touchdown.

As painful as it was, I could hardly accept the losing season that the Vallejo Apaches had that season. There was little I could do about that. The hardest thing for me to accept was the fact that of all the plays during my high school football career, the one I remember most is that one play when I was taken out of the game and had to painfully watch as the cross-town rivals were victorious by running over my position played by and inexperienced freshman. I couldn't help but feel partly responsible or letting not only my teammates down, but for letting the alumni down that season as well. I didn't think I would ever live that down until a few years later. Redemption was mine while at a class reunion, one of my former teammates, introduced me to his wife as the guy who was the hardest hitting player on the football team.

As I began to spend more time listening to the Beatles and my parents spent more time drinking and getting drunk, a rift began to form between us. They began to bring their drinking friends home from the bar more frequently. While watching television, I overheard my dad, boasting with some of his friends that someone "was much better off now than he would have been if he had he still been living back there." Dad made references to the back hills and mountain people on more than one occasion. Mom always tried to keep him quiet, but he always said, "Oh, he doesn't know what I'm talking about." He was right about that. I didn't know and I really didn't care. I didn't pay much attention to what I thought was just alcohol induced audacity and storytelling. Little did I know that my parents told Michelle's mother, that while they were living in Virginia, Dad got mixed up with another woman, got her pregnant, and I was the result of that pregnancy.

After graduating from high school, Geno moved back to Ohio with his family and enrolled in a college back there. After only a few months in Ohio, he returned to marry Charmaine and take her back with him this time.

On the evening of their wedding rehearsal, we were all sitting around talking when the subject of catholic school came up. I mentioned that I had started school while living in Japan. Charmaine chimed in and said that she too lived there and attended a Catholic school as well. As we compared notes we discovered that we both attended Cherry Blossom Elementary School during the same time period. She then asked if I was the blonde kid that they had a sendoff for just before he was to return to the States. I couldn't believe my ears. I had almost forgotten about that party. Confirming that I was indeed that person, we had even more to celebrate that evening.

The next day, I stood proudly by Geno's side, his best man, as he and Charmaine became husband and wife. Charmaine's maid of honor, Doreen, had been dating Geno's brother throughout high school and were engaged. Pam was very jealous of her and she let it get the best of her at the wedding reception where she got into the champagne and drank too much. When it was brought to my attention, Geno and I took her outside, away from the party. His former boss offered the backseat of his car to let her sleep it off. As soon as we got her comfortable in the backseat, she passed out. We left her there to sleep it off and returned to the reception celebration.

Later, someone went out to check on her and discovered that she had gotten sick all over the backseat and floor of the car. That upset me even more than the fact that she got drunk -- however, it was bittersweet as well. The guy who owned the car was the same guy that fired me from Taco Bell and then told the other employees that he did it because I ate too much. I cleaned it up but was unable to get the smell out of his car. I just figured that he and I were now even.

Doreen and I sat next to each other in English our senior year. Both sitting in the front row, her desk was the closest to the door and I sat to her left. The teacher, Mrs. Sandals, sat at the rear of the classroom where she could keep a watchful eye on her class. Strictly business, she didn't allow any talking during class time. The school bell rang, signaling that class was to begin. I was quietly talking to a gum-chewing Doreen. I continued only long enough to finish my thought. Hearing my whispers, Mrs. Sandals looked up to see where it was coming from. When she saw Doreen's lips moving, she said, "Doreen, that's enough talking. Get back to work." Doreen tried to explain that she wasn't doing the talking, but Mrs. Sandals said that she saw her talking and there was no use in denying it. In an attempt to set the record straight, I spoke up. Mrs. Sandals told me to mind my own business. Stating that Doreen never said a word, I was cut off when Mrs. Sandals insisted that she heard and saw Dorene's mouth moving I again, tried to explain that she saw Doreen chewing gum and it was my voice that she heard.

The stand off ended and the room got relatively quiet before Mrs. Sandals called me back to her desk. Getting up, I walked back her desk at the rear of the room. She handed me a pass to the dean's office. While I couldn't believe what was going on, I was every bit as happy to get out of that atmosphere. As I returned to my desk to gather my things, I read what she had written. Turning to Mrs. Sandals, I said loudly, "You've got to be kidding!" She ordered me to be quiet and leave the classroom.

The entire class was begging to know what was going on. What she had written was so incredible that I had to read it out loud. "Ted is being disruptive in class and very argumentative. He must be on drugs or something." A roaring laughter came from the classroom, then I read the rest of her note. "I don't want him back in my classroom." My classmates responded in a bit of a protest, knowing that I didn't do drugs and that I was only trying to be accountable for my own actions. They were then ordered to be quiet and she once again ordered me to leave.

I went directly to the dean's office not knowing what to expect, but confident that I had done nothing wrong. Knowing me better than any of the teachers on campus, the Dean of Boys asked me what really happened in class. I pleaded my case and Mr. Bell just shook his head while looking at what Mrs. Sandals had written. Mr. Bell said, "I think I know you well enough to know that you aren't on drugs. You're a fine athlete and an honest student who always tried to avoid trouble." I simply sat quietly, nodding my head as he continued, "She says here that she doesn't want you back in her class. Do you want out of her class?" When I told him that I would prefer to stay, he promised that he would talk to her and that I should expect to be back in her class the following day. "I don't think it's a good idea to send you back to class today," Mr. Bell said, "I'm going to ask you what you'd like to do with the remainder of the hour." I requested to go to the library and Mr. Bell wrote me a pass and dismissed me.

The following day, I was back in class and everything was as if nothing had ever happened. I thought it was all settled until the last day of school when she called me back to her desk. She was telling everyone what their final grade was for the semester. As I sat down in the chair next to her desk, she looked me right in the eye and asked if I needed the credits from this class to graduate. I told her that I had enough credits to graduate midterm, but my parents practically begged me to stick it out and graduate with the rest of my class. Appearing a bit uncomfortable and nervous, she quietly informed me that I was receiving an *F* for the semester. I had no doubt that she was settling the score, but I didn't challenge the grade, nor did I care. I quietly let her know what I thought and returned to my desk.

Just before graduation, my parents surprised me by saying that they'd like to send me back to Virginia to meet the Taylor family. I didn't really know them, but they had mentioned who they were once or twice. They were a couple they knew when they were stationed in Norfolk. Their daughter was named Inga Jo, for my mom, so I knew that they must have been close, but didn't quite understand why all of a sudden, they wanted me to go back there and meet them when the last time they saw me was when I was just a baby. They told me that the Taylors would love to see me and would enjoy having me for a week, adding that they thought I'd get along well with their daughter. I had never gone so far away from home by myself and thought it might be an adventure, and reluctantly agreed to go.

My high school graduation was a blur. I didn't want to be there. I just wanted out of school. Pam's sister, Candy was also graduating that day. Their grandmother had come all the way from Iowa for her graduation. After the ceremony ended, I began looking for Pam when I happened upon Robin. It had been a long time since we had seen each other and I was happy to have a few moments to talk to her. I congratulated her and we spoke briefly before going our separate ways. My parents were there, but they didn't stay long. As soon as the ceremony ended, they were off to the bar.

I had no idea what I was going to do with the rest of my life. Some of Dad's friends had tried to tell me what I should do with my life including radio broadcasting and going into plastics. I never thought that radio was something I could make a living at and plastics just seemed to me to have no future. Back then, plastics were used primarily for cheap little toys. Without any idea of what I was going to do, I only knew that I didn't want four more years of academics. Once again, I began to feel that loneliness returning. I decided to continue working at

McDonald's cooking and serving hamburgers, until something better came along. Moving to Ohio was an option that Dad Shepherd had offered, explaining that there was always work to be found there and I was welcomed to come back anytime.

Arriving in Virginia, I found the Taylor family very accommodating and hospitable. A bikini clad Inga Jo looked as though she could have just walked off the set of one of those Beach Party movies from the early sixties. Things seemed to be going pretty well until her mother asked her to take me to the beach with her and her boyfriend one evening. Feeling like I was interfering, I excused myself to give them some time alone once we were at the beach. Inga Jo also took me to the mall where I ran into a girl that I knew in high school. I couldn't believe my eyes. Here I was, thousands of miles away from home and I ran into someone I knew in high school. What are the odds? That would only be the beginning of many years of running into people I knew wherever I traveled.

While flying back home, I never figured out why my parents really wanted me to go back there to visit the Taylors and they never offered any other explanation.

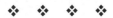

Younger than my classmates and only seventeen when I graduated, I was torn about going into the military. The Vietnam War was nearing an end, and I didn't feel I was ready for the military. I believed that staying in high school for that last semester was probably the worst thing I could have done. Of course, Mom and Dad were disappointed in me, but not as much as they were when I told them that I decided not to go to college. I hated school, and didn't feel I was college material by any stretch of the imagination. I moved out of the house as soon as I graduated and temporarily lived with Pam's oldest sister, Cindy. Understanding my situation, she allowed me to move in if I would help her with things around the apartment. Pregnant with her second child, Cindy's husband was in the Air Force and stationed in South Korea at the time. I moved into a place of my own as soon as she had her baby and assured me that she was capable of taking care of things on her own. I continued to work very long hours to pay my rent and buy groceries. Fortunately, I didn't need many groceries since I often ate at work.

While visiting my parents one afternoon, they brought up the subject of college once again. They pitched to me that if I moved back home, they would help me with college expenses, but they wanted me to continue working to help out with some of the costs. I gracefully declined.

The following week, they offered me yet another chance to go to college on their dime. This time they said that they wouldn't expect me to work so I could focus on my studies. Cautiously agreeing, I moved back home on the Sunday before Thanksgiving. Mom and Dad had been drinking and I had only been home for a few hours when they told me that they decided to change the terms of the agreement. Dropping the bomb, they told me that they did in fact expect me to continue working while going to college. I couldn't believe that they would do that to me. I lost my apartment and moved back home for what? Feeling betrayed, I went to my room and gathered all my things that I could fit in to my small Toyota. Walking out the front door, I told Mom that I was going to Ohio, and wouldn't be back. I was gone before she could reply.

Before leaving town, I drove to Pam's house and told her what happened and that I was moving to Ohio to get a job and live there. Crying, she begged me not to go. I told her I'd be back for her but she didn't want to believe it. I then promised that I would come back for her as soon as she graduated from high school.

Driving most of the way with very little sleep, I only ate when I needed to stop at a rest stop or to gas up the car. I had become so weary that I found myself squinting to see out the windshield. It was anybody's guess how long I'd been doing that. I finally realized that it was snowing when I lost control of the car when the bald tires caused it to slide out of control. Fortunately, I was the only one on the road and there were no patrol cars on the highway. I pulled off at the next rest stop and slept until the weather cleared and the roads were once again safe enough to drive on.

Four days after leaving California, I arrived at the Shepherd's house in Dayton, Ohio. It was especially significant because it was Thanksgiving Day. It seemed we all had plenty to be thankful for upon my arrival. It was hard to tell who was happier to see who. With a broad smile and open arms, Dad Shepherd offered their house to me as long as I began looking for a job immediately.

I helped out wherever and whenever I could until I got a job. I even went to the school where Dad Shepherd was the night janitor and helped him with his duties there. I didn't know it, but Dad had called Mr. Shepherd several times and asked him to talk me into joining the military. Even though Mr. Shepherd had been the army recruiter in Vallejo for a number of years, he didn't think it was his place to do that. He was, however, instrumental in helping me get a job in a machine shop where several of his old friends and family worked.

Hired as an entry level shipping clerk, I worked hard and learned quickly. When the opportunity to work in the adjacent machine shop came my way, I eagerly accepted the position. The hours were long -- 7:00 a.m. to 5:00 p.m. with no time off for lunch. We ate while we worked Monday through Friday. Working Saturdays was mandatory, but only from 7:00 a.m. until noon.

The following summer, Pam's parents allowed her to come visit me on one condition -- she stayed with the Shepherd family. They knew the Shepherds since Mike had dated Pam's older sister, Cindy in high school a couple times. While on a date during her visit, I proposed to Pam with a diamond ring. She accepted on the condition that I write a letter to her dad and ask him for her hand in marriage, which I gladly did after she returned to California. Pam and I began looking for an apartment right away. We found one that overlooked a river and a park on Riverside Drive, not far from where I worked.

During the following year, I saved all the money I could. Rarely going out on weekends, I was able to save a nice sum of money before going back to California for our wedding. I did, however, spend enough to go back to California for one Christmas.

Fishing was one of the things I could do without much cost and it would sometimes put food on the table. One day, I drove around until I found a stream that looked pretty inviting. Pulling my car off the road, I parked it near a barbed wire fence that separated the road from a field. Getting my gear out of the trunk, I climbed over the fence and walked about twenty yards to the stream where I baited the hook and tossed a line. Enjoying the peace and quiet, my mind began to wander. I began to doze off when I heard a voice from behind. I turned around to find an elderly man in bib overalls standing at the top of the embankment. He was the farmer who owned the property I was on. He asked if that was my blue Toyota up on the road. Confirming that it was, I asked him if he objected to me fishing there. Without any objections, he said that the reason he asked about the car was because he had noticed the Twelfth Naval District decal on the window.

When I asked him if he was familiar with that area, he said that he knew it quite well. Telling me that he was stationed in San Francisco back in the late '30s and early '40s, he and all his buddies used to go to Vallejo to party. "Georgia Street," he said, "was nothing but bars and a red light district back then. Every weekend, the party was on." I laughed with him and said that I had heard some stories about downtown Vallejo much like that from others, but it wasn't like that anymore.

When I started thinking about who I was going to ask to be in my wedding, Mom Shepherd asked if I would do her a favor. I told her that I would do whatever I could, of course. After all they had done for me, I did feel an obligation. Then she lowered the boom. She requested that I ask Mike instead of Geno to be my best man. This was going to be the most difficult decision I had ever made in my nineteen years. I wanted to respect her wishes, but at the same time, I didn't want to betray Geno. She assured me that Mike would not accept, giving me the opportunity to ask Geno. I didn't think I could live with myself if it ever got back to Geno that he had not been at the top of my list. I didn't know how I could make everyone happy, so I did what I knew I had to do.

Valuing my friendship with Geno more than anything, it broke my heart to disappoint Mom Shepherd because I knew that she wasn't going to be very happy with my decision. Telling her that I just couldn't do as she asked, she pleaded with me to change my mind, but I stood my ground. I thought it was over until she asked me one more favor. She wanted me to cut my shoulder length hair, saying that I would look back on my wedding pictures and hate them if I didn't cut it. It was the style and I liked it that way. I gave my word that I would think about it, but wouldn't make a decision right away.

The week before I was to return to California, I went to the bank to withdraw enough money to make my flight reservations for the trip, only to learn that there wasn't enough money in my account. The bank clerk informed me that there had been a withdrawal just a few weeks earlier that all but closed the account. Overcome with a sick feeling in the pit of my stomach, I told the teller that I hadn't made any withdrawals since the account was opened. Excusing herself, she returned with copies of the withdrawal transaction and presented them to me. The first thing I noticed was the obvious. The signature on the withdrawal slip wasn't mine and it didn't match the one that they had on file. She also noticed the difference. It was quite clear that the clerk who handled the withdrawal didn't compare them before completing the transaction. The bank initiated an investigation and I didn't know what I was going to do.

Parking my car next to my apartment building, I noticed the painting contractor outside. I struck up a conversation with him and he told me that my roommate had locked himself out of the apartment and he let him use his ladder to gain access through an unlocked window on the parking lot side of the building. The guy he described to me actually lived with a couple of women in the building next door. I knew their names and reported what I had learned to the bank. They assured me that they would have him investigated.

I decided that I should call my parents and explain my situation, hoping they would loan me enough to cover my expenses. Never in my wildest dreams did I think they wouldn't help me, but things only got worse when they told me that they didn't believe my story, "You'll have to figure something else out," they said. I couldn't believe what I was hearing. I pleaded with them, but they weren't buying my story.

Desperate now, I turned to the only ones I knew could help. Explaining to Mom and Dad Shepherd what had happened, I showed them the documents I got from the bank. They in turn called my parents and confirmed my story. Still, they didn't believe it. Dad Shepherd told me that they thought I had gone out and partied the money away so they would not loan any amount to me. Mom and Dad Shepherd then talked it over between themselves and decided that they would loan me the money.

Once in California, I stayed with my parents before the wedding. Nothing was ever said about their unwillingness to help me with a loan. A few days before the wedding, Pam and I got a couple of cots out of the garage and set them up in the living room. I wanted to get some sleep before getting up in the middle of the night to pick up Geno and Charmaine at the

San Francisco Airport. To ensure that we didn't oversleep, I borrowed the alarm clock from the nightstand on Mom's side of the bed. Since it was only for a couple hours, I didn't think it would be missed and I didn't say anything to her. Wrong again! We were abruptly awakened when Mom came storming out from her bedroom in a rage. Awakened from a sound sleep, I was taken aback at what could possibly have ignited such a frenzy. "Where's my clock?" she shouted with profanity. I don't know for the life of me how she did that without stumbling, as inebriated as she was. Still half asleep, I tried to explain why I had it, but she wasn't having any of it. She stood directly over me, pointing her finger, saying, "I don't care why you need it. When I wake up in the middle of the night, I want to know what time it is, so put it back! Right now!" Was this the same woman who knocked me across the room years prior for innocently using that very same word she was now using to dramatically make her point? Knowing that it was useless trying to argue with a drunk, I returned the clock to her nightstand. Pam and I didn't dare go back to sleep for fear we would not wake up in time to pick up Geno and Charmaine.

We got married in St. Peter's Chapel on Mare Island Naval Shipyard, where Pam's two older sisters had also married. The reception was held at the Vallejo Women's Club. While everyone was eating, Auntie Barb asked us what we liked to drink. I looked at her a bit confused and she said "I'm going to get you whatever you would like to have on your honeymoon." I told her we liked orange juice and vodka. I couldn't believe it when she came back a short while later and put it in the car for us. She trusted us to drink it responsibly and we honored her trust. Before we could mingle with all the guests, the photographer rushed us through our photographs and sent us on our way before either of us even knew what happened.

As we drove away in Cindy's, orange Volkswagen, we heard the racket of cans behind us. Charmaine and Kevin had ducked out of the reception unnoticed and tied them to the bumper of the car. On our way out of town, we stopped by my parents' house to remove the cans from the bumper. Mr. Lundquist noticed what was going on and walked over to congratulate us both with a $20 bill. We were both pleasantly surprised by his kindness and thanked him before continuing on our way. We stopped in Santa Rosa the first night, on our way to the Little River Inn, up the coast.

Wasting little time to get there, I didn't want to miss my favorite television show, *All In The Family*. Arriving at the Little River Inn on the second day, we checked in and began drinking the orange juice and vodka. While taking a shower that evening, I slipped and fell, cutting my tailbone wide open on the faucet. It bled profusely and I didn't think I'd ever get it to stop. Even more embarrassing, I didn't know how I was going to hide it from Pam. She didn't hear the fall and since she didn't ask, I didn't tell her until after the honeymoon was over.

We lived our first year in Ohio. Less than a week after we got back, I went to the barber shop, owned by Geno's Uncle Gene, and got all my hair cut off. When I got home, Pam wasn't very happy about it and I promised her that I would let it grow back out. She got a job in a local pharmacy close enough to our apartment for her to ride a bicycle to work. I drove the car to and from my job. We both worked hard, long hours. I continued working ten hour days, five days a week, plus five hours every Saturday morning. We spent the remainder of our weekends up at Lake Shawnee with our friends Larry and Linda, water skiing, fishing and having fun on the lake. Having known Larry before he even knew me, Geno had introduced me to him after I moved back there. He and Charmaine joined us when they could afford the break from his college studies in Kentucky.

I learned that Mom was anxious for grandchildren when every Saturday morning, around 2:00 or 3:00 a.m., we received a call after she'd spent the day drinking with Dad down at the bar. Every phone call was the same. "We miss you two," was always followed by "Is Pam pregnant yet?" My answer was always the same and Mom always ended each conversation by saying that she was going to hang up so we could get to work on it. Pam and I had just spent the last two years apart and we weren't ready to start a family. For almost one year, like clock work, the same phone call, the same questions and the same frustrated response from Mom took place until she finally said to me, "Well, don't you know what that thing is for?"

I later learned that the person who broke into my apartment and stole my savings book, had taken his girlfriend to Disneyworld in Florida with my hard earned money. After hearing that he had been arrested, I returned to the bank to get my money back. Much to my dismay, I learned that they wouldn't reimburse me until the alleged suspect was tried and convicted. Realizing how long that could take, I told the bank president that Pam needed to have a life saving surgical procedure and that money was needed to help pay for it. "If you don't give me my money right here and now," I continued with my totally fabricated story, "I will hold you personally responsible for anything that happens to her if she isn't able to have this surgery." Excusing himself, he quickly returned with a check for all the money that had been stolen from my account. Proceeding immediately to cash the check, I also closed my account. I then drove directly to Mom and Dad Shepherd's to pay them back the money they had so graciously loaned me.

While visiting her mother in Ketchikan, Alaska, Mom called me to tell me that Dad had fallen asleep on the couch at home and a couple of men broke in and beat him up pretty badly. He never got a good look at either of them, but was sure that there were only two. At one point, he remembers hearing them arguing with each other. One told the other to kill him, but he didn't want to. A few items were taken from the house before they left him lying in a pool of blood, battered and bruised with a badly broken jaw.

Mike Lindke had since gotten married and was now living across the street from Mom and Dad, in the same house that Michelle had grown up in. Coming home late that night, he noticed the front door of Dad's house was wide open and the lights on. He went over to make sure everything was all right and discovered Dad unconscious on the floor and called an ambulance.

His jaw had to be wired shut and remained that way for months. His face had been beaten so badly, it looked like hamburger. Dad was a kind and gentle man who never bothered anyone and wouldn't harm a fly. After it healed, his face was so tender that he could never shave again.

April 3, 1974, a big storm was coming to Dayton. While I was in my car, stopped at a very large and busy intersection on my way home from work, I noticed a young woman sitting in a car facing the opposite direction. I couldn't believe what I was seeing through the heavy rain. She looked a lot like Robin. When the traffic signal turned green, we drove in different directions. Almost sure it was her, there was no way I could get turned around and catch up to her, especially with the storm as bad as it was. It was a big one and I had to get home to Pam. She had never been in a storm like this and I didn't want her to be alone any longer than was necessary.

Sitting on the couch with a blanket over us, we watched the *Sonny and Cher Show* on television that evening. A news bulletin interrupted the show. A tornado had just touched down in Xenia, not far from Larry and Linda's home in Lake Shawnee. Touching down at 4:30 pm, nine miles away from Xenia, it hit Xenia ten minutes later. Continuing on a path that was 32 miles long, it killed 32 people, but left Larry and Linda and their families alive and well. I often thought back upon that day for years to come, wondering if it truly was Robin I saw at that intersection in the storm while praying that she had survived if it was, indeed, her.

Every once in a while, someone would play a practical joke on another employee in the machine shop. One of the favorites was always played on anyone who left their safety glasses laying unattended on the work bench. Someone would always dip them in the sulfur oil that was used as coolant in the machines. It was not only hard to clean off the glasses, but it was pretty smelly. On one occasion, one of the older machinists had brought in a small bottle of whiskey. Showing it to me, he said, "watch this." Walking over to the 30-cup coffee pot, he opened it up and poured it all into the coffee without anyone else seeing him. When he came back, he and I waited to see if anyone would notice. As luck would have it, the first person to get a cup of coffee was a Christian man who didn't drink. We got a pretty good laugh as he took a sip right after he filled his cup. Still standing at the coffee pot, he looked into his cup then drank the rest of it right down and walked away. We laughed for the rest of the afternoon about that.

Lavelle was one of my coworkers and friends at Lenz Company. Considerably older than myself, he was well liked by everyone who worked with him. I looked up to him with great admiration and during one of our conversations, I brought up the subject of pay. Even though I knew it was forbidden to discuss pay with the other employees, I asked him how much he made. He had been a faithful employee for over twenty years. I was relatively new and curious about how I could expect to be treated if I remained there for any length of time.

Lavelle appeared somewhat embarrassed and reluctant to talk about it. "Oh, you wouldn't believe me if I told you," he said. An excellent machinist, he had an exceptional work ethic to go along with his great skills. He taught me how to grind and sharpen drill bits by hand, a rare and valuable skill that few others had. Like everyone else in the machine shop, he worked extremely hard every day, ten hours a day, plus five hours every Saturday, with one exception. When everyone clocked out at the end of our work day, we all went home. All but Lavelle. He immediately clocked back in on a different time card and performed janitorial duties at night, for less pay and without benefit of overtime.

We didn't work in a union shop, but the advantage we had over the union shops was that we never experienced lost time due to the occasional strikes or layoffs like they did. That was the tradeoff. After more prodding, Lavelle finally gave in and told me that he made only three dollars an hour. It was hard to tell which of us was more embarrassed, I'm sure. I felt horrible that anyone would take advantage of a man just because of his skin color and I was sure that was the case. I was earning $2.70 an hour and as a machinist helper. There obviously was no fairly established pay scale in that machine shop. The writing was on the wall and I took note.

After giving it a great deal of thought, I decided to test the waters with my supervisor. He was not only the vice president of the company, but he was also Dad Shepherd's brother-in-law. I was hoping that the latter gave me an advantage. Realizing that this could be a very sticky situation, I didn't want to look like I didn't appreciate what they had all done for me thus far. However, I had to look out for my best interest and now Pam's as well.

After having spent some time looking around at other machine shops to see what they had available and how much they were willing to pay, I went into Harry's office and explained to him that Pam and I had decided that we wanted to start a family, but I needed to make a little more money in order to do that. Appearing a bit uncomfortable, Harry told me that he knew that I had been looking around, and he couldn't justify it. He did however, promise to give me a ten cent increase in January, when everyone else got theirs. Pressing a little more, I explained that I was hoping for thirty cents an hour a bit sooner and that I didn't feel ten cents an hour would work for me. Shrugging his shoulders, Harry said that he just couldn't do that.

I continued looking around. Pam and I had talked to her mother about what we wanted to do. She worked at a naval shipyard in California and told me to send her an application with my work experience. When she received it, she took it to the machine shop on the base. It wasn't long before I received and accepted an offer that I couldn't refuse. Of course, Pam was excited to know that she was going to be back with her friends and family once again. My friends and family were in Ohio as far as I was concerned.

When I gave my two week notice to Harry, he asked if there was anything he could do or say to change my mind. Explaining that I was going to earn more than double my current wage in California and that Pam and I would not only be able to start our family, we would both be closer to our own families. Harry's hands were tied. There was nothing he could do but let me go at that point.

The following week, Harry and I had a disagreement. He returned to his office and came back out about a half-hour later carrying an envelope. Handing it to me, he said that I wouldn't be needed anymore, then turned and walked away. I opened it to find my final paycheck and notice of termination inside. Not surprised, I was however disappointed by the way Harry was behaving. I began cleaning up my work area, wiping down my tools, and putting them away one final time.

Before I was done, Harry returned with his head down. Unable to look me in the eye, he said that he had spoken a little hastily and told me that I could stay if I wanted to. "If I wanted to?" I asked myself. I wondered why he couldn't just come out and say it. "Who would want to after all this?" I thought. I told

Harry that I didn't need the extra money, adding, "I gave you two weeks' notice, so you would have plenty of time to hire someone to replace me." I was really waiting for an apology and I was now determined not to stay without one. When I told Harry that I didn't understand what he was trying to say, Harry told me that he was sorry for talking to me the way he did and asked me to stay that final week. I accepted his apology and remained for that second week.

The following week went pretty smoothly. Saturday was my last day, I left work at noon and Pam and I were off to California with trailer in tow, behind our 1973 Ford Maverick Grabber. We shipped our furniture and towed what we could. We agreed not to drive more than five hundred miles each day and stop to rest each night. When we reached Nevada, Pam got behind the wheel while I napped. When I woke up, I realized we were a lot closer to home than I expected to be at that time. She had driven most of the state well over the speed limit while I slept. One of my first observations was a frightening one as we came out of the Sierra Mountains, on the California side. The sky was thick with smog. I had only been gone for three years and I had forgotten how smoggy it could be. It bothered me to think we would be breathing that and probably raising our children in all that dirty air.

Three days after leaving Ohio, we arrived at Pam's parents' house in Napa. We ended up living with them during the following year until finding a place of our own. My first day of work was Friday, September 6, 1974, my twenty-first birthday. I didn't want to start on my birthday, but it was my good fortune as it turned out. President Nixon put a freeze on all civil service hiring the following day.

Pam's parents were season ticket holders for the MIRA Theater Group in Vallejo. They had four seats reserved for each of the four productions during the season. Pam and I became their guests at those plays. They were usually older productions, stories from the forties and fifties, but always fun. Dolly was still running the theatre and during the intermissions she made sure to talk to Pam's dad, Lou and myself about getting involved in future productions. He and I agreed that it would be a lot of fun, but neither of us managed to take the time to do it that season. I don't know how he ever thought that he would have the time for that as heavily involved as he was with the Masons. The following season, I finally decided to try out for one of the productions. Much to my surprise, I got the lead role. I didn't even expect to get a second look since I had never done anything like that before and there were others that had a great deal more experience.

After several rehearsals I became pretty comfortable with my role until my wisdom teeth became impacted. I had put it off until I couldn't stand it anymore. They were removed on Monday, just before the Friday night opening. Making my debut and grand entrance, I looked like a chipmunk and if that wasn't bad enough, I crashed and burned moments after walking onto the stage. Unable to recall my opening line, terror struck. I became petrified in front of the sold-out house. If not for the veteran actress onstage with me, I probably would have experienced complete meltdown. She picked me up with part of my line and I quickly recovered. I was so embarrassed by that very first show, I never missed another queue.

Following one of the performances, I received a note backstage. Much to my surprise, it was from a girl I knew in high school. She had written that she was in the audience that night and enjoyed my performance. Much to my dismay, she said that I seemed so confident onstage that she was embarrassed to go backstage to visit with me. I never saw or heard from her again.

After the play finished its run, I tried out for a part in the next production, *White Sheep of the Family,* about a high society family of thieves, well respected in their British community. Everyone was instructed to try out with British accents. I felt pretty comfortable with that since I always clowned around, imitating the Beatles. I tried out for the title roll, the forger son who was having to make the very difficult decision of going straight, hence "white sheep." I attended all three tryouts, critically watching all the others I was competing with for the same part. On the third and final night, following the last of the tryouts, the director announced who his choices were for the various characters. When I heard him say that someone else had been selected for the title character, my heart dropped. Had I once again become the victim of overconfidence? Although not as embarrassed as I was that day on the football field when I was crowned with the leather helmet for a week, I was so disappointed that I immediately started thinking that maybe my first play might be my last. I was frozen, but remained as I listened to all the other announcements even though I didn't know any of the other actors.

When the director announced his choice for the patriarch, I couldn't believe my ears. Immediate fear struck. At only twenty-three-years of age, not only had I been selected to play the middle-aged father, but I had to play alongside a much older woman who would be playing my wife. I thought that it could look pretty ridiculous, but the most intimidating fact was that my character was required to be on stage nearly every minute of the two hour play and had as many lines as everyone else combined. Flattered, and happy that the director had the confidence in me, I kept thinking about the poor woman who would be playing the part of my wife. Not only was she in her mid fifties, she was also a very accomplished actress. To make matters worse, she intimidated me by saying that the success of the play was riding on my performance. I would either make or break the show.

A dialect coach was brought in to help us with our accents early on during the rehearsal schedule. Near the end of the first rehearsal, the dialect coach had coached everyone but me. Out of character, I timidly approached her and asked if she had any advice for me. She began to blush as she said to me, "I thought you were British."

With a sigh of relief, I thanked her for the compliment and continued by saying, "But there must be some advice you can give me." She insisted that I needed no coaching whatsoever and to continue what I was doing. Makeup helped me look the part, including the white shoe polish that was put in my hair and beard to make it look gray.

This was a role that I could really excel in. I had a lot of fun with it and ended up enjoying every line and every moment on stage. I was surprised to learn that Mom and Dad attended opening night. Knowing that this really wasn't the kind of thing they went for, I was even more surprised upon learning that he had returned for each and every performance afterward. Sitting in the back of the theater, he delighted in listening to what the people in the audience were saying as they critiqued the actors. He couldn't help but laugh as he told me that I was the only actor that the audience members believed was from England.

As usual, following each performance, the audience was invited to come backstage for a meet-and-greet with the cast members. As soon as each show ended, I couldn't wait to get backstage and wash off my makeup and get the shoe polish out of my hair. As the visitors filed through, they chatted with all the other cast members while staring at me. Not one of them ever stopped to talk with me. When I finally realized that no one recognized me without the makeup and the accent, the production had already finished its run.

At the end of the season, I was again pleasantly surprised upon learning that I had been nominated for best actor for both of my performances during the season. I lost to the actor who played in the more popular show that season, *Butterflies Are Free*. Satisfied with my achievements, those two plays were the beginning and end of my stage career. Having become a new father during that time, I found the rewards of being a father were much more gratifying than acting had been. I decided to dedicate all my available time to being a loving husband and father from then on.

In 1976 our nation celebrated its bicentennial for much of the year. Everywhere you looked everything reflected the anniversary of our nations independence. Deciding to have a little fun with that, Pam and I decided to tell my mom and dad that if our baby was born on July 4 and it was a girl, she would be named Betsy Ross Haskins. A son would be named George Washington Haskins. For some reason, they didn't share the same enthusiasm that we had over our choice of names. Dad was the more outspoken of the two. "Why would you do that to a kid?" he'd ask. Pam and I kept the joke going until July 15, 1976.

Pam and I had attended natural childbirth classes and nearly two years after returning to California, our first son was born. Pam contracted gestational diabetes, and the medical team had to induce labor one month early. I remained at her side, coaching her through the delivery. After twenty plus hours of hard labor, they took her to x-ray to see what was going on. The doctor showed us the images and explained that the baby was breach. He didn't want to perform a cesarean because of her diabetes and said he would give her every opportunity he could to deliver naturally. On our way back to our room, I thought about the x-ray image of the baby. Still not knowing what sex it was, I was struck at how perfect its teeth were.

The doctor was determined to deliver the baby before the end of his shift. As that time approached, he decided to be a little more aggressive in one final attempt to avoid a cesarean. Standing over Pam, the nurses took turns pushing down on her abdomen until the baby came out. She ended up in hard labor for nearly twenty-four hours. We had chosen the name of our son when we were dating in high school, but on our way to the hospital, I asked Pam if she would mind if we named our baby, after myself if it was a boy. She had no objections and we gave him the name that I had been given by my parents but decided to call him Little Ted. To no surprise, Mom and Dad were much happier with that choice than they were with George Washington Haskins.

I was beaming proud of her and our newborn son who weighed in at nine pounds, three and one-half ounces. Pam had such a difficult time in delivery that the doctors advised us against having additional children. Upon receiving our first baby pictures, we thought that he looked like a little Eskimo baby. After all, Mom was an Alaskan native. His skin and hair were dark, and his chubby cheeks were just like those of a little Alaskan Indian. Upon sharing that observation with Mom and Dad, neither of them commented. As odd as we thought that was, we both left it alone.

Right after Little Ted's birth, I began working twelve hour days, seven days a week. Two months later, it ended. Exhausted, I just wanted to get away and relax. Mom called me and said she wanted to take the three of us to Alaska for the weekend so that her mom could see the baby. I thought this was the perfect opportunity. Ketchikan is beautiful this time of year. When I pitched it to Pam, she didn't get very excited about the idea. Knowing very little about Alaska, all she could imagine was a land that was nothing but ice and snow. Sunny ocean beaches were her idea of the perfect getaway. I explained to her that Ketchikan was nothing like she imagined and she eventually gave in. The following Friday, we were boarding a plane to Ketchikan, Alaska.

Little Ted cried the entire way. Nothing we could do would stop his crying. We both felt awful for him as well as for the other passengers who had to put up with his constant crying. Upon arriving in Ketchikan, we registered in a downtown hotel. Mom had a separate room no doubt after having flown all the way next to a crying baby, she needed some time to herself. After settling in, I walked to the local pizzeria about a mile away and brought back a small cheese pizza to eat in the room for dinner. Little Ted finally went to sleep that night and that was the first night that he slept without waking up. The following morning, Pam and I went for a walk in the brisk Ketchikan air. Walking down to the river that ran through the town, we got to see the salmon run. The river was so thick with fish that there appeared to be little room for the water. The weather was beautiful as the days were warm and the nights were brisk. Pam fell in love with Ketchikan as I knew she would. Of course the most memorable part of the visit was my grandmother and the way she interacted with her first great grandchild. Grandma never spoke much. English was her second language, but I'm not sure why she was always so quiet. I loved hearing her talk because she always sounded like a little girl as she always spoke in broken sentences. She just sat in her rocking chair looking at her first great grandson with tremendous pride.

The doctors told Pam that because her diabetes was gestational, it might go away after the baby was born. Unfortunately, that wasn't the case, Little Ted was such a blessing that we decided to risk having a second. Three years after Little Ted was born, we had a second son. He was given the name that Little Ted was supposed to have, Joshua. Pam's labor was much easier the second time. Her water broke at home one evening while we were watching television. We went to the hospital where she had a much easier delivery this time. Instead, it was harder on me this time around and I didn't know why. I sat next to Pam in delivery and nearly passed out from all the excitement.

Life was good. My career was going well. Pam stayed home taking care of the kids until she decided to apply for a part-time job at a nearby pizzeria. Expressing my objections, I told her that we didn't need the extra money, but we would probably become dependent on the additional income and she wouldn't be able to quit if she wanted to. She decided to apply for the job and got it. She worked there long enough to move up to night manager. Eventually deciding that she wanted more, she went to work at Mare Island Naval Shipyard with me so that we could work the same hours and have the same days off and paid vacations together. Several years later, we learned that Little Ted nearly didn't survive when he was born after ingesting a germ that nearly killed him.

In the late 1970s, I joined the Jim Fix running revolution that was grasping America. I was never much of a runner, but I was determined. I got myself in great physical condition as I ran daily until I could run three or four miles without any trouble. I ran in the evenings after the boys went to bed and during my forty minute lunch time at work. Shower stalls upstairs allowed me to freshen up before returning to work.

It was about this time that I started a weight training regimen to give my now stringy physique a little shape. I had been running in local events around the bay area when one of the marathon runners I knew at work, talked me into training for an upcoming marathon in the Napa Valley. It sounded like fun, so I started training for it.

I entered the Devil Mountain Run in Danville while Josh was still a newborn. We brought both the boys and while Little Ted was big enough to walk, Josh was carried in a cane basket while he slept. Crossing an intersection, I went to change hands with the basket. I missed grabbing one of the two handles and out rolled Josh. Wrapped in his blanket, he landed right on the asphalt, in the middle of the crosswalk.

Pam saw the basket begin to open, but Josh rolled out faster than she could do or say anything. I, of course, felt awful and was worried that he may have been seriously injured. A nearby volunteer nurse came running to his aid. Following a quick examination, she assured us that he was unscathed and would be just fine. Fortunately, the basket was only inches above the ground and he landed softly. He never even woke up during all the commotion.

Not long after the event, I began to develop shin splints and eventually decided to give up running and devote my physical activity to body building. It was during this same time period that I had begun working out in a nearby gym. It led to a lifestyle change for health reasons, but I thought that I might be able to lead by example where my sons were concerned. Never expecting that they might reject it, after all, I always admired and wanted to be like my own dad when I was growing up until they became alcoholics.

Hoping that my children would follow in my footsteps for the good example I was setting, I tried to keep them focused from the harmful lifestyle of illicit drugs and alcohol abuse that they might become exposed to while remembering how poorly my dad had handled that situation. I did everything I could to avoid repeating his mistakes.

While visiting my parents, they were pretty surprised to see my new fit appearance. While Mom couldn't get over the size that I had achieved, it was Dad who appeared upset by it. He told me that he didn't think it was a good thing to be training with the intensity that resulted in such body mass. I assured them that I wasn't taking any performance-enhancing supplements and that my diet was very healthy. That didn't go over well. Mentioning the healthy eating habits seemed only to throw fuel on the fire. They asked what I thought was so healthy about my diet and when I told them that I was eating mostly complex carbohydrates, very lean protein -- no red meats, nothing with processed sugar, no saturated fats, bleached flower, and only chicken without the skin. Dad went off, "So you think that what we fed you was wrong?" he asked. When our discussion felt more like an argument, I dropped it and let them know how much I enjoyed working out as hard as I was and did it in part to set a good example for my sons. That probably didn't help either as I thought they might misunderstand me to say that I thought they didn't set good examples for me growing up. Somehow, I managed to dodge that bullet.

Pam and I attended bodybuilding competitions and I really got into that. Having never competed in a sport that wasn't a team sport, I decided to give it a try. I began training for my first bodybuilding competition. I was so happy with my progress, that I gave serious thought to going professional sooner or later. But, that wasn't to be.

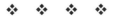

We enjoyed taking the boys camping where Geno and I had spent much of our childhood summers camping near Truckee. We bought an old Chevy truck and put a camper on it. We enjoyed many family outings in that old cab over camper. It was not only ideal for long trips, but it was perfect for weekend getaways. One year, when the lake was lower than usual, we noticed a truck and camper pull in and park just a few feet from the water's edge at sunset. The man driving the truck got out of the cab and retreated to his camper for the evening. Up early the following morning, as we always were, Pam and I were sitting by the campfire enjoying the cool crisp mountain air, and a hot cup of coffee. We could hardly keep from laughing as we watched for that guy to come out of his camper. No longer at the water's edge, the lake had risen overnight and the truck was now axle deep in water. When the camper door opened, the man began to step out. He immediately clung to the door as it swung out over the water. We got a pretty good laugh out of it because it looked so cartoonish. Lucky for him, his truck was a four-wheel drive, and he didn't have any trouble driving it out after scaling around the camper and shimmying into the cab of the truck.

One year, while camping down at Pinecrest Campgrounds, Pam's diabetes went out of control and she ended up in the hospital. I tried to keep the boys occupied while she recovered in the hospital the next couple days. We fished, hiked, and went swimming until she was released at which point we drove back home. That was the last time we all went camping as a family. She refused to go so far away from her doctor from then on and we ended up selling the truck and camper. It was then that I began taking the boys on my backpacking trips. We always had a great time and I loved teaching them about the outdoors and how to respect mother nature by always cleaning up your campsite to look like it did before we arrived and pack everything out that we brought in with us.

While I never played organized baseball as a kid, Pam and I wanted give the boys every opportunity to do that. We talked it over between ourselves and agreed to be as supportive as we could without becoming overbearing bleacher parents. When Little Ted became old enough, we asked him if he'd like to be a Little Leaguer. He was more excited about playing baseball than we ever expected. More fortunate than most other Little

League parents, my job allowed me to attend nearly every practice and every game.

Little Ted had a natural athletic ability and while his body type was probably more fitting for a football player, he took advantage of that and realized that he was a natural behind the plate. Although, very enthusiastic about playing baseball initially, he later confided to us that he didn't really want to be the catcher. He told me that the catcher's position was where they put the kids who had the least talent and interest in the game and he wanted to play where there was more action. I then shared a different perspective, explaining that catching was the most important position on the field, "Not only is the catcher the only player that can see every other player on the field, but he is involved in each and every play." I continued to point out that each play begins with the catcher and every pitch depends on him. From then on, Little Ted took to that position and played it with renewed enthusiasm and energy, becoming a true leader on the field.

Over the years, he honed his catching skills while learning how to take control and dictate every play of every game from behind the plate. One of my proudest moments was when he initiated a triple play and had to explain it to the home plate umpire before he would eventually make the proper call. A double steal was on and the batter struck out. Little Ted threw to third base, getting the runner out and then the ball went to second base to prevent the double steal attempt. As I said, the plate umpire didn't catch on until Little Ted explained it to him.

I couldn't have been more proud as I watched my son mature as a player and as a young man all the way through high school. Then to see his name listed as one of the top three catchers in Northern California his senior year was more than I ever could have imagined. It's the dream of every father to see his son excel and surpass his father's achievements. Little Ted had done all that in my eyes. My son was a better student and a better athlete than I ever was. He had the world in his hands as he was being scouted by several pro teams. It didn't get much better than that as far as I was concerned.

Josh emulated his big brother so much that one day while he was outside playing with the other kids in the neighborhood he came running into the house crying at the top of his lungs. When I asked him what was wrong, he could hardly catch his breath between each sob, he was that upset. In short choppy statements, he said that they were playing baseball and the other kids wouldn't let him be the squatter. Amused at his reference to the catcher's position, I told Josh that there would be plenty more opportunities to be a catcher. I gave him a popsicle and that seemed to take care of his problems.

Both Little Ted and Josh became very involved in youth sports at early ages. Josh, however, would discover his calling for football more so than baseball, but insisted on playing both sports. Pam and I remained supportive and active in their activities. I even became an assistant coach to fill the void of volunteer coaches.

Josh became an exceptional athlete in his own right. In just his second year as a football player, he took his youth football team to the state championships after replacing the first string quarterback, whose season ended early due to an injury sustained on the field. At the young age of only nine years old, he was a Joe Montana protégé. Able to read the defensive lineups from the line of scrimmage, he also had an uncanny running ability which made him a double threat as a quarterback. If he was ever flushed out of the pocket, he didn't think twice about running it, often for a touchdown. The opposition always wanted to keep him inside the pocket whenever he dropped back to pass because he was so hard to tackle as a runner. There were numerous times that he'd take off in a sprint when he couldn't find an open receiver. With legs like rubber, he bounced off the defenders and left them in the dust. Because his talent was overlooked in high school, he became very bitter and resentful. I remained proud of the way he gave it everything he had, but it didn't seem to help matters. Those were some of the best times of my life as I watched proudly from the bleachers, my sons excelling on the field that dreams are made of.

Music was still a very important part of my life and I still enjoyed listening to the music of my favorite 60s bands, the Beatles and Paul Revere and the Raiders. Upon learning that Paul Revere and the Raiders were going to be in concert in a community park in Elk Grove, about an hour away from where we lived, Pam and I decided to take the boys to share the band's unique music experience with them. The boys had a good time as some girls at the concert were flirting with them, albeit attending a Paul Revere and the Raiders concert wasn't what they would have preferred doing. They did, however, enjoy the live performance of the band. I brought one of their LP albums to try and get it autographed by Paul Revere. After the band was finished performing, they came out for autographs. Upon handing the album to Paul Revere, he said, "Wow! This is an old album." A bit embarrassed, I thought to myself, "Yeah, but aren't they all?" Not sure of how he might react to such a comment, I kept it to myself.

Thinking that I might want to get into teaching, I decided to take some classes out at the community college. I wanted to learn more about health and fitness and thought maybe I'd like to become a gym teacher. In spite of being much more physically advanced than my fellow classmates, I was also lacking confidence with the level of my fitness. While in one of my gym classes, the instructor approached me and said that the art class was looking for an anatomical subject to paint. Pointing out my exceptional physical condition, she believed that I would be the best student she had for such a project. Very flattered by her recommendation and a bit embarrassed, I also realized that it wasn't every day that anyone was offered such an opportunity. After all, I was always the one behind the camera whenever pictures were taken. Rarely was I ever the subject. I thought it over and talked to Pam about it. When she asked if I would be nude, I said that it was not required and it would be my decision. She wasn't very happy about me being a nude model and asked that I not do it. Disappointed, I honored her request and declined the invitation.

While working dayshift, I had been putting up with one of the backshift employees who would never clean up his machine at the end of his shift. He instead left the mess for the next guy to clean. That guy was usually me. Because it always delayed my work, I reported the problem to my supervisor. Unfortunately, he never brought it up to the other employee so I decided to take matters into my own hands.

After coming in at the beginning of my shift, I noticed all the metal chips and shavings left spread all over the machine. I had to clean the chips out before I could start my own job. After cleaning up all the metal chips that the other guy had left, I gathered them and poured them through a hole on the side of that guy's toolbox. It not only dirtied up all the tools inside, it left quite an oily, dirty mess throughout. Of course, he wasn't happy upon finding the mess inside his toolbox. When someone told him that I had done it, he walked up to me while I was talking to one of the senior machinists in the section.

Holding a hot cup of coffee in my left hand, I noticed that the other guy was clinching his fist at his side while yelling at me. Calmly switching my cup of coffee to my other hand, I admitted to having put all those metal shavings in the toolbox. I continued to explain that I was tired of cleaning up the mess that he'd left every night. Almost able to see the raging fire in his eyes, I was prepared to defend myself. The other guy brought his arm full circle, up and around as I threw my left arm up, blocking the telegraphed blow. Freezing in his tracks, there was undeniable fear in his eyes as I calmly placed the cup of coffee down and asked him if he wished to continue now that I had both hands free. I was ready to defend myself without throwing a punch and was determined to keep the other guy from hurting me and himself in the process. He wisely turned and walked away and I never had any trouble with him again. It would have been too easy for either of us to seriously injure or kill the other in that environment. My calm and disciplined deportment prevented any serious harm to come from the disturbance.

Over all, I was happy with the progress of my career. I was transferred to work in the nuclear section of the shop, manufacturing parts for the nuclear reactors on submarines. It was a privilege to work in that specialized field. Only the most disciplined machinists were invited to become nuclear machinists. Always up for a challenge, I spent most of my machinist career working in the nuclear department. Over the years, I accepted temporary positions as work leader, supervisor, and apprentice instructor. When rework became a problem in the shop, I believed that much of it could be avoided through better training. As supervisor, I proudly reduced workplace errors and the unacceptably high rework rates that were affecting production, as well as moral in the machine shop.

Achieving my goals as a supervisor, I figured out that I could have a much greater impact if I could reach the machinists at the beginning of their careers. As an apprentice instructor, one of the first things I did was create an objective method of grading apprentices in the shop, after they left the apprentice school. One day, the director of the apprentice school asked me if I would like to teach in the vestibule. I confessed that I was self taught and knew nothing about trade theory and didn't think I could teach in a classroom setting. He just said to let him take care of that. Not long after, I was transferred to the vestibule, where I was given the challenge of not only writing curriculum but also teaching in a classroom setting as well as practical hands-on work. Teaching trade theory also taught me a lot more things that I didn't know as a self-taught machinist. I brought fresh ideas and some techniques that had never been taught before my arrival at the apprentice school.

Deciding that we needed a 4-wheel drive, Pam and I bought a 1993 Ford Explorer to get us up to our mountain property near Alturas, California. Every 4th of July, the nearby buffalo ranch would barbeque a buffalo as part of the Independence Day celebration. The boys enjoyed going up for that that holiday. There was plenty for the kids to do, including good trout fishing, a playground, tennis courts, swimming and of course during the 4th of July, there were always extra activities for everyone. One year, we also took Pam's sister, Candy and her children. As a single mother, she worked a lot of hours to support them.

Therefore, they didn't have much time for these kinds of things and they enjoyed it as much as we did.

While visiting my parents one day, I informed them that I had been experiencing some lower back pain. Dad had always encouraged me to work out and stay fit when I was growing up, but that was about to change. They were both quick to blame my pains on my workouts. They didn't like seeing my now 18 inch biceps and 15 inch taper in my torso. I had been making great gains at the gym. Besides having an 8 percent body fat count, I was curling 100 pound dumbbells and bench pressing over 500 pounds. I knew right away where that conversation was going. After all, they already thought that I believed they didn't feed me right as a kid and I wanted to avoid all confrontations with them.

Knowing that the pain I was experiencing wasn't muscle pain, I was sure that it was much deeper. I did however make it a point to mention it to my chiropractor, who only confirmed my belief that my back problems were not muscle related and that my muscles were stronger and supporting the weak area of my lower back better than ever before. There was no doubt that my workouts were postponing the obvious -- my inevitable date with a neurosurgeon.

While never having felt threatened in my chiropractor's office, I did feel some strange vibes at times, but I couldn't quite figure it out. As time went by, I began to feel increasingly uncomfortable during my appointments. Two young nurses assisted the chiropractor in his office. One evening, while I was on one of the treatment tables, with the room door wide open, I heard some rustling in another part of the office. Turning to look through the open door, I saw one of the nurses rushing past my room, followed by the sound of the front door opening and closing. After my treatment, the nurse was nowhere to be found so I let myself out. A few days later, there was a story in the newspaper about a chiropractor being arrested after a teenaged patient accused him of touching her inappropriately during an examination. I was subsequently notified that I was being referred to another chiropractor while my current chiropractor took some time off to deal with some legal matters.

Every Friday was cleanup day at work. After lunch, everyone was expected to spend an hour cleaning up the work area before any work could resume. As the acting supervisor; I was responsible for cleaning the supervisor's office. After sweeping the floor, I leaned over to sweep the dirt into a dustpan. Bent over, I sneezed and felt an excruciating pain shoot from my lower back, down the right leg. Immediately dropping the broom,

I fell to my hands and knees. The pain was so unbearable that I couldn't stand up. Crawling to my desk a few feet away, I managed to pull myself up. Trying to avoid a scene, I managed to walk from my office, inside the secured industrial area, out to my car in the parking lot located about a half mile away. Not since losing that high school football drill and my helmet, had I ever felt so humiliated, even though, this time, it wasn't my fault.

There I was, the picture of health -- less than nine percent body fat and in the best shape of my life—and I could hardly stand, let alone walk. I was quite a sight to behold as I hobbled down the sidewalk to the parking lot. It took everything I had to stay on my feet. That walk seemed like an eternity. When I finally reached my car, I very slowly and carefully got in and drove thirty miles to the chiropractor's office in Vacaville. This new chiropractor had been treating me for a year now. Following his examination, I was diagnosed with a subluxation of the lower vertebrae. My lower back had twisted in opposite directions, leading to three herniated discs, pinching the nerve that travels down the leg. After the examination, my chiropractor shook his head and told me that the time had come that surgery could not be avoided in his opinion. He then recommended a neurosurgeon in nearby Fairfield. Collapsing on the floor when I finally arrived home, I laid there for several hours before I could get up on my hands and knees and crawl to bed.

After several weeks without being able to get out of bed, I felt devastated as everything I had worked for seemed to be coming to a screeching halt. My career as a machinist with a possible future in bodybuilding all seemed to be fading away. Devastation turned to depression. It spiraled downward as I began to realize that I wasn't going to be able to compete in my first competition. After three months in bed, the Workers' Compensation Board finally authorized the neurosurgeon to proceed with a laminectomy discectomy to correct my debilitated state.

It turned out that the advanced stage of my degenerative disc disease had put me at high risk for such an injury, but was only diagnosed after my on the job injury. Apparently, it was advanced by the demands of my profession as a machinist. My neurosurgeon informed me that my condition was a genetic disorder so there were probably other family members who've had the same back problems and may have had a similar procedure to correct it.

This news came as quite a shock. I'd never heard of anyone in my family who'd had such problems. When I mentioned it to my parents, they seemed every bit as surprised as I was. They quickly changed the subject as Dad placed the blame on my bodybuilding, explaining that no one on either side of the family had ever had back problems. I concluded that, once again, I was that one in a million chance that you always hear about. Another red flag that I never gave a thought to.

Coming out of surgery, I was pain free and felt like a new man. After three months of constant pain, I couldn't believe how great it felt after the drugs wore off. I never felt a need to take any pain medications. Within hours, I was out of the bed and walking the hallways of the hospital. After being released from the hospital, I was eager to get back in shape. I continued a walking regimen recommended by the physical therapy department until I was allowed to return to work, part time, in a light duty capacity. I wasn't allowed to lift, push or pull more than 20 pounds until my surgeon approved my full-time return.

I had fond memories of being a kid when Mom took me across town to visit Lucille Perry and her family. One of the things I remember most was the fun we had when her husband, Frank, brought out the old 8mm film projector and we'd watch home movies. Thinking that it would be fun to create our own family movies now as an adult, I decided to buy a video camcorder to videotape our sons' sporting events. I not only recorded what the boys did, I videotaped the entire game. When others realized what I was doing, I began to field their many requests for copies. Making so many copies didn't leave me with much time of my own. Upon learning about Public

Access Television, the light went on and I looked into it. It could save me a lot of time by broadcasting the games while the parents made their own copies right off the local cable channel.

I enrolled in the Volunteer Public Access program and became a certified volunteer public access producer. It wasn't long after I had been broadcasting the videotaped games that people within the cable company started talking about what I was doing. As they got to know me, they made me feel like part of the team. Walking into the cable office to do some editing one day, I was stopped by one of the cable company employees. She informed me that they were receiving calls from subscribers who were not only watching the games, but they were requesting more of that type of programming.

Giving it some thought, over the next couple of weeks, I decided to make a formatted show in which I would host a weekly two-hour program featuring one game each week. Wanting to include my sons, I asked them for suggestions on what to call the show. We came up with *Heroes Youth Sports Television*. The popularity of the show continued to grow and I decided to produce local high school games long before high school sports had become popular on television. It wasn't long before I began to receive awards and recognition for promoting the local youth in a positive light, including recognition from the California State Senate and the United States Congress.

One evening, Pam and I decided to take the boys out to dinner at a local Mexican restaurant. It was a busy night there when we arrived. After giving the hostess my name, we sat in the waiting area. Looking around the room, I noticed a woman sitting with a man on the other side. Pointing her out to Pam, I asked if she thought the woman resembled Robin. Pam didn't think so, but I was pretty sure it was her. A few minutes later, the hostess called the next person on the waiting list, "Robin," she said, and sure enough she stood up with the man she was with and they were shown into the dining room. I couldn't believe my ears. I remembered how I worried about her in that storm back in Ohio and was now happy to see that she was okay.

When it came time for us to be seated, I handed a business card to the server and asked her to give it to the woman sitting across the room. When she was handed the card, Robin excused herself from the table. I stood up as she approached. We gave each other a big hug before I introduced her to my family. We spoke for a few minutes before she returned to her table. Sitting back down with Pam and the kids, there was an unusual silence around the table that I didn't notice. All I could think of was how happy I was to know that Robin was well. When I asked Pam what she thought about inviting her over for lunch or dinner to catch up on things, she responded with a resounding no. You'd have thought I was asking for her permission to take Robin out on a date or something. I only wanted to catch up with Robin and find out how her family was. She and I had grown very close and I got to know her sisters and her parents very well back then. I didn't see anything wrong with wanting to know how they were all doing and what she had been up to since high school. Much to my dismay, Pam didn't budge an inch.

When we returned home, Little Ted, about ten years old, told me that I should have seen the look on Mom's face when I was hugging that woman. She obviously wasn't very happy about it. Against Pam's wishes and without her knowledge, I took Robin out to lunch a few weeks later. We talked about our families and we brought each other up to date on everything when I could no longer resist asking her if her ex-husband had been good to her. She told me that he hadn't. I was crushed. That was the last thing I wanted to hear. After telling her that I was sorry, we finished our lunches and I drove her back to her office. I let her out of my car, thanked her for seeing me and we never saw each other again.

Mom had been a lifetime smoker and decided one day to quit just before she was diagnosed with lung cancer. Mom and Dad chose not to share the doctor's prognosis with me, but I knew from what they were telling me that it wasn't good. She agreed to chemotherapy at her doctor's recommendation, but following her initial treatment, she decided not to continue. When Dad confided that she didn't have more than a few months to live, he also said that he didn't feel he could take care of her in her condition. Pam and I talked it over. We both agreed that it would be best for me to move back in with them long enough to take care of her.

I hadn't been there long when Mom gave me her diamond engagement ring along with a couple other diamond rings that belonged to her mother. She told me that she wanted to pay to have a ring made from the diamonds that I would wear. She also stipulated that the ring be passed on to the oldest child of each generation. Pam and I found a local jeweler in Vacaville who designed a nugget style gold ring to accommodate the five diamonds. When I took it back to show Mom what the jeweler had done, she was very pleased.

Living with my parents during Mom's last three months, I worked nights and took care of her during the day while sneaking in short naps as time allowed. She was amazing. Not once did she ever complain about anything including her pain. Getting to the point where she no longer even had the strength to get out of bed, I noticed that she was no longer comfortable. Realizing that there was nothing more I could do to comfort her, I asked if she wanted to go to the hospital where they could treat her and make her final days more comfortable. She decided it was time to go. Before leaving the house, Mom removed her wedding band and her gold necklace with her gold cross. Handing the necklace to me, she asked me to hang on to it until she died. She requested that I place it around her neck before anyone saw her in her casket and be present when it was sealed to make sure that it was still around her neck when she was buried.

Before leaving the house, I called David Grant Hospital and let them know that she was on her way. Hospice had previously alerted them a few days before I had called. During the 40-minute drive, I kept a keen eye on her. She never took her eyes off the green rolling hills and wide open countryside between Vallejo and Fairfield. It was obvious that she was taking it all in, knowing it was the last time she'd ever see it. She was admitted upon arrival and I never left her side after she was assigned a private room.

The next couple of days, the nursing staff came in like clockwork to suction her lungs. I agonized as I watched Mom fight the tube that was forced up her nose and into her lungs. Flailing her arms, she jumped and squirmed as the pump sucked the fluid that had built up in her lungs between each suctioning. As painful as it was to watch, I couldn't begin to imagine how painful it was for her to have to endure such treatment. There was little solace in knowing that she could breathe easier afterwards, at least for a few hours, until the next treatment. On the third day, the treatment was discontinued at Mom's request.

Pam came by one evening with a quick meal from the local fast food restaurant. While I watched over Mom, we ate our hamburger and fries. Making a gesture, Mom no longer had the strength to even whisper. I struggled to understand what she was trying to say then Pam said "I think she wants some of your fries." Asking her if that's what she wanted, she nodded. Having been fed through an IV, she hadn't had a bite to eat for at least a week. The smell of the fries must have made her want some. I placed a short, single french fry in her mouth. She sucked on it and made a pleasurable moan with a smile that must have taken all the energy she could muster. She clearly enjoyed the taste of some real food. When she could no longer get anything out of it, she spit out what she couldn't chew and I disposed of it.

Early the next morning, April 11, 1986, Mom opened her eyes as the sun lit the room. She gazed through the window from her bed with a stare unlike I had ever seen before. Her breathing was now shallow and rapid. Her skin had become pale. I felt a strong sense that Mom was in her final hours. Leaving the room briefly, I found a phone and called Dad to tell him to get to the hospital as soon as he could. He asked what was going on. Becoming too emotional to explain, I only said, "Hurry" before quickly returning to her room. I sat at her side, holding her hand as she continued to gaze through the window with an absent stare. She was at peace and seemed to anticipate what was coming. It had been a long time since I had seen her so at ease. She then took her last breath, exhaled, and died peacefully.

Leaning back in my chair, I was relieved that her suffering had finally ended. She was now embarking on her final journey, a journey that would at long last put her at her brother's side and in the love and glory of her Savior. A few moments later, I got up and notified the nurse on duty. Shortly after returning to her room, Dad walked in and sat in the chair next to me. I couldn't find it within myself to even acknowledge that he was there. We both just sat in silence. A few minutes passed before he asked, "Is she breathing?" Still all choked up, it was all I could do to simply shake my head as the tears ran down my cheeks.

At Mom's request, I put her small gold cross back around her neck just before the funeral home viewing began. She was given the modest funeral she had requested and pre-arranged with the funeral home. After the service, everyone went to her favorite bar at the bottom of the hill, across the street from the cemetery. Mom and Dad had decided to be buried together on that hill so they could keep an eye on their friends at the bar. As everyone gathered there, at the bar, it felt as though Mom was indeed overlooking the celebration of her life from atop the hill. Never having felt comfortable with the bar scene, Pam and I stayed only long enough to meet and greet Mom's friends and have a couple of drinks with them before leaving.

After everything was settled in California, I went to Alaska to visit Grandma and let her know that I would be handling her affairs from then on. While we were talking, she asked me what Mom had died from. I didn't want to tell her, but I couldn't lie, either. She was her mother, and she deserved the truth. After I told her that she died of lung cancer, she asked if Mom smoked. Hanging my head, I said, "Yes, she did." Obviously, disappointed, she just shook her head. It never occurred to me that Mom had never smoked when Grandma was around.

Handling her affairs from California for the following year, everything was going rather smoothly until I received a phone call, informing me that she was dying. I told the nurse that I was going to catch a flight out the following morning and be there as soon as I could. She told me not to expect to see the woman I had known. "Your grandmother had quit eating some time ago and has lost a lot of weight," she said. I arrived the following morning to find Grandma in bed and very frail, breathing deeply as she slept. Sitting down at her side, I spoke to her softly. "Grandma, it's Ted," I told her, "I'm here to take care of everything." Without opening her eyes, she simply nodded her head, smiled and took her final breath. She died peacefully one year after her daughter.

Rumors were rampant about Mare Island Naval Shipyard having been targeted by Congress for shutdown. Barbara Boxer accompanied San Francisco Mayor Diane Feinstein to Mare Island Naval Shipyard during a congressional run. They addressed the shipyard employees and promised that if Diane Feinstein was elected to the United States Congress, neither of them would ever vote to shut the shipyard down. After winning the election, one of the first votes she cast was in favor of closing the shipyard.

Mare Island employees were consequently notified that the shipyard was slated for closure as part of the congressional mandate. The closure impacted not only the City of Vallejo, but it seriously impacted the entire San Francisco Bay Area. I had worked there for eighteen years and would be only one of the thousands of employees losing their jobs. A relocation program was set up for the employees who were interested in relocating in another government job or in the private sector. Much to my dismay, I wasn't allowed to take part because even though I had returned to work, I was still receiving workers' compensation while working part-time. After being let go, I returned to full time workers' compensation.

My neurosurgeon then informed me that I would not be allowed to return to work in my trade as a machinist and was subsequently placed in a vocational rehabilitation program. After one month of testing, I was enrolled into the respiratory therapy program at Napa Valley College after taking some prerequisite classes at Solano Community College. Excited to be going into the health care field, I was eager to once again be a productive member of the workforce.

Subsequently diagnosed with lung cancer, Dad was given no more than three months to live. When he shared the news with me, he told me that Betty, a very close friend of Mom and Dad had agreed to live in and take care of him so I could continue school. Unfortunately, after a month or so, she told me that she couldn't do it anymore, "I just can't take sitting here and watching him die," she explained. Disappointed, Pam and I talked it over. We agreed that it would be in everyone's best interest to have Dad come live with us. He could have his own room and round the clock care by Pam and I in Vacaville. Never did we think he would refuse, but he did. "I want to die at home," he explained. Respecting his wishes we agreed to do whatever was necessary. Again, I moved back to Vallejo and in with my dad this time, leaving my family once again for what they thought would be only a few months.

Three months passed with little change in Dad except his resentment that turned to anger. Our arrangement had grown increasingly difficult when he needed supervision around the clock. He didn't want anyone around, including me. When I explained that we would have to hire someone to come in and sit with him I knew it wasn't going to be easy. My academic obligations were beginning to require more of my time. He worried that things would come up missing as a result. Unfortunately, it wasn't until after he died that we learned that it was a close friend that had taken from him before he died.

Six months after his diagnosis, he continued to hang on. Wanting his life to end, he asked me to contact Dr. Kevorkian. He had been in the news a lot during that time and was offering terminal patients a dignified and humane way to die instead of suffering long and painful deaths at the hands of terminal diseases. About that same time, school was breaking for the summer and we released the woman sitter that we had hired. On Sundays, Pam brought the boys down to visit. Since they were still playing sports, Sundays were most convenient since no sports were played on Sundays back then.

The word processor that helped me with my studies became a wedge that further divided the two of us. Spending much of his time on the couch, Dad watched television while I studied at my word processor in the dining area, behind him. The built-in monitor looked much like a small television screen so he believed that I was working on my video production instead of my studies. I never understood why he disapproved of my interest in video production while always seemingly proud of my years in the trades and he made that clear every chance he got.

As summer drew to an end, so did his struggle with lung cancer. Hospice was now helping out a couple of times a week and when the nurse suggested he begin taking morphine for the pain, Dad insisted that it wasn't necessary. "Besides," he added, "I don't want to become addicted to it." It was all I could do to keep from laughing at the irony of it all. Managing to contain myself. I tried to explain to him that he probably wouldn't live long enough to have to deal with the addiction. Unfortunately, I was just the son and Dad knows best. This was a stubborn alcoholic, worried about becoming addicted to drugs. It was a battle within the war that he was determined to win. No matter what the nurse or I told him. He wouldn't agree and refused the morphine.

As Dad began to sleep more, I spent more time with him. He slept in the room that used to be my childhood bedroom. He hadn't slept in his own bedroom since Mom died. He had now battled his lung cancer for a year, and continued to fight right up to the bitter end. One night, while sitting quietly at his side, Dad opened his eyes. After panning the room, he looked as though he was trying to focus on me. Without saying a word, he closed his eyes for the last time. I knew that look all too well, remembering Mom's final minutes. Moving from my chair to Dad's bed, I sat closer to him. Speaking calmly as he lay there fighting for each breath, I attempted to put him at ease by telling him to let it go. "Everything will be all right," I said. His breathing grew shallow as his lungs began to fill with fluid. Each exhaled breath brought an all too familiar gurgling sound. I pleaded with him to end his fight and be at peace. The pulsating vein in his neck seemed to decrease in strength. Thirty minutes later, I placed my hand on his neck to check his pulse. It was no longer detectable, but he continued to breathe. Again, I pleaded with him to give in and be at peace. A few moments later, his breathing stopped and the color in his face washed away. Relieved that Dad's pain and suffering had finally ended, I bowed my head and cried.

It was late September. Dad had died in his own bed, at home, as he had wanted. The World War II veteran's body was cremated. His ashes were buried with Mom as they had requested -- without a funeral service, or any kind of fanfare. Reluctantly, I followed my parents' wishes and gave them exactly what they wanted, even though I believed that he was worthy of so much more. I never got over the fact that despite all our differences, I hadn't told my dad that I loved him before he died.

Retuning to my respiratory therapy classes, I began to struggle as an intern in a Santa Rosa hospital. While witnessing a cancer patient being suctioned, I stood tall, behind my fellow classmates as we were all crowded in the patient's room. Beginning to feel weak, I broke out into a cold sweat as they pumped the fluid from the patient's lungs. They struggled to get the tube up the patient's nose and down into her lungs just like they had with Mom.

Realizing that I had quit breathing, I exited the room to get some air and avoid the embarrassment of passing out in front of my fellow classmates. While walking around the corridors, one of the other interns found me and asked if I was okay. Admitting that, while things got a little bizarre for me, I was now feeling much better.

The reality was that I wasn't well. I had begun to experience flashbacks of my mother being suctioned and I was finding it increasingly difficult to deal with. Time went by and things weren't getting better. My heart told me to change my major. I finally gave in and decided to leave RT and pursue the career that I felt better suited for. Returning to Solano Community College, I began my quest for an AA degree in television production.

Continuing to suffer with bouts of depression, I hadn't fully recovered after my original on the job injury. When the doctors began treating me with Prozac, I began to have disturbing nightmares. Two of the more distressing and recurring nightmares included dark silhouetted images of hooded spirits standing over me as I lay in bed. In my many attempts to resist, I pulled the covers over my head as they bumped the bed and tried to take me away with them. I was an infant in the other lurid nightmare who was victimized by sexual abuse. To complicate matters, I was also experiencing seizures for a lack of better terms where my body would convulse with a single rapid burst of blackouts. Each episode lasted less than a second. If I were holding something in my hands, I would drop it, but recover fast enough to catch it before it hit the floor. Upon explaining these symptoms to my doctor, he notified DMV, which resulted in the suspension of my driver's license. That only made things even more difficult for me. As if I wasn't having enough trouble, I was not unable to drive so I couldn't continue with my classes.

Our older son, now going by LT -- too big to be called Little Ted, was now playing baseball for a nearby community college. When he shared their weight training program techniques with me, I was stunned. Being a very knowledgeable trainer and well versed in kinesiology and nutrition, I felt an obligation to tell him that he was being taught poor training techniques and that would eventually lead to serious injury if he continued. Stuck between a rock and hard spot, he couldn't very well tell his trainer that his weight training techniques were improper. He said nothing and continued following the baseball weight training program.

When he received an offer from Nebraska State I told him that it was a great opportunity and encouraged him to take it. He was torn. He didn't want to leave and risk losing his girlfriend. Explaining to LT that if his girlfriend truly loved him, I felt sure that she would wait for him, just like his mother had done when I went to Ohio.

He declined the invitation and stayed close to home. It wasn't long before he began to experience pain in his shoulder. When he went to the doctor, he learned that he had a serious rotator cuff injury that would require corrective surgery. He wasn't very thrilled about the thought of having surgery and agonized over his options. In the middle of the night, LT walked into our bedroom. Standing near the foot of the bed, in tears, he told me that he couldn't go through with the surgery and decided to quit baseball. Knowing how important baseball was to him and how difficult such a decision must have been, I was disheartened, but accepted his decision. Pam and I never forced him to play, and we never thought that a career in baseball might become a possibility when we first gave him the choice to play ball. Of course, we were thrilled when he had done so well and that some pro scouts were seriously looking at him. We were proud of our son and remained proud of his accomplishments. Not long after he left baseball, his girlfriend left him.

One year after having my drivers' license suspended I got it back, but not without a fight with DMV. I returned to school where I excelled in television production. In my element, this seemed like a natural fit for me. I studied hard and became a teacher's aide at the local community college while I was taking on less responsibilities at the local public access station.

It was August of 1997 and I was now interning with Comcast Cable in Vacaville. While at home, on my computer, I was in a chat room chatting with someone I only knew as Deb. When she asked me what line of work I was in, I told her that I produced videos. She then asked if I would be interested in shooting a video of her husband. My immediate reaction was, "Why would I want to produce a video of this woman's husband?" Not wanting to be rude, I asked her what she had in mind. Deb said that her husband was a musician and was going to be performing in Santa Maria in a few weeks. Well Santa Maria was in southern California, a full days drive from my home in northern California. When she said that her husband's name was Mark Lindsay, I couldn't believe my ears. "You've got to be kidding me!" I exclaimed. Well, I wasn't about to let this rare opportunity get away. "Of course, I will," adding, "I've been a big fan of his ever since Louie, Louie."

It was September 6, my birthday, when I woke up in a motel in Santa Maria the morning of the concert. It was one of the brightest days of my life. I was going to work for one of my teen idols. On the other hand, this was a dark day for much of the rest of the world. Great Britain was burying Princess Diana, who had lost her life in an automobile accident the week before. Getting out of bed, I looked out the window, onto the parking lot and noticed a big bus parked there. On the side of the bus was the word "Arizona," Mark's big hit single. Wondering if it was his touring bus, I got on the phone and called the front desk. When the woman answered, I asked to be connected to Mark Lindsay's room. Before I knew it, I was talking to Mark himself. We spoke for a few minutes as I got detailed information about what time to be at the park and what exactly Mark wanted as far as video was concerned. Upon my arrival at Pioneer Park, Deb was there to meet me. She showed me around and introduced me to everyone. I videotaped the concert and edited it later, before sending it to Mark.

A couple of years later, Pam and I met Deb and Mark at River Cat Stadium in Sacramento during a concert tour where Mark was appearing with the likes of Tommy James, the Grassroots, Herman's Hermits, and Mickey Dolenz of the Monkees. They treated us like family and I will never forget how genuine and down to earth they were. There was not a trace of show biz snobbery to be found. We kept in touch through the internet and we would meet again, a couple of more times after that while Mark continued to tour. To her credit, Deb always acted like she truly remembered me and always made me feel like a close friend during our visits.

The following semester, I interviewed at the Sacramento NBC-TV affiliate station, hoping to intern there. During the interview process, I provided my resume and a sample of my award-winning work. Very impressed with my portfolio, the interviewer apologized, explaining that all the intern positions had been filled. My initial disappointment was short-lived as he continued to say that he was impressed with my work before offering me a paid position as a video editor in the news department. I had just a few months left before I would be graduating with an AA degree, but the offer was tempting. Flattered and encouraged, I gracefully declined. Finishing school was my priority. He interrupted me as I began to thank him for the opportunity. Picking up his phone, he made an internal call. A few minutes later, he told me that because he so admired my work and determination, he created a spot for me to intern in the commercial production department. I gratefully thanked him as we shook hands and I was welcomed to KCRA-TV.

It was a thrill as much as it was an honor to be interning at the television station that was the best in their market. I would be learning from some of the best in the business. Becoming a sponge, I absorbed as much as I possibly could from Ron, the only full time camera operator and lighting specialist in the commercial production department. Steve and Denny were the only two directors and I took every opportunity to observe and ask questions of them. Not only was Ron the head cameraman, but he was also the one responsible for maintaining all the lighting in the news studio. I was very fortunate to be working with them and learning all those things including lighting the news set and maintaining the lights in the overhead light grid.

At the end of the semester, I graduated with honors at the top of my class and was subsequently hired by the TV station as a commercial photographer. Because it was a part-time position, I also started my own video production business in Vacaville. Seven years later, the station was sold to Hearst-Argyle Corporation. One year after that, I once again fell victim to corporate downsizing. Realizing that Vacaville was perfectly located between San Francisco and Sacramento, I decided to work full time at my small business. That location provided opportunities to work in both the Sacramento and San Francisco regions as well as the entire area between them.

Not only did I look a lot like my dad growing up, I also looked like a number of Hollywood celebrities over the years. As a young kid, people used to tell me I looked like Wally Cleaver on the *Leave It To Beaver* television show. As a young teenager, I would often hear that I looked like the movie star, Ryan O'Neal. As a young adult and for many years, I used to hear people say that I looked like Wayne Rogers who played Trapper John on the TV show, *MASH*. After both my parents passed away, I began to notice changes that no longer resembled either of them. Ignoring it initially, as time passed, I began to wonder why I no longer looked like either of my parents.

I began to question the circumstances of my birth and one question led to another. Nothing made sense anymore. Keeping all those questions and concerns inside, I was cautious about sharing any of my thoughts with anyone, including Pam. She knew me, my mom and dad and my history as well as anyone. I wasn't sure of my heritage anymore and if I talked about that, I'm sure that my sanity would be in question. It got worse when I started to feel like someone was looking for me. Those feelings took on yet another dimension when I began to feel that this person was very possibly my sister. Then, while watching a movie that took place in the 1940s, it occurred to me that women spent seven to ten days in the hospital after delivering a baby back then. It didn't make sense that Mom and Dad wouldn't stay close to home as she was closer to delivering their baby.

Mom and Dad enjoyed life to the fullest, but they weren't risk takers by any means. They were, in fact, pretty reasonable people. They had tried for nine years to conceive. They had even lost one by their own admission. Why then would they drive hours from civilization when they knew that Mom could go into labor any time? The risk of doing just that seemed implausible. I always took my parents at their word. Not once did I ever question them about those things. I had no reason to doubt them until now.

My business began to grow until the unimaginable happened. Everything came to a standstill when four coordinated suicide attacks in New York and Washington DC, killed nearly three thousand Americans and trashed the nation's economy. It was a long struggle to get back to the economic position everyone had before the 9/11 attacks. As things began to look up, the housing industry crisis struck and took many businesses with it. My business suffered further. Believing that I was being tested like never before, my business was really struggling. To make matters worse, Pam was working very long hours, six or seven days a week, which left little time, if any, for the two of us. I began to spend more hours at the office so I wouldn't have to spend the evenings alone at home.

When a seat on the board of directors of the Downtown Vacaville Business Improvement District had been vacated, I was invited to fill it for the remainder of the year. Accepting the invitation, I thought that it would be a great opportunity, although I wasn't sure about the amount of time that it would require. At the end of the year, I was elected to a two year term on the board. Then much to my surprise, I was elected by the board members to serve the first year as the vice president. I would go on to become president of the Vacaville DVBID the following two years. As a result, I had a much greater presence on the internet through my business and as a BID board member.

VI

THE PHONE CALL

SEASON'S GREETINGS

from our house to your house

*The Christmas card that Mom and Dad sent
to Dot in late December, 1953.*

It was a chilly afternoon in northern California, having just officially become winter in 2008. Only a few days remained before Christmas. This was normally a very busy time of year for my business. Having worked right up and into Christmas Eve in past years, business was slower than usual now, and had been since September 11, 2001. As slow as it was, however, I still felt I had a lot to be thankful for. After all, my business was doing better than most in the slumping economy that had put a lot of people out of work throughout the country.

The phone rang, breaking the silence in the office. Little did I know that my life was about to experience a change of grand proportions. The voice on the other end was that of a man with a Southern dialect. Introducing himself as a private investigator on the East Coast, he said that he would like to ask me a few questions about my parents.

He told me that he knew I was born in Virginia but wasn't sure which county. "I was born in Albemarle County," I replied with conviction. Mr. Tonker said that he believed that Madison or Green County was more accurate. Keeping it to myself, I thought that this guy was pretty bold to be telling me that I didn't even know where I was born. When I told him that I was born out in the country away from any town, Mr. Tonker shifted gears and began to ask about my mother. He had learned that her name was Bobbie and knew that she was from Alaska, but was unable to find anything else about her. Feeling a bit uneasy, I chose not to give this stranger too much information. He said that he had been looking for a Roberta so I explained that while Bobbie was her nickname, it had nothing to do with her birth name and left it at that.

Dad, on the other hand, had several different nicknames, from Bus to Buck, to Skinny, to Dad. Dad is what all his shipmates called him because he was so much older than they were. Bus is what his family called him growing up before changing it to Buck. I never knew why.

Mr. Tonker continued with trepidation, telling me that what he had to say might sound pretty strange. I assured him that I had seen and heard some pretty strange things in my line of work and doubted that what he might say would be any worse. Then he said that he believed I was the half-brother of his client. His client, it seems, had spent much of the last forty-five years searching for her long lost half-brother, adding that he was the second PI she had hired over the years. Taken aback, I said nothing while hanging on to each and every word. Tonker methodically explained that his client's half-brother had been given up for adoption only a couple weeks after being born to a mother who couldn't keep him. As he understood it, this half-brother was given to a childless couple who wanted children, but couldn't have any. So far, this story could have applied to almost anyone, but I wanted to hear something definitive— something that was going to slap me in the face. Unfortunately, it wasn't happening. As a matter of fact, I was sure that this guy had the wrong person and I told him so. Letting him know that I was intrigued, not so much by his story, but how he came to believe that I was the one he was looking for. I wanted more. I needed more.

Mr. Tonker explained that his client was one of three children whose mother had left with their grandparents to raise. She subsequently had more children, but he didn't feel they were very close to the older three. He wasn't very clear about any of those details which made me even more suspicious. Trying to remain low key, straightforward, and more importantly, monotone, I wanted to conceal my true feelings of optimism and most importantly, my vulnerability. I told Mr. Tonker that I needed more time to absorb all the information and requested that his client not contact me for the time being. Again, Mr. Tonker was very gracious and understanding, telling me to take my time and he'd be back in touch in a few days.

Driving home from work, an emotional roller coaster swept me away. "Did I really have a sister? Why did my parents keep that from me? What else did they keep from me? How did it happen? What were the lives of my parents really like before I was born? Was one of my parents unfaithful to the other?" Those were only a few of the things running through my mind. The two-and-a-half mile drive home seemed like an eternity that evening. I had a lot more questions than answers, but one thing was certain; I was jubilant about the possibility of finally having the family I had always wanted, needed and craved.

Then I began to wonder how I was going to break the news to Pam and how she might react. We knew each other as well as anyone who had known one another for so long, but how can anyone predict how another might react to such news? Was everything we thought we knew, suddenly, completely false? The one thing that I never told her was that I had spent much of my childhood wanting brothers and sisters. Mom and Dad were the only ones who knew that. Unsure of how she was going to react to this astonishing revelation, I did know that she was going to be as surprised as I was. To say she knew me well would be a huge understatement. I'd never shared the anguish and isolation I felt growing up as an only child with her. And now there seemed to be so much more to be learned by what, on the surface, seemed like a simple phone call on an otherwise cold and dreary winter's day. Feelings that I had hidden about my childhood—feelings that I managed to put away and keep locked up for so many years—were beginning to resurface and have their way with me.

Arriving home, I was greeted by our seventeen-year-old Yorkshire terrier, Baby. At her advanced age, she was no longer the vivacious pet she was for so many years, but no less a very loving part of our family. She was now very fragile as she approached the end of her life. She came into our lives as a very young puppy, during my recovery from lower back surgery. It was also not long after my mom had lost her battle with lung cancer. Pam and I often joked about how the dog was possessed by Mom's spirit, basing that on the way she reacted to certain situations. Because Baby and I had such a long time to bond, we became very attached.

I gave her my love before proceeding to the kitchen. I then opened a bottle of wine and placed two glasses on the table— one for myself and one for Pam, even though I was pretty sure she wouldn't have any, but the way things had gone on this day, nothing else would have surprised me more. I was pouring my second glass when she came home. Offering her a glass of wine, I told her to sit down because I had something to tell her.

An insulin-dependent diabetic, Pam didn't drink alcoholic beverages. She did, however, sense something was seriously wrong. She always asked compound questions making it impossible to answer just yes or no. Before I could respond to her question, "What's wrong," she immediately followed with "Did the dog die?" Assuring her that the dog was fine, I told her that I thought she should sit down before she hears what I had to say. For a second time, I offered her a glass of wine as I was still trying to figure out how to proceed.

Again, an upheaval of emotions that had been locked away for over forty years began to consume me. Taking another sip of wine, I desperately searched for the right words. They weren't coming easily, and I began to crumble under the overwhelming emotions that were now rampantly running amuck. I could hardly imagine how she must have felt or what she might have been thinking.

After several failed attempts, I finally got it all out in bits and pieces, followed by her silence and astonished gaze. She was speechless, but who wouldn't be after hearing such news? It's the absolute last thing either of us ever expected. We had both grown up knowing a much different truth. Suddenly, out of nowhere, after fifty-five years, my past wasn't what we thought it was. Or was it?

Knowing that I needed some help, neither of us knew where to begin. I suggested we call her parents to see if they would mind having some company for a little while that evening. I was sure that her mother, an ardent genealogist, would have a few suggestions on how to proceed.

We drove to her parents' house, about a mile and a half away. They offered us something to drink when we arrived. After we were all settled in the back room, Pam told her parents that I had something to tell them. Sensing her serious tone, they both turned to face me. Looking from Pam to her parents and back to Pam again, my feelings of helplessness once again overcame me. Finding it increasingly difficult to speak, I took a deep breath, tried to relax and regain my composure. Looking up, facing her parents, Lou and Carol, I once again tried to talk when the words seemed to get caught up in my throat. Words were replaced with a shiver in my lip and a choking sensation. Feeling as embarrassed as I was helpless, I turned back to Pam. Recognizing my anguish and frustration, she asked if I wanted her to tell them. Now, nearly in tears, I once again managed only a simple nod.

She began to tell them about the phone call I'd received from someone who claimed to be a private investigator in Virginia. Their faces were now twisted and contracted in total confusion as she continued to repeat what I'd been told by Mr. Tonker. Lou immediately thought it was some kind of hoax. Carol jumped to her feet and jetted into the adjacent computer room to research Wayne Tonker and Jeanette Meade. Not one, but two Jeanettes came up. There was no information on one of them and little about the other.

We tried to come up with as many scenarios as possible, trying to figure out how I could have other siblings. We began with what we already knew to be true. My parents were married nine years before I was born, and we were sure there were no other children afterward. Coming up with very few viable explanations, we concluded that we definitely needed more information. They assured me that they were there for us if either of us needed anything. Lou and Carol had always been very good to me. There was nothing we couldn't talk about with them. They'd always made me feel like one of their own. I knew that there was absolutely nothing that they wouldn't do for me.

Over the following couple of weeks, Mr. Tonker continued to talk to me, adding to my confusion with each conversation. He seemed to be getting his facts mixed up, and I in turn began doubting his integrity. Tonker described his client as a very nice lady, whose family no longer supported her efforts to find her long lost half-brother. He also thought that she might be doing this without her husband's knowledge or approval. Then, as an almost by-the-way statement, he commented that he didn't think she had much money since she had paid him his entire fee in rolled quarters she had saved. He also added that he had performed his investigation for much less than he would have for anyone else because she came to him with not only what he considered an extraordinary story, but she was referred to him by a mutual acquaintance and felt somewhat obligated. Okay, this guy is a good Samaritan. I wondered if he was trying to set me up for a gotcha moment. Why would he think I cared if she was looking for someone without her husband's approval or that she had paid this guy in quarters?

Between our phone conversations, much of my time was spent trying to figure out all the angles and possibilities, including which one of my parents might be in the mix, if not both of them. Had their failed attempts to conceive been made successful by a surrogate? If so, had my dad acted alone with another woman or did one of them have an affair that resulted in my birth and subsequent adoption? My mind ran wild with countless possibilities.

There was no doubt in my mind that I was in fact the son of my dad. The family resemblance was obvious. It was only during the recent years that I failed to see any physical similarities between myself and either of my parents. That family resemblance could be seen in the third generation as well. Several years prior, Pam and I discovered an old photo of Dad right after he entered the United States Navy. We were amazed at the likeness Josh had to my dad at approximately the same age. If not for the obvious age difference in both photos, we would have sworn that the persons in both pictures were the same. When we shared that with my parents, we thought their reaction was rather strange. Neither Mom nor Dad ever reacted one way or another. It was much like the time I asked them about health issues so I could know what to watch for over time. They discounted my need to know without ever offering an explanation. I had always thought that was strange, to say the least. In retrospect, it was one of the few red flags that I should have paid attention to, but never did.

The math just wasn't adding up for me. I was fifty-five years old. If Mr. Tonker's client was only a couple years older than me, she would be fifty-seven. That wouldn't allow time enough for two other siblings between us, assuming that I was the youngest of the siblings. Mr. Tonker's story became increasingly confusing the more we spoke. Disappointed, to say the least, I finally told him that we really needed to face the facts and bring this to an end. I was positive that I wasn't the person he was looking for. I grew up an only child three thousand miles away, and I was pretty sure that my parents weren't the kind to have been unfaithful. He pleaded with me to give his client just one chance. "She can explain this a lot better than I can," he said. Begrudgingly, I agreed to accept a call from his client. I had become determined to put an end to all the nonsense once and for all, for my own sanity. I needed to get my life back—the sooner, the better!

Deciding to take a walk around the downtown area, I dropped by the Business Improvement District office to share what was going on with Downtown Bob, the director and his secretary, Judy. Neither of them believed it was anything but a hoax. It was then that Judy shared her own story of losing her only brother several years prior and how it had affected her life. It was clear from the tears in her eyes that it still upset her as she talked about it. I confided that I grew up an only child and always wanted siblings and deep down inside, I wanted this to be true.

Nearly one month had passed. We were now three weeks into the new year. I still hadn't heard back from the investigator or his so-called client. My early suspicions were beginning to be realized, or so I thought. Beginning to feel foolish, I thought I had been an easy target for some jokester.

At 11:30 AM the phone in my office rang. Looking at the caller ID, I didn't recognize the number. I did, however, notice that it was a long distance number, possibly from the East Coast. Taking a deep breath, I picked up the receiver. On the other end was the voice of a woman with a Southern dialect. Apologetic, she almost sounded embarrassed to be calling. She told me that she was calling from work and that her supervisor had been kind enough to let her call from the privacy of her office. She apologized for all the emotional upset that I and my family must have been going through. After a brief pause, she tried to assure me that no matter how bad my life may have been, it was better than it would have been had my mother not given me up for adoption.

Sitting silently, I didn't know quite what to make of it all. Her voice sounded too sweet to be anything less than honest and sincere, but I was still on the defensive. What she said next was like a double-dose jolt of adrenaline. She explained that she had hired not one, but two investigators to aid her in her search. The first one was unsuccessful. She then went on to explain that she and two sisters had been raised by her grandparents. Their mother had two more daughters who were born long after me. I was the result of an affair that our mother had while her military husband was stationed in Germany and she had to get rid of me before he came home.

She said that a woman named Dot Schumaker, now living in Michigan, used to be her mother's neighbor in Madison County. Her brother, Tommy, was in the Navy, stationed in Norfolk, approximately two hundred miles away. He would often come home on the weekends and bring a shipmate and his wife along. It was during one of those visits that Dot told them about a neighbor who was going to deliver a baby any time, but she couldn't keep it. The couple talked it over and agreed to take the baby. When they got word that the baby was born, they drove from the naval base to the foot of the mountain where our mother walked up to the car and handed me through the window to the woman inside.

I couldn't believe what I had just heard. Totally taken aback, I fought tears of joy. I didn't dare let on that she had touched a nerve. I thought to myself, "So, in Mom and Dad's eyes, I was born in that car." How fortuitous that my parents had always told me their own personalized version of that same sequence of events!

This woman's version was just too familiar to ignore. Furthermore, it made more sense to me than the one I'd always been told. I began to get excited by the prospect that I now might actually have siblings out there. Trying to remain calm, I told her that there were some things I needed to do, and I'd be in touch.

After arriving home that evening, I wrote a letter to Aunt Blanche. I explained what I had learned and asked her to tell me what she knew, if anything. I assured her that no matter what she said, she would always be my aunt and my cousins would always be my cousins. Nothing would change that.

The following day, I attempted to write Jeanette an email. Unable to put what was in my heart, into words, I gave up. The same thing happened on the second day. It was the third day that it all finally came together. I wrote:

Jeanette

This is the third time in as many days that I've tried to write this email (something new to me as I am usually never at a loss for words when writing.)

First of all, I don't know where to start so let me begin by saying thank you for calling me Tuesday. It says a lot about your character. I'm sure it took a lot of courage. As I sat in my studio moments before your call, I was thinking about the anxiety I would be feeling if the shoe was on the other foot. I'm a better listener than I am speaker as I'm sure you know. That is probably why I'm a video producer because I have to listen first and express myself through my productions. It's one of my shortcomings and I hope you'll forgive me for that.

After my initial conversation with Mr. Tonker, my emotional state was quite rampant and I felt like I was on an emotional rollercoaster throughout the holidays. Please don't feel that I blame you or anyone else. I am not one to point fingers. I accept responsibility for my actions and I'm not afraid to take credit for what I do. It wouldn't be fair to blame anyone for the way I process information.

It took several attempts to explain to my wife that night what I had learned. I never told anyone this until recently when I revealed to my wife of many years. I pleaded with my mother for siblings whenever I was asked what I wanted for my birthday or Christmas or any other occasion. And now after all this time I'm finally realizing that you were always there, but beyond my world. Even though my parents had their shortcomings, I have no doubt that they loved me very much and provided for me (an only child) very well, but something inside me wanted more than you'll ever know, to believe Mr. Tonker's story was factual. I'm getting away from where I intended to go. I'm sure you get my drift so I will return to where I was going earlier.

After a little time passed following my initial conversation with Mr. Tonker and we continued speaking, it wasn't long before I began to realize that his facts weren't adding up. I was sure that you were misled and I was not the person you've been looking for. He assured me that if I spoke to you, it would make better sense and I was rapidly growing tired of his being a third party to our conversations and I'm sure he was too.

You struck a chord more than once during our telephone conversation and now I believe that it's very possible we are siblings. I know that a DNA *test will confirm what we both already suspect. However, I need for you to be patient with me right now while I sort things out on my end. What I've had only days to learn, you've had a lifetime to digest. Rest assured I won't take so long; besides since we're both well into our 50s, we don't have a lot of time. I will do the best I can to expedite what I need to do. These things I need to do before I can move forward with you right now. Again, I hope this has a positive outcome and I look forward to meeting you and all my other siblings and relatives. Thank you again for that renewed hope.*

By the way, feel free to contact me either by phone or email. I am truly looking forward to a life-long relationship and celebration. One more tidbit... I brew my own beer. Just thought you should know since you work for a brewery. I've also attached a picture that I just took moments ago. Any family resemblance that you can see? Hope you'll send me a picture or two so I can see you. Bye for now.

The next time I heard from Jeanette, she told me that she couldn't bring herself to read my email. Instead, she asked a friend at work to read it to her. Her friend first began to read it to herself. Telling Jeanette that is was very good, she also said that she needed to read it herself. She then told me that she didn't really recognize any familiar features in the photos I had sent but when she asked her daughters to take a look at them, they told her that they could clearly see Grandma Sugarloaf in my face. I could hardly contain the excitement I was now feeling. I wanted so badly to meet my biological mother and see for myself.

I was prepared to hear my Aunt Blanche say that she knew nothing about an adoption when a couple of days later, much to my surprise, I received a phone call from her. We talked for a few minutes, laughing about the good times we all used to have and then she said, "I guess it's okay to tell you now." My heart was in my throat as I listened intently. She confirmed that I had been adopted and that everyone in the family knew. She continued to explain that when Mom and Dad adopted a son in Virginia, they all believed that he had really gotten mixed up with another woman who had his child, then adopted it. Sworn to secrecy, all my aunts and uncles promised that they would never tell me that I was in fact adopted.

It seems that some of Dad's sisters and brothers were sitting around talking about it one day when Aunt Donna's older daughter walked into the room. The adults stopped talking so she wouldn't hear their conversation. Unbeknownst to them, she already heard enough to know what they were talking about. "Oh yeah, I know. We all know that Teddy was adopted," she said quite frankly. They were all stunned but no one ever knew how all the kids knew the family secret.

How they kept that secret, I'll never know. My cousin Mark had the best opportunities, although we lived hundreds of miles apart. We were the closest of the cousins growing up. We also did our share of teasing and fighting. How he kept from blurting out in one of our heated arguments, "well, you're not even my cousin, you're adopted!" is beyond me.

Aunt Blanche added that they all had thought I was really Dad's son because I always looked so much like him. I agreed and said that the next step would be to arrange DNA tests with this woman who claimed to be my half-sister. I asked her if she thought her son, Jim, would mind doing a DNA test with me to see if Dad was my biological father. She said that she would talk to him and let me know.

The following day, I wrote another email to Jeanette.

Hi Jeanette-

Just wanted you to know that I got some information that was quite an eye-opener for me. Seems I am the last to know that the woman whom I thought was my mother wasn't my biological mother. All my aunts and uncles knew this but were sworn to secrecy. This I just learned from a reliable source. Do you remember my asking if you knew if my father could have been my biological father? Too many things point me in that direction even though I can't prove infidelity on his part. Not only do I have strong suspicions about this, so do all his brothers and sisters. So, it looks like we not only need the DNA test at this point to confirm what we both believe will absolutely prove that you and I are indeed half-siblings. So I have another question for you and don't think it will be the last. As I tear up one more time - can I call you Sis? We have so much time to make up and I look forward to meeting you and the rest of the family.

Continuing our dialogue on the phone, Jeanette and I exchanged stories, information, and pictures through the Internet. The most unbelievable coincidence was that she had named her first daughter Pam. I told her that my wife's name was Pam as well. I could hardly believe my ears when she said that her daughter was Pamela Denese. I replied, "You're not going to believe this, but my wife is also Pamela Denise." We would later figure out that her Pam was born about the same time that my Pam and I had started dating in junior high school.

The parallels seemed never-ending, growing with each conversation. Our grandfather, who raised her, was a mountain man, farmer, and bootlegger. She worked as a setup machinist before going to work in a brewery. Of course, my first career was as a machinist and I had begun brewing my own beer in a few years earlier. We both even drove 1993 Ford Explorers that we had purchased new.

Soon after, Jeanette wrote me saying her heart goes out to Pam and myself for what this has done to us, but believed it would all be a blessing for everyone in the end. She also explained that she already knew who her father was after only having recently found out after he came forward and they agreed to DNA tests. It was therefore impossible that the man who was her biological dad could also be my biological father since he was a thirty-three month POW in the Korean War, overlapping the dates that I was conceived and born.

Jeanette had already made the necessary arrangements for the DNA testing. She mailed my part of the kit to me and I was to send my swab to the lab of her choice. Feeling uncomfortable with that arrangement and wanting more control, I asked Jeanette to cancel the test so I could contract with the lab of my choice. After I explained that I was doing a Y-chromosome DNA test with a cousin to find out if my adopted dad was my biological father, she graciously agreed.

Upon receiving the results, I opened them with nervous anticipation. The results were clear. Jim was not my biological cousin therefore the man who raised me could not be my biological dad. I notified Jim, and although we were both disappointed in the results, we agreed that it wouldn't change anything as far as we were concerned.

The following week, I received the results for the half-siblingship DNA tests. The final numbers revealed that there was a 99.97 percent possibility that we were, in fact, half siblings. The perplexing part was the full siblingship results which revealed a 99.961 percent chance that we were full siblings. When I called Jeanette, she and Haywood were out and about together. I told her that I'd received the DNA test results. "Give it to me," she said. I told her about the half-siblingship results first and then I said, "But there's more." She asked what I was talking about and I told her that the full siblingship test revealed a 99.961 percent chance that we were full siblings. She couldn't believe her ears.

Her dad was audible in the back ground, wanting to know what was going on. When she told him that the test results indicated that we were full siblings. I could tell that he was upset. I heard him cry out that it was impossible. Jeanette told me once again that the DNA tests performed a few years earlier confirmed Haywood was her biological father. She made it clear that because he was a Korean POW when I was conceived and born, he could not be my father too. Asking Jeanette to contact the lab, I wanted to know if there could have been an error in their findings.

Upon contacting the lab, Jeanette learned that there could have been some cross contamination because they performed the swab tests on each other at the same time, in the same room, and without wearing surgical gloves. The lab also didn't know before performing the test, that Haywood was her third cousin which very well could have compounded the error.

Since the DNA tests between Jeanette, Jim, and myself were performed in separate locations, the risks of cross contamination were not likely.

The time had come to break the news to the sisters. My first call was to Darlene on a Sunday afternoon since she lived the closest. Darlene was in the middle of cooking a big dinner for a house full of grandchildren. That was routine for her after returning from church. When she answered the phone, I said "Come on down here. I got something to tell you." Darlene couldn't leave right then. She asked if it could wait until everyone left the house. I was so excited, I was ready to burst. "No. Come now," I said.

"I'll be down in a few minutes," Darlene said. She hung the phone up and told Big C to come with her to my house.

Just a mile down the road, it was a short drive to my house. Darlene told Big C that she knew what I was so excited about.

"What might that be," he asked. She said that I was going to say "she's found our brother."

When he asked her why she thought that, Darlene told him that she didn't know how to explain it, "I just know that's what it is."

Walking through the garage and into the kitchen when they arrived, I blurted out that I had found our brother. With a broad smile, Darlene said "I knew that's what you were going to tell me." I was as surprised by Darlene's response as I thought Darlene would be by my news. When I showed her the picture on my computer, Darlene said, "Oh my God! He looks like Uncle Bullpuncher—the mouth, the teeth..." Sharing more details with her now, I explained that my first phone call came in December when the investigator told me that he thought he had located our half-brother and was pretty sure he had the right person.

Darlene's mind wandered back to when she was in the eighth grade and Bullpuncher told her for the first time that she had a brother. She wasn't sure whether or not to believe him since he wasn't above telling some pretty tall tales. Granny confirmed what Bullpuncher had said. "Yes, you do have a brother," Granny told her. "Sugarloaf gave him away when he was very small." When she asked Granny how that could have happened, she said that Granddaddy had begged Sugarloaf not to give her baby away, insisting that she would be sorry for the rest of her life. "But you know your mother," she said, "She did what she wanted to do. Nobody influenced her very much."

I called Dinah only to learn that she couldn't come right then. Susan lived farther away, so I told her over the phone. Caught off guard, her response was simply,

"Oh wow!" but managed to say that she looked forward to meeting him.

Knowing that Cheryl would be home, I called her and said that I needed to talk to her. Immediately thinking that something terrible had happened, she asked what was wrong. "I don't want to tell you over the phone," I said. Cheryl quickly drove over. Walking through the kitchen door, she looked right at me." Unable to contain myself, I again blurted out, "I've found our brother!"

Bemused, Cheryl said, "Well, damn! I thought something was wrong with Mike or one of the kids" before saying that she had to have more time to think it through.

I told her to take her time and "let me know."

It was in high school that Dinah remembered first learning from me that she had a brother, and she never gave it much thought afterward. She had even forgotten about it until now. When I finally got to speak to her, Dinah was bewildered to say the least. Her emotions ran wild, feeling excited and then scared. She managed to finally settle down enough to ask how he was. I said that everything was great and that I thought it would be "good for Momma to see him. Maybe this is what she is hanging on for."

Meeting with Momma's doctor, I told him that her son she had given away at the young age of two weeks, was coming out from California to meet her. Asking him how he thought I should approach it, he advised against springing it on her at the last minute.

VII

A NEW BEGINNING

The cabin where it all began, on Berry Mountain.

On a Sunday, early in April, 2009, Haywood, Darlene, and I took Momma out to breakfast. Shortly after we finished eating, I told her that someone from California was coming to visit and wanted to meet her. Well, Momma

354

had no idea what I was talking about and asked, "What would someone in California want to meet me for?"

Still unsure how she was going to respond, I just said, "He's your son."

A nervous quiet loomed over the table. All eyes focused on Momma as she stared into space for a moment and then a second or two longer before she said, "Oh, Jeanette, you come up with the dumbest things!"

Looking Momma right in her eyes, I said, "Now don't you sit there and deny that you had a son that you gave away when he was just two weeks old." The tension began to ratchet up as Momma sat silently in defiance. I continued, "Let me tell you a little bit about him. He lives in California and holds no grudges against you. He's had a good life. He's been married for thirty-five years, and he wants to meet you."

True to character, Momma snapped back and said, "Bring him on!" During the following weeks, she gave no indication as to how she was going to accept him -- or even if she would accept him. I don't reckon anyone knew what to expect -- most of all, Momma.

Wanting to present Jeanette with a special gift and knowing very little about her, I began to consider what might be most appropriate. It had to be something that she would forever cherish. Looking at the fifty year old, personalized Christmas card for ideas, it hit me. I walked into one of the shops in the local mall and made a personalized teddy bear for her. There were many styles and accessories, each making the teddy bear all the more personal and precious. It would be something that could be held with a sense of love and appreciation and provide a certain level of security as well. I gave it a heart that would beat when she hugged it. Made with love and special care and attention to detail, that's the way it was going to be treated until it was in Jeanette's possession. To make sure it survived the trip unscathed, I boarded the plane with it as one of my personal carry-ons.

While in the mall, my cell phone rang. Looking at the caller ID, I noticed it was a call from back east. Too noisy to try and carry on a phone conversation, I let it go into my voicemail. Arriving back at my van, it was quiet enough to listen to the message. "This is your sister, Cheryl," it began. Much more than that was difficult for me to understand because of her southern accent. She said something about playing golf after I arrived and that she mostly drove the golf cart and drank the beer while her husband golfed. I liked how she started her message out by saying she was "Sister Cheryl."

When I called her back, I got her voicemail. I decided to have a little fun with her by saying "Hi Sister Cheryl, this is your brother Ted, calling from the California convent." I told her that I didn't play golf, but I would be more than happy to ride along and drink beer with her. My opening line was either not as funny as I thought or she had as much difficulty understanding me as I did with her message since she never said anything about it afterwards.

On May 2, 2009, Pam and I flew to Virginia to meet my new family. Boarding the plane in Sacramento, California, we were bound for Richmond, Virginia via Atlanta, Georgia. It was just another flight for me until the plane approached Richmond. Staring out the plane window, I began to get a bit emotional.

I was finally going to see and touch someone who had the same blood running through their veins -- the same genes and DNA. After fifty-five years, I would be able to look at someone else's face and see my eyes, among other likenesses. I would finally see others with similar features as mine. No longer would I feel that sense of loneliness that I'd grown up with all my life.

After exiting the plane, Pam and I weaved our way to the receiving area of the terminal. My eyes searched the busy lobby of scurrying bodies. Anxiously, I looked between and around all the heads of others that were so frantically doing the same. Suddenly, through the crowd, flashed Jeanette's welcoming smile. Our eyes connected and locked on each other. Her face lit up with the warm glow of an angel. Her eyes began to well up as I got closer. Reaching out with extended arms, we embraced with a hug -- a long hug that seemed to be trying to make up for all those lost years. I began to feel a building succession of upheavals as I heard Jeanette beginning to cry. Still, we held on, more tightly than before as if our lives depended on it. The rest of the world vanished, if only for the moment. It was just Jeanette and me, her long lost little brother,

Reluctantly pulling ourselves apart, we said our hellos as she wiped her tears away. Turning to my wife, Pam, I proudly introduced her to my older sister before we proceeded to claim our luggage and go out to the car where Jeanette's husband, Mike, sat waiting. He drove us home where the rest of Jeanette's family was anxiously waiting. Pulling into the driveway, there were miles of smiles as everyone made their way to the Escalade. An energized little Whitney, Pamela Denese's youngest daughter, emerged from the middle of the crowd congregated in front of the garage. Rushing to greet us, a determined Whitney was anxiously prepared to give us a tour of the house.

We met Jeanette's and Mike's children, my nieces and nephew, Pamela Denese, Chastity, and David. My Pamela Denise, met Jeanette's Pamela Denese. Eventually, Dinah, Darlene, Cheryl, Susan, and their families all filtered into the house.

Giving Pam and I a personal tour of Jeanette's house, Whitney was very thorough. She didn't miss a detail as she told us about each room throughout. In the basement, Whitney told us that we were in the television room next to the bedroom. Quickly pointing out the string dangling from the ceiling light in the middle of the room, she said, "This is the string that turns on the light. Just pull it to turn it on." Then she said, "Be careful. Don't bump your head on it." The rest of the day was filled with hugs, kisses, and stories while snapping what must have been thousands of pictures. A stranger would have thought that royalty was visiting or there was a Hollywood premiere going on with all the flashes that were going off.

All my life, it had always been someone else's family doing this or hosting that. Now, this time, it was mine. The siblings that I had always wanted were finally a reality. I felt a sincere sense of love and belonging that there were no words for. These were my people. I couldn't imagine how they must have felt all those years knowing they had a brother and not knowing who he was, where he was, or how he was. What was once a dull and seemingly pointless life was now enriched and renewed after 55 years. Now with a sense of total fulfillment, my soul was finally at ease, thanks to all these wonderful people, and most particularly, Jeanette. Thank God she never gave up on her lifelong search for her half-brother, who, as it turned out, was actually her full brother. That was the icing on the cake as far as Jeanette and I were concerned.

I had always tried to teach my sons the value of family and how important siblings are through my unique perspective after having grown up an only child. Thank God my sons did not and would never know the loneliness I had grown up with. I didn't want that for anyone -- most importantly my own children. It was beginning to occur to me that I had underestimated that significance as I was beginning to experience a sense of sibling love that was nothing like I had ever experienced before.

I wondered what my sisters were feeling as we exchanged glances that turned into longer gazes while we nervously checked each other out. Cheryl seemed to be the elusive one. As we all gathered in Jeanette's kitchen, she spent much of the time in the adjacent garage, watching out the other door, into the yard. Wanting to reach out to her and invite her to join us, I reluctantly gave her time, hoping that she would eventually appreciate my tolerance and warm up to me. At the end of the day, I felt a sincere connection with all my sisters except for Cheryl. She remained distant and that bothered me. We would eventually bond, but on that day, the dreams of two other people were once and for all realized.

The following morning, Jeanette drove us to the convalescent home to meet Sugarloaf, the woman who had twice given me life. I couldn't help but wonder how she would react. How would she feel after fifty-five years?

Entering the room first, Jeanette told Sugarloaf that she had brought someone from California to meet her. "This is your son, Ted," she said as Pam and I entered the room.

With failing vision, Sugarloaf strained her eyes before they finally focused as well as they could. Did she see something she recognized? From her bed, she smiled and reached out for me. Squeezing my hand, she pulled me closer. Her face lit up as she pulled me in for a great big hug.

I wondered what was going through her mind at that very moment. How was it different this time from the last? What was different from that day she held me and walked down the mountain with Virgie, her dear friend, to deliver her infant son wrapped in a blue blanket and blue cap, through the window of the waiting car, into the arms of a couple she didn't know and had never met? Would she once again turn away and reject the man the same way she did the infant son?

Holding my hand ever so tightly, as if to never let me go this time, Sugarloaf told me that she loved me and that she was proud of me. We talked and took pictures before Jeanette returned and it was time to leave. Needless to say, parting this time was very different from the first, back in 1953.

Jeanette had already told me that Sugarloaf had never been one to show her affectionate side to anyone, except a man. Had it all been an act to cover up and protect the insecure person within, or was she truly the heartless and thick-skinned woman she always led everyone to believe she was? Would this turn of events soften her, or would she change at all?

Sugarloaf and "the boy." Their first meeting since she gave him away fifty-five years earlier.

❖   ❖   ❖   ❖

The next morning started early as Susan, Darlene, and her son, Bino, journeyed with Jeanette and I to the cabin on Berry Mountain, where life began for me fifty-five years before. It was a beautiful, sunny spring day -- cool and partly cloudy with a threat of rain looming. In two separate trucks, we drove as far as the road would allow. Parking the vehicles on the side of the road, we got out and walked back into the wild for at least a mile to the cabin. It had recently been restored and bore little resemblance to what it looked like then. While the timbers, floor, fireplace, and chimney were still original, a kitchen had been added in back and a new roof replaced the original.

The Cabin, before it was restored. Notice the poor condition of the chinking between the timbers. Also the deck area on the back which has been replaced by a kitchen in the remodel.

This was God's country, if ever there was one. The surrounding area was no longer like it was fifty-five years ago. Neatly cultivated trees and vegetation now surrounded the cabin making the view from the porch absolutely breathtaking. It was as though God had blessed the land and prepared it for this homecoming. We spent about an hour looking around and taking pictures while Jeanette described what it was like back when Ohmer and Granny lived there. Instead of being in the back of the cabin, as it is now, the kitchen was detached and adjacent, to the north side of the house. Of course, there still is no indoor plumbing and the outhouse was about twenty yards to the north.

From there, we proceeded to the house in the hollow, where Jeanette, Dinah, and Darlene were raised by Granny and Ohmer. We didn't get far when it began to rain, and we sought the shelter of the taller trees like Jeanette and Darlene had done when they were kids.

When the rain let up, we continued our hike. Upon our descent to the white house, as they called it, Jeanette pointed out what remained of the spring box in the mountain stream.

The house in the hollow had been abandoned for years and was now home to the cows that freely roamed the area and few other animals. As Jeanette opened the door, a bird flew out and away. The floors were muddied throughout and rotted in places. The stairs leading to the second story weren't safe enough to climb, so we remained on the ground floor. We discovered a nest near the ceiling in a corner, with baby swallows chirping for their mother. I wondered what Jeanette and Darlene must have thought as they saw the deteriorating condition of the home in which they spent many of their childhood years. I never asked, preferring to use this time to celebrate and bond. Cherishing every moment, I was satisfied learning of my origins and discovering that I once had a life as brief as it was, that was much like I had fancied as a child.

Virgie and I reunited for the first time in fifty-five years.

Darlene and Dinah, respectively, circa 1960.

Teddy, circa 1957.
Bobbie delighted in making every effort to give
Teddy what he would have never had otherwise,
often referring to him as her "little man."

Jeanette's bedroom in the hollow.

The day before Pam and I left to return to California, we stopped in to visit Sugarloaf one last time. Jeanette showed us in but didn't stay, preferring to give us some time alone. Wanting to ask her if she could tell me anything about my biological father, I didn't feel comfortable with such inquiries so early in our relationship. When it became obvious that I wasn't going to ask, Pam broke the silence and asked the question. Staring at the floor for a few moments, Sugarloaf looked up at her and said, "I really don't remember." Turning away, Sugarloaf paused and thought a little more before she continued. "I think his name was Dan and he was in the military." The room once again became uncomfortably quiet before Jeanette returned. We all talked for a while longer, then it was time to leave.

As we said our good-byes, Sugarloaf squeezed my hand firmly and lovingly. We exchanged hugs and a kiss. As she looked into my eyes, she said, "I love you." I told her that I loved her too then we left. I wondered if I would ever see her again. I hoped that if she had ever regretted giving me up, that she now had closure and was satisfied with the way her son turned out. I believe that she probably did feel a void in her life after giving me up. The identity of our biological father still remains a mystery even though we are reasonably sure of who he is.

Jeanette flew to California the following September for my birthday. It was Labor Day weekend and Pam and I took her to the Art, Wine and Brew Festival in historic downtown Vacaville's town square. I proudly introduced her to everyone I knew and much to my surprise, one of the musicians on the stage stopped playing long enough to tell everyone in the square our story and that Jeanette was in attendance, helping me celebrate my birthday. It was followed by a very long applause by the people in attendance.

Vowing to be with each other on our birthdays from then on, we next met in Denver for her birthday near the end of October. Our little celebration, however, was dampened by illness. She had become sick and ended up spending much of her time in bed during that extended weekend, but we did manage a nice dinner at an old fort that had been converted into a restaurant not far away. It was cold when we arrived, but cozy and warm inside. We were seated at a window that overlooked the courtyard that had been restored to look like it must have looked all those years ago in the old west. As we began to eat a wonderful meal, it began to snow outside, making the scene that much more beautiful and picturesque." It was certainly an occasion to be remembered.

I returned to Virginia six months after our initial visit. On Christmas Day 2009, one year after the initial phone call from Wayne Tonker, the entire family gathered at Jeanette's house for a festive holiday dinner. Finally with the family I had always wanted, it was more than I could ever have imagined, a dream come true for both her and I. It was big news in the Charlottesville area, as NBC29 was there to cover the Christmas homecoming. It made for the perfect Christmas story that not only aired on the local news, but it also aired on the NBC television affiliate in Sacramento, where I had once worked.

Later in the day, the children were running around the house, playing, and having a good time while the adults were in the kitchen and dining area, celebrating, talking, and eating. A couple of the grandchildren darted through the kitchen, right past Sugarloaf, as she sat at the end of the dining table. Chastity turned to her and asked what she thought of all these kids. With a sigh of relief and a smirk on her face, Sugarloaf said, "I'm glad all mine are grown and gone."

Across the room, I couldn't resist the opportunity to chime in. Smiling, I said, "Yeah, but they're starting to come back." Chastity seemed to hang on to that remark as the room filled with laughter. All eyes turned to Sugarloaf as everyone expected her to come back with something else. She simply sat there at the table, smiling warmly, looking at me. She didn't need to say anything more. Her face said it all.

EPILOGUE

Back row: Jeanette, Darlene, me; Front row:
Cheryl, Susan, Dinah; Seated: Sugarloaf

Although many questions have been answered since that first phone call in 2009, many still remain. We still don't know if I was legally adopted or if I was just given away. Virginia is a closed adoption state so any records that may exist are sealed.

We think that it is very likely that there was an exchange of money before I was given away. We question whether or not documents were forged to show that I was born to the parents who raised me. If that was the case, we wonder who may have been involved and what motivated them. Who would have risked their medical career by doing such a thing and what did he have to gain by doing so? What if the doctor who forged the documents had much more to hide and was trying to cover up his trail?

Dad must have been pretty confident that their secret would never catch up to them. It was obvious by the way he sometimes flaunted what they'd done, even right under my nose. He and Mom had done a pretty good job of convincing me when I was little that I was in fact their biological son, making sure that I had seen my birth certificate numerous times as a very young and impressionable child. They made sure that I knew about their great difficulty conceiving their first child, going as far to say that they had a baby that didn't survive before I was born. Then almost by a miracle, after nine years of marriage, they succeeded and I was born.

I am elated to finally know that after all those years of yearning for siblings, I now have them. Maybe the day will come when I will want to know more about how my parents managed to keep everything such a well kept secret, not only from me, but also from the military. I wonder why there were no questions asked about Mom's condition, before and after supposedly having delivered me. What military doctor risked his career by filing false documents? Did a military doctor actually claim to have delivered me before giving Mom a clear bill of health? How did they explain that all of a sudden, Bobbie had this baby without any prenatal care and no ubiquitous signs after delivery? Did a country doctor forge the documents to cover any involvement he may have had with Sugarloaf's pregnancy?

Mom and Dad took many photographs while they were married. Always keeping them neatly organized in the family photo albums, she often wrote captions and or dates under many of them to identify people and situations. Not once did It ever occur to me that I never saw one picture of my mother when she was pregnant, even though there were many of both Mom and Dad before Mom was supposedly pregnant and after I was born.

As a young woman, I had an appointment with Dr. Roberts. He had been the family doctor ever since I was a little girl. This time, however, was different than all the other times. Feeling rather uncomfortable about it, I went to Granny. When I told her that I wasn't going back to see him again, she asked why I would say such a thing. I said "Well, he's never been out of the way with me, but his line of questioning was just too personal this time."

I further explained that after the exam, he proceeded to ask me personal questions, like "How are things at home? Where are you living? Where are you working, and are you happy?" And then when I got ready to leave, I asked him how much I owed him.

Instead of charging me, he said, "I'll catch you next time."

Shrugging her shoulders, Granny said, "Maybe he has a guilty conscience. The doctor was one of the men your mother had been seeing back then, and when you play in the briar patch, you never know which one sticks you." If I had false teeth, they would have fallen to the floor.

Occasionally, someone would tell me that I resembled one of Dr. Robert's children, enough to be related. Honestly, I heard it so many times that I eventually responded by saying, "Oh no, not you too."

Eventually, I decided that I wanted to know for sure, if only for my own peace of mind. When Dr. Roberts died, I went to his oldest son and asked if I could have a DNA test done with his father before they buried him.

Demanding that I put my wishes in writing, he wanted me to explain my objectives, and have the official request back to him the following morning. I did exactly as he asked. Writing a request for a DNA, I explained that I only wanted peace of mind and nothing more. When I delivered it to him in person the following morning, he told me that he couldn't believe that I would come to him with such a request before denying me without further explanation.

Time had passed and I ran into Dr. Roberts' daughter one day, and she told me that she felt a special connection with me and if there was anything I ever needed, I need only ask. With nothing left to lose, I asked her if she'd consider doing a DNA test with me. I was pleasantly surprised to hear her say that she didn't see why not. After making all the arrangements, I called her to set up a convenient time and date with her. Unable to talk to her directly, I left a message on her phone. It was days before she finally returned my call. When she did, she said that she had changed her mind and wouldn't explain why.

When Jeanette and I were interviewing relatives for our book, we learned a lot of interesting facts. One of the most interesting comments was from a second cousin the first time we met. Before anyone could say anything, he asked me, "Has anyone ever told you that you look just like Dr. Roberts?"

I have always believed and I continue to believe that Momma was aware of what Gordon had done to me. A mother knows her child and can tell if and when something is wrong.

The DNA test between Haywood and me changed our lives, and we have become very close since then. While there were conflicting results in our DNA test, it hasn't changed what is in our hearts. To further solidify our love, Haywood officially adopted me in my early 60s. While my search for my half-brother concluded with extraordinary results, I continue my search to try to learn who my biological father is, with the support of my newly found full brother.

There are many interesting coincidental parallels in our stories. That is one of the fun things about it. Worth mentioning is the coincidental naming of my first granddaughter, 14 year old Madison Paige. My birthplace was not Albemarle County, but actually *Madison* County. Aunt *Paige* was one of Ohmer's sisters.

The list goes on. It's fun to try and see how many you can count. How many did you make note of while reading our book? It's okay to go back through it again. Let us know how many you found by visiting us on our Facebook page: www.facebook.com/twicedelivered.

ACKNOWLEGEMENTS

We would like to thank the following people whom without their support, this story could not have been told:

Charles Beahm	Jim Haskins	Mary Stanley
John Beahm	Inga Hines	Sarah Thomas
Dot Benham	Susan Jones	Wayne Tonker
Bradley Berry	Shirley Kite	Dinah Williamson
Cluster Berry	Arlene Krebs	
James Berry	Virginia Lewis	
Tommy Berry	Debbie McMinds	
Carol Carsner	Darlene Meade	
Louis Carsner	Richard Rico	
Beulah Cason	Billy Schumaker	
Nan Coppedge	Phil Shepherd	
Mavis Elkins	Virgie Shifflett	
Cheryl Evans	Dan Simms	
Blanche Haskins	Kevin Stanley	

Made in the USA
Monee, IL
14 August 2023

41000619R00225